TRANSFORMING UNIONISM

Also by Michael Kerr:

Imposing Power-Sharing:
Conflict and Coexistence in Northern Ireland and Lebanon

Published by Irish Academic Press 2005

TRANSFORMING UNIONISM

David Trimble
and the
2005 General Election

MICHAEL KERR

IRISH ACADEMIC PRESS
DUBLIN • PORTLAND, OR

First published in 2006 by
IRISH ACADEMIC PRESS
44, Northumberland Road, Dublin 4, Ireland

and in the United States of America by
IRISH ACADEMIC PRESS
c/o ISBS, Suite 300, 920 NE 58th Avenue
Portland, Oregon 97213-3644

WEBSITE: www.iap.ie

British Library Cataloguing in Publication Data
An entry can be found on request

ISBN 0-7165-3388-X (cloth)
ISBN 0-7165-3389-8 (paper)

Library of Congress Cataloging-in-Publication Data
An entry can be found on request

Typeset in 10.5/13 Palatino by FiSH Books, Enfield, Middx.
Printed by Creative Print and Design, Gwent, Wales

For The Ulster Unionist Party

Contents

Acknowledgements

There are two people I have to thank before anyone else. The first is Lisa Hyde of Irish Academic Press, who came up with the idea for this book and who worked tirelessly on the project from start to finish. The second is my colleague and friend, Claire Kirk, without whose support and assistance at every stage, writing this book would have been an impossible task. For their support and enthusiasm I am extremely grateful. I would also like to thank Geoffrey McGimpsey for reminding me of all the things I had forgotten and for reading successive drafts. I am very grateful to Dr Rory Miller for all his help, advice and enthusiasm along the way. Thanks also to Frank Cass, Dr Shelley Deane, Professor Keith Jeffery, Dr Bill Kissane, Andrew Lynch, Professor Brendan O'Leary and Dr Kirsten Schulze.

I am deeply grateful to Alderman Roy Beggs, Alex Benjamin, David Burnside MLA, David Campbell CBE, Tom Elliott MLA, Sir Reg Empey MLA, Lady Sylvia Hermon, Lord Kilclooney MLA, Dr Steven King, Tim Lemon, Lord Maginnis, Rodney McCune, Alan McFarland MLA, Lord Rogan, the Rev. Martin Smyth and The Rt. Hon. David Trimble MLA for granting me interviews at such short notice. I also sincerely apologize to all those involved whom I did not get the opportunity to speak with. Many thanks and best wishes to all those in Cunningham House who shared their hopes and fears with me before, during and after the election: Jack Allen OBE, Stephen Barr, Dr Ken Bishop, David Christopher, Will Corry, Dr Brian Crowe, Cyril Donnan, Dorothy Downey, Barbra Knox, Alison Laird, Hazel Legge, Anne McCormack, Peter Munce, Steven Knott, Mark Neale, Barry White, Andy Wilson and Jonathan Cain of Conservative Central Office. I must also thank David Kerr.

ix

I am deeply indebted to the 'Celebrity Chefs', who took part in our Healthy Eating Campaign in East Antrim. They were Nick Price, Paul Rankin, Jenny Bristow and Robbie Millar, who tragically lost his life in a car accident not far from his famous 'Shanks Restaurant' on 13 August 2005. He was a great credit to Northern Ireland.

I would like to take the opportunity to show my appreciation to the Ulster Unionist East Antrim canvassing team, led by the indefatigable May Steele MBE, JP. In some parts of the world when things do not go your own way it is never for the want of trying.

Many thanks to Robert, Valerie, Richard, Gillian, Fred and Julia, who all helped me in terms of support, both during the election and while writing this book, as did Sarah. The same, as ever, can be said for Dave McClay and Willie.

And thank you to Daniel for helping me pick the title for this book.

Dramatis Personæ

The Leadership
David Trimble, UUP Leader
Denis Rogan, President
James Cooper, Chairman
David Campbell,
    Vice-Chairman

The Westminster Candidates
Roy Beggs, East Antrim
Rodney McCune, North Antrim
David Burnside, South Antrim
David Trimble, Upper Bann
Sylvia Hermon, North Down
Dermot Nesbitt, South Down
Tom Elliott, Fermanagh and
    South Tyrone
Earl Storey, Foyle
Reg Empey, East Belfast
Fred Cobain, North Belfast
Michael McGimpsey, South
    Belfast
Chris McGimpsey, West Belfast
Basil McCrea, Lagan Valley
David McClarty, East
    Londonderry
Danny Kennedy, Newry and
    Armagh

Gareth McGimpsey, Strangford
Derek Hussey, West Tyrone
Billy Armstrong, Mid Ulster

Outgoing MPs
Rev. Martin Smyth, South Belfast
Jeffery Donaldson, Lagan Valley
    (defected to DUP)
Sylvia Hermon, North Down
David Trimble, Upper Bann
David Burnside, South Antrim
Roy Beggs, East Antrim

War Room Team
Will Corry, Chief Executive
Tim Lemon, Campaigns Director
Alex Benjamin,
    Communications Director
Brian Crowe, Policy Officer
Alison Laird, Policy Officer
Steven King, Speech-writer
Geoffrey McGimpsey, Press
    Officer
Michael Kerr, Campaigns
    Officer
Claire Kirk, Campaigns Officer
Peter Munce, Press Officer

Leadership Contenders
Reg Empey
Alan McFarland
David McNarry
Lady Sylvia Hermon
Lord Kilclooney
Lord Maginniss

Barbra Knox, Campaigns Diary
David Christopher, Website
   Manager

List of Abbreviations

AIA	Anglo-Irish Agreement
APNI	Alliance Party of Northern Ireland
BBC	British Broadcasting Company
CLMC	Combined Loyalist Military Corporation
DSD	Downing Street Declaration
DUP	Democratic Unionist Party
EU	European Union
HMSO	Her Majesty's Stationery Office
IICD	Independent International Commission on Decommissioning
IMC	International Monitoring Commission
IRA	Irish Republican Army
MEP	Member of the European Parliament
MLA	Member of the Legislative Assembly
MP	Member of Parliament
NILP	Northern Ireland Labour Party
PEB	Party Election Broadcast
PR	Proportional Representation
PSNI	Police Service of Northern Ireland
PUP	Progressive Unionist Party
RTE	Radio Telefís Éireann
RUC	Royal Ulster Constabulary
SDLP	Social Democratic and Labour Party
STV	Single Transferable Vote
TD	Member of the Irish Parliament
UDA	Ulster Defence Association
UDP	Ulster Democratic Party

UDR	Ulster Defence Regiment
UK	United Kingdom
UKUP	United Kingdom Unionist Party
US	United States
UUC	Ulster Unionist Council
UUP	Ulster Unionist Party
UUUC	United Ulster Unionist Council
UVF	Ulster Volunteer Force
UWC	Ulster Workers' Council
VULC	Vanguard Unionist Loyalist Coalition
VUPP	Vanguard Unionist Progressive Party

Prologue

It was 24 June 2005, and the Ulster Unionist Party (UUP) had just lost a general election to Ian Paisley's Democratic Unionist Party (DUP). The delegates to the UUP's one-hundred-year-old ruling council had gathered in Belfast's Ramada Hotel to elect a leader to replace David Trimble. It was indeed an historic moment in the Ulster Unionist Council's (UUC) long and tumultuous history, and I felt glad to be a part of it. It did strike me as ironic, however, that for the first time in a decade the outcome of the Council's proceedings would not be determined by whether the grumpy old men in grey suits, plotting to get rid of David Trimble, outnumbered those he could still count on for support. Alas, there was no such entertainment to be found on that occasion.

As I stood at the back of the hall watching the delegates take their places, I wondered how the UUP would cope without the man so many of its members had spent the best years of their lives trying to undermine. On entering the building I had heard the same three questions whispered over and over again. Who do you think will win? Will it make any difference? Is David Trimble here? The third question was the only one for which I had a definite answer. For the first time since I had begun working for the party at Westminster in 1999, its controversial, courageous and always contentious leader was absent without leave.

David Trimble had lost his direction in the political process over the last eighteen months, and during that time it became painfully obvious that he had also outgrown his party. He had carried Ulster Unionism a considerable distance in his ten years at the helm, but for many delegates it had been in a direction in which they had no desire

1

to go. David Trimble had challenged the dynamics of politics in Northern Ireland and in doing so brought steely realism and proactive engagement to Unionism's liberal position. He had put Northern Ireland's union with Britain before party politicking, swapped intransigence for political dynamism and altered the perception of Unionism in the eyes of the international community. On his long political journey David Trimble had rubbed salt into old wounds and pitched modernists against 'not an inch' Unionists across the Province. He was also the first Unionist leader in decades to have significantly influenced the British government's approach to politics in Northern Ireland. In recent months, I had often wondered why Prime Minister Tony Blair, who had invested so much time and effort in Northern Ireland's political process, had abandoned the man who had made it all possible.

As the Party President, Lord Rogan, rose to introduce the first of this evening's contenders, I thought of David Trimble at his last UUP conference in Newcastle, County Down the previous year. While I knew then that his time as Northern Ireland's most complex politician was drawing to a close, the speech he gave that afternoon reminded me of why I had joined the party in the first place. His performance and delivery matched that of any world statesman and what he said was as challenging and inspiring as it was out of place and out of touch. He spoke of bringing the distinction of being both Irish and Unionist back into British political life, of a forward-looking Northern Ireland whose pluralism had become its strength, and of the achievements of Unionism in helping to raise up a new Northern Ireland. The problem David Trimble faced that day, and thereafter, was that nobody in his part of the world seemed to be listening to him anymore.

As Lord Rogan stood to announce the result of the leadership election, one of David Trimble's most ardent opponents whispered to me that the three men before us that night were a damning indictment of how low the party had sunk in its centenary year. I laughed to myself in the thought that among all of David Trimble's enemies, not one of them had had the guile to play the role of Brutus in the tragi-comedy that was his undoing. Mind you, it did seem more fitting to me for the red-faced, stubborn Ulsterman to fall on his own sword.

I had begun working in David Trimble's office in October 1999 as an intern while studying for a PhD in ethnic conflict regulation at the

London School of Economics and Political Science. My supervisor, and erstwhile critic of Unionism, Professor Brendan O'Leary, had informed me that his Government Department ran a House of Commons placement scheme, sending students to cut their political teeth among the great and the good in the nation's parliament. He pointed out, however, that while the LSE was a broad international church, as far as he was aware nobody had yet come forward to join the UUP. While somewhat perturbed by his Irish wit, I left content in the knowledge that I should stand a fair chance of gaining employment with David Trimble's Ulster Unionists. The thought of working for the man excited me, and while I had always voted for his party in Northern Ireland, the positive approach he brought to the whole political process filled me with enthusiasm.

A couple of weeks passed before I received a letter from the party's then Chief Whip, the Rev. Martin Smyth, seeking my attendance at an informal interview in the House of Commons. When I arrived I found the South Belfast MP hidden away in a small but ornate oak office just off parliament's central lobby. I assumed my academic credentials would stand me in good stead, but sticking to my father's advice I took the opportunity to tell him that my grandfather, Cecil Kerr, had been the Archdeacon of the Church of Ireland in the Diocese of Elphin and Ardagh in the 1950s and 1960s, and that many of my relations had fought gallantly in both world wars. Having kept my brief and avoided any mention of the Orange Order – a weak point since none of my immediate family are members – Smyth seemed happy enough and told me to report for duty every Wednesday at 9.30 am.

I was born in East Belfast and grew up in its leafy suburbs attending Campbell College on the Belmont Road. Ultimately, such an upbringing sheltered me from worst of the conflict raging only two miles down the road and the sectarianism it brought with it. My father's side of the family all came from what became the Republic and lived mostly in the border counties until the end of the 1960s. To some extent this history set my family life apart from that of the average Belfast boy, as few of my peers had parents from the south. This was not true of Campbell College in general, however, as there were boarders from mixed backgrounds in the Republic and a good number of Catholics enrolled from both jurisdictions. To its credit the school successfully fostered a totally non-sectarian environment and one that undoubtedly influenced my view of Unionist politics in later life. It was, however, a typically British schooling so much so, that it did nothing to prepare its unsuspecting pupils for the ethnic conflict taking place outside its gates.

My mother's side of my family are from Londonderry (or Derry as my grandmother referred to it). While my father's relations co-existed happily and comfortably alongside their Catholic neighbours in the border counties, my mother's family had a different experience of life in Northern Ireland's second city. They originated from a Scots Presbyterian–English background, settling in counties Armagh and Derry. They came from a different Unionist perspective in the sense that they lived within the six counties that became Northern Ireland in 1920. Their experience of the Troubles was tempered by being held hostage at gunpoint by the IRA during a bank robbery at a branch in Warrenpoint where my grandfather was Manager.

My father, too, had similar experiences at the hands of both Loyalist and Republican paramilitaries during his long career in the bank. Such was life in Northern Ireland. It was not that my relations from the Republic were not Unionists, for they certainly were. My great aunt, Julia Kerr, was decorated for her services in North Africa during World War Two and this was something that my family were extremely proud of. Their distinction, at least to me, was that they had a Unionist perspective that was shaped by being part of a minority Protestant community in the Irish Republic.

I left Northern Ireland in the mid-1990s to attend university in England, but retained my interest in Northern Ireland's developing political process. It came as no surprise to my friends or family when I began working for the UUP. Like many of David Trimble's supporters I had become disillusioned with the representation of Unionism on the mainland and its inability to influence the political situation in Northern Ireland – not just for the benefit of Protestants or Unionists, but for everyone living there. What motivated me to become involved in Unionist politics was in fact my experience of living in Britain, and not Northern Ireland. I was shocked that Unionism had won practically no support with either the government or fellow citizens for the maintenance of the political union between Northern Ireland and Britain. I was deeply ashamed and embarrassed that the first thing many English people spoke of after I told them I was an Ulster Unionist was the DUP leader Ian Paisley and his attitude towards Catholics in Northern Ireland. Consequently, it was not long after David Trimble began transforming such perceptions and engaging positively with the British government that I renewed my enthusiasm for Ulster Unionism and support for his party.

During my first two years working part-time for the UUP I wrote speeches for East Antrim MP Roy Beggs and learnt how to run a political press office. After two years I went to live in Lebanon before completing my Doctorate at the LSE. That done, I returned to work full time for David Trimble and Roy Beggs running the party's Westminster office with my colleague from Saintfield, County Down, Claire Kirk. Our tasks included writing political speeches and briefs for the parliamentary party team of MPs and Peers as Northern Ireland legislation passed through both houses. We would also liaise with junior members and, when not so busy, MPs from other political parties. I enjoyed most aspects of the job, but never tired of giving visitors from Northern Ireland and our MP's acquaintances tours of the Palace of Westminster. It is a visually stunning place to work in and I never took for granted the sight of Big Ben telling me I was late in the morning or bleary-eyed MPs shuffling into the debating chamber when a late-night division was called. In the evenings we did PR work for the party, which, if we were lucky, might entail the odd champagne reception. There we would lobby on behalf of the UUP and make contacts with important people from other parties and organizations. Working at Westminster is something that completely takes over your life. Before you know it, you have become a part of the political furniture alongside all the other elected representatives, Peers, officials and staff. Well, at least until the next general election that is.

I had often thought of writing about modern Unionism and what the UUP had been trying to achieve in negotiating the Belfast Agreement in 1998, but somehow never seemed to find the time. As fortune would have it, the 2005 election result provided me with plenty of spare time and I began work on this book having returned to London shortly after the poll. At the outset I must state that this is not the inside story of David Trimble's decline and fall written by a disgruntled former employee. Neither is it an authorized or official book on behalf of the UUP or anyone affiliated with the party. What it is, however, is an unsolicited contribution to the lengthy learning process that party must now undergo if it is to recover its electoral fortunes in the wake of the 2005 defeat. This book provides a serious and fresh analysis of how the UUP arrived at the 2005 election and what that election result holds for modern Unionism, seen from the perspective of someone sitting inside and looking out. Moreover, it is an attempt to ignite a much-needed debate within Ulster Unionism regarding its role in Northern Ireland and the UK in the post-Trimble era.

When I took up employment in the nation's parliament the UUP had ten MPs. By March 2005, when I packed my bags to fly back to Belfast to fight my second general election campaign with the party, we had been reduced to just five. I knew we were going to have a fight on our hands if we were to hold any of them. But before I tell you the story of the 2005 Westminster general election campaign, and offer an explanation of what its outcome means for Unionism, I had better explain to you where the UUP was coming from and how we got there.

If I ever go looking for my heart's desire again,
I won't look any further than my own backyard.
Because if it isn't there, I never really
lost it to begin with!

Dorothy,
The Wizard of Oz.[1]

1 Maintaining the Union

> For us Britishness is not just a flag too often waved to annoy others. It is a living organic relationship with our fellow citizens elsewhere in the Kingdom. We are for a big United Kingdom, not a little Ulster. Such Britishness is inclusive. Emerson Tennant, one of the MPs for Belfast in the mid-nineteenth century put it as follows: 'we wish to add to the glory of being British, the distinction of being Irish'.
>
> David Trimble, 13 November 2004

By early 1920 Ulster Unionist leaders had negotiated a settlement with the British government that partitioned Ireland. This created Northern Ireland and secured a form of political union with Britain that lasted until direct rule was imposed in 1972. At the beginning of its second century, the Ulster Unionist Party had recently experienced what will be regarded historically as an equally significant and critical period in its history. In 1998 UUP leader David Trimble had maintained Northern Ireland's position within the UK through a negotiated settlement with the British and Irish governments known as the Belfast Constitutional Agreement.[2] This Agreement came after almost 30 years of conflict, terrorism and political stalemate and marked the end of that period of the conflict, or 'the Troubles', as it had become commonly known. But the year 2005 had its own historic significance. It was the year when the Agreement's failed implementation phase had come to an end. It was also the year when the man who had carried Unionism to that agreement fell spectacularly from power.

Not enough has been written about Ulster Unionism during this period, or indeed about what its leaders have been trying to achieve over this last decade. Not enough is known about Northern Ireland's oldest political party and how it faced the transition thrust upon it during the recent political process. Of what is available, John

Harbinson's analysis of Ulster Unionism is the most useful.[3] Much has been written about Unionist politics and history, from A.T.Q. Stewart's *The Narrow Ground: Aspects of Ulster 1609–1969*, to Arthur Aughey's *Under Siege: Ulster Unionism and the Anglo–Irish Agreement*.[4] On David Trimble himself, there is Dean Godson's monolithic account of the Ulsterman's rise to power (which does not chart his last days as UUP leader) among several others.[5] It is my intention not to fill the gaps in this literature in a generic sense, but to offer both an academic analysis and an insider's account of where the UUP leader was coming from in negotiating the Belfast Agreement. In doing so, I shall endeavour to address many of the unanswered questions surrounding David Trimble's role in the political process and his downfall in Upper Bann. Only through an analysis of the UUP's electoral defeat in 2005 can a serious evaluation be made of the causes and consequences of David Trimble's fall from power, its implications for Unionism as a whole and indeed the flagging political process in Northern Ireland. As 2005 was a critical movement in that process there is uncertainty, in the election's aftermath, as to whether the process or the UUP can actually survive. Before addressing these issues a brief historical narrative of how Ulster Unionism arrived at this crossroads will be beneficial in understanding recent events. There is unfortunately no place in this book for a detailed narrative of the history of Ulster Unionism or the political process, so I offer only a short digression in order to contextualize David Trimble's contribution to British and Irish history.

The Ulster Unionist Party, or the Official Unionists as many people still call them, emerged from a body named the Ulster Unionist Council. This organization was created in 1905 and was made up of Ulster and Irish Unionists who were at that time opposed to the British government's home rule legislation, which sought to provide self-government for Ireland as a whole. The term 'Ulster Unionist' came into existence as Irish Unionists looked to the northern province of Ulster as a territorial entity where Unionism could retreat in the event of Irish Nationalists gaining some form of independence from Britain. Ulster was the part of Ireland where the Unionist, or Protestant, community were demographically superior to the Nationalist or Catholic community.

After Edward Carson became UUC leader in 1910, Unionist

thoughts had already turned to Ulster as the British government's Third Home Rule Bill gathered momentum on the mainland. Irish Unionists soon divided in their opposition to this Bill. Those living outside Ulster, in the provinces of Connaught, Leinster and Munster, made up at most ten per cent of the total population of Ireland.[6] In 1911 Ulster Unionists agreed to draw up a provisional constitution for government in Ulster to counter the Third Home Rule Bill, should it pass through Parliament. In November of that year an ardent Unionist of Ulster–Scots descent, Andrew Bonar Law, became leader of the British Conservative and Unionist Party, giving the UUC's cause a significant boost. Ulster Unionists then legally forged the Ulster Volunteer Force (UVF), in what could only be seen as a warning to the government that they intended to defend their union, even if that meant defending it against Westminster.

During the British government's third attempt to pass the Home Rule Bill through parliament, the UUC held an 'Ulster Day' on 28 September 1912, when 218,206 males signed 'Ulster's Solemn League and Covenant', declaring their opposition to the Bill.[7] As Irish historian Patrick Buckland wrote, 'by demonstrating the incompatibility of Ulster Unionism and Irish Nationalism, the crisis over the third Home Rule Bill paved the way for the partition of Ireland'.[8] Amendments were then put to the Bill to allow for the exclusion of some, or all, of Ulster's counties. However, a settlement and a potential civil war was offset by the outbreak of World War One in 1914.[9]

The division between Ireland's two main communities stemmed from their differeing national identities. For Irish Nationalists, the root cause of conflict in their country was British colonialism and the continued British presence on Irish soil. They demanded independence from the British Crown in the form of a united Ireland within which Unionists would become a political minority within the Irish nation.[10] In contrast, Unionists viewed themselves as part of the British nation and loyal to its Crown. Consequently the Unionists sought to maintain Ireland's position within the UK and, while rigidly opposed to any form of Irish home rule, when faced with a *fait accompli*, they opted for partition.[11]

Following the onset of war and the Easter Rising of 1916, the UUC negotiated the partition of Ireland with the British government. This allowed for six of Ulster's nine counties to remain within the UK.

11

Partition was legislated for under the fourth Home Rule Bill, which subsequently became the Government of Ireland Act, 1920. While Unionists had never desired such a settlement, they accepted the 'Hobson's choice' of partition as it granted them devolved government in Belfast and allowed them to set up a government within the United Kingdom which they could control. The UUC abandoned their compatriots in Ulster's most westerly and southerly counties – Cavan, Donegal and Monaghan. Had these counties of Ulster been included in what became Northern Ireland the demographic balance between Catholics and Protestants would have been considerably less favourable to the Unionist élite.[12]

The ideological origins of Ulster Unionism were based on political pragmatism. The history and concentration of Protestant settlers in Ulster made the idea that Ulster, or part of it, should forge its own separate identity and union with Britain, a concept Unionists in the six counties that became Northern Ireland could easily accept. The realism of early Ulster Unionist thinking was premised on the fact that Irish Nationalists looked certain to gain some form of independence. For the mass of Protestants living in those six counties Ulster Unionism made geopolitical sense. Furthermore, Irish Nationalism had done little to persuade Irish Unionists that a united Irish Republic would be a place where Protestants would be accepted, treated equally under the constitution or enjoy the same cultural privileges as their fellow countrymen. But regardless of these points, Protestants would have been a minority in any united Ireland, as they made up just over a quarter of the total population according to the 1911 census.[13]

It was not only the fear of Irish Nationalism dominating the Unionist tradition that fuelled Ulster Unionism in its early years, but also a deep-seated fear of betrayal from Westminster. Sections of the British political establishment viewed Irish Unionists as expendable and their position within the United Kingdom conditional. They thought of Unionists in terms of the 'Irish question' or 'Irish problem', as opposed to part of the British nation. This uncomfortable relationship between Irish Unionists and their government at Westminster, as much as anything else, is what created the 'siege mentality' that developed among Ulster Protestants during the remainder of the twentieth century. This was a dilemma David Trimble would constantly grapple with during his ten years as

UUP leader and this is discussed at length in the final chapter of this book.

Northern Ireland's first elections were held in 1921, and Sir James Craig, who had succeeded Edward Carson as UUC leader, became its first Prime Minister. Irish Unionists had failed in their opposition to Home Rule. Ulster Unionists, however, had gained a state within a state from which they could defend both their position in Ireland from Republicanism and their position within the United Kingdom from those within the British government who wished to withdraw completely from Northern Ireland. Northern Ireland did not experience an easy birth and the immediate challenges Ulster Unionism faced from Irish Republicanism marked out the ethno-national divisions between the two communities that would lead to future conflict. The Irish Republican Army's (IRA) assault on Northern Ireland that followed partition, Dublin's attitude towards that movement and the Ulster Unionist Government's response ensured that Northern Ireland developed as 'a place apart' within the United Kingdom, rather than as a unified region of it.[14] The parameters of ethno-national division were therefore indelibly drawn between Unionists and Nationalists from the inception of Northern Ireland. Consequently, Ulster Unionists excluded Irish Nationalists from the government of their new political homeland.

In the inter-war years Northern Ireland did not meet its potential within the United Kingdom to become a prosperous and economically stable region. Relations with the south remained frosty and the contrast between Irish Taoiseach Eamon de Valera's Catholic Nationalist Ireland and Craig's Protestant Parliament for a Protestant people did not bode well for any political détente between Ireland's two ethno-national groups. Dublin's neutrality in World War Two further symbolized the long-held animosity between the two states which Northern Ireland had come to represent.

After the war, the Ulster Unionist Party exercised control over Northern Ireland and its Protestant majority ensured it won all major elections before Stormont was prorogued following the outbreak of widespread violence in 1972. Ulster Unionism had successfully dealt with the IRA's 1956–62 border campaign, which was also ruthlessly suppressed by the Dublin government.[15] Yet by the time the civil rights movement emerged in the late 1960s, the moment had passed when the UUP might have successfully taken initiatives that would have reformed Northern Ireland in a peaceful fashion. As such, the belated attempts at reform by Ulster Unionist leader, Terence O'Neill, undermined the stability of Northern Ireland.[16] By that stage minor reforms were not going to transform Northern Ireland into a place where Nationalists could comfortably co-exist with Unionists. Introducing socio-economic reforms in the face of a civil rights movement led O'Neill to be attacked by 'not an inch' Unionists for pandering to Nationalist demands and for not going far enough by the Nationalists making those demands. (This was, of course, the unenviable position that any Unionist leader attempting reform would become accustomed to throughout the remainder of the twentieth century and beyond. Such were the challenges facing David Trimble from those opposed to any shift in the idea of Unionist dominance over Nationalism after he unveiled his reformist agenda.)

Despite this, O'Neill was successful in implementing some reforms and promoting better community relations before being displaced as UUP leader. He did, however, fail to 'transform Ulster' in the way he had hoped.[17] Opposition to his plans swelled from within the ranks of his own party and around prominent Unionists outside it, such as the aspiring politician and Protestant preacher, Ian Paisley. By 1967 the movement against Unionist rule had manifested itself in the form of a Northern Ireland Civil Rights Association (NICRA). Catholics lobbied for the same rights within Northern Ireland as they would receive anywhere else within the United Kingdom.[18] Modelling itself on the civil rights movement challenging the US government on the other side of the Atlantic, NICRA demanded radical political and social reform within Northern Ireland, as well as equal rights and citizenship for Catholics. Nationalist leader Gerry Fitt compared Unionism's response to the civil rights movement to the Soviet Union's reaction to the uprising in Czechoslovakia occuring at the same time.[19]

O'Neill's reforms were viewed as too little too late by Nationalists. With hindsight it seems obvious that there was little he could have done to undo the years of Unionist misrule in the eyes of the Nationalist community. But by 1969, Nationalist leaders dominated the civil rights movement and had shifted its agenda from civil rights towards meeting Nationalist Republican political goals. The Unionist government met this challenge with brute force, the IRA renewed its terror campaign against British rule in Northern Ireland, and the British deployed troops to protect the Catholic community from Loyalist mobs to prevent the outbreak of civil war. These events posed an insurmountable challenge to Unionist rule in Northern Ireland and the situation came to a head in 1972, when the British Government gave Northern Ireland Prime Minister Brian Faulkner a choice between maintaining his government at Stormont without security powers or accepting direct rule from Westminster. For Faulkner who had come to power having earned a hard-line reputation as Home Affairs Minister in the last government there was no choice, as Unionist control without security control was no control at all, and direct rule was imposed from Westminster in March 1972.[20]

Having distanced itself from Northern Ireland's political affairs for decades Britain was suddenly faced with regulating a rapidly escalating ethnic conflict within its state. The outbreak of violence between Northern Ireland's Unionist and Nationalist communities brought the British and Irish governments to reconsider both their diplomatic relations with each other and their attitude towards Northern Ireland. Consequently, in January 1974, Northern Ireland's first power-sharing government between Unionists and Nationalists was established following the Sunningdale Agreement of December 1973. This venture did not survive the tide of anti-Agreement Unionism that swept the Province in its wake, and the power-sharing government collapsing after only five months in office under the weight of the Ulster Workers' Council (UWC) strike in May 1974.[21]

Sunningdale brought a new form of devolved government to Northern Ireland. Power was shared between Unionists and Nationalists through an Assembly elected by proportional representation. To assuage Nationalist demands there was to be a 'Council of Ireland' where representatives of the Assembly and the Irish parliament would meet. Like the Belfast Agreement of 1998,[22] Sunningdale gave the Assembly powers to legislate on most regional matters, while Westminster retained control over security and foreign affairs. The Executive, which was formed on 22 November 1973, consisted of six Ulster Unionists, four Social Democratic and Labour Party (SDLP) Nationalists, and one Alliance Party member. Brian Faulkner and the SDLP leader, Gerry Fitt, headed the Executive, taking up the positions of Chief and Deputy Chief Executive, respectively.

Many Ulster Unionists rejected Sunningdale on the basis of their opposition to the concept of power-sharing and the Agreement's Irish dimension. It was the latter point, however, around which they fostered support amongst the Unionist community to undermine it. The Agreement envisaged an all-Ireland ministerial council, whereby the two Irish governments would 'consult and co-ordinate' on issues of mutual interest, such as agriculture, tourism and transport.[23] The problem for Unionists was that this dimension had the potential to develop and expand after devolution had taken place.[24]

Ian Paisley, Vanguard leader William Craig and other Unionist leaders immediately rejected the British government's proposals in the belief that resistance could force a return to the old Stormont government.[25] Under pressure from the British Prime Minister, Edward Heath, Brian Faulkner cautiously welcomed the government's power-sharing proposals. The UUP leader then made a fatal mistake by allowing his party to split over whether to accept them or not. Before Northern Ireland Assembly elections were held his party divided between those 'pledged' and 'unpledged' in their support.[26] The jostling for position had begun within the Unionist camp. O'Neill's demise was fresh in the minds of all those considering whether to back the government's reforms or try to take control of the UUP while its leader was exposed.[27]

When the Assembly elections were held on 28 June 1973, anti-Agreement Unionists picked up 26 seats to Brian Faulkner's 24, severely constraining his room for manœuvre before devolution took place. If he was going to sell the idea of a Council of Ireland to Unionists as something harmless to their interests, Faulkner desperately needed the Irish government to publicly accept Northern Ireland's constitutional position within the United Kingdom. When the Sunningdale negotiations took place on 6 to 9 December 1973, Brian Faulkner made it clear to both governments that he was going to have grave trouble advocating the Council of Ireland to the Unionist electorate. The problem for Faulkner at Sunningdale was that he had previously agreed to have an Irish dimension in Northern Ireland's devolved government during talks with Secretary of State Willie Whitelaw and the SDLP. He failed to significantly alter that position or the public's perception of it during the Sunningdale negotiations.[28] As soon as the parties emerged from the talks the anti-Agreement coalition leaders dismissed it as a sell-out to Nationalism. This was a key lesson David Trimble learnt while negotiating the Belfast Agreement. In 1998 nothing was agreed until everything was agreed.

The anti-Agreement Unionists who had been excluded from the Sunningdale negotiations by Prime Minister Heath quickly gained support around their opposition to the Irish dimension. It was a 'Catch 22' situation for the British government. Had the opposition been included at Sunningdale they would have undoubtedly disrupted the talks. Excluding them, however, meant they could claim the British government was ignoring the majority of Unionist opinion, which it was. Such was their anger during the talks that members of the DUP and William Craig's Vanguard Unionist Loyalist Coalition (VULC)[29] physically assaulted Brian Faulkner's 'pledged' Unionists at the Stormont Assembly.[30]

Just as devolution was taking place, Brian Faulkner's party had split beyond his control and he resigned as UUP leader on 7 January 1974. The Sunningdale question was then put to the Northern Ireland electorate as Prime Minister Heath called an early election on 28 February.[31] Standing as the United Ulster Unionist Council (UUUC) and under the slogan of 'Dublin is just a Sunningdale away',[32] the anti-Agreement candidates won 11 of 12 seats, polling just over 51 per cent of the vote. Consequently, they claimed a popular mandate for the rejection of Heath's power-sharing Agreement.[33]

Regardless of democratic setbacks such as the general election defeat, the power-sharing Executive and devolved government continued to function well despite the weight of opposition against it. Consequently, by Easter 1974, the UUUC's constitutional opposition to Brian Faulkner's power-sharing venture was running out of steam. Another form of opposition then emerged in the unlikely form of an Ulster Workers' Council (UWC).[34] This grouping, which was largely under the control of the Protestant paramilitary force, the Ulster Defence Association (UDA), had the backing of the new UUP leader, Harry West, Vanguard leader, William Craig, and Ian Paisley. As its chairman, Glen Barr, put it, membership of the two bodies was 'synonymous'.[35] The Unionist leaders were subsequently co-opted onto the UWC to give it political legitimacy.[36] However, they only threw their full weight behind it when it looked like becoming a vehicle for popular Protestant opinion.[37]

A vote still had to be taken in the Stormont Assembly on the ratification of the Council of Ireland, and to coincide with it the UWC leaders announced that a strike would begin at 6pm on 14 May. Once the Assembly had passed an amendment endorsing Sunningdale – by 44 votes to 28 – the UWC, whose supporters controlled Northern Ireland's electricity power stations, slowly began to reduce output across the province. The following day they declared a provisional government, inserting roadblocks on major road arteries across Northen Ireland and preventing people from going to work with a mixture of intimidation and grass roots Loyalist support. As the strike gained momentum the UUUC leaders met the new Secretary of State, Merlyn Rees, at Stormont to warn him that the stoppage could bring Northern Ireland to its knees. During talks they demanded that the government negotiate with the UWC but Rees, who could not, would not.[38] By the end of the strike's first week Northern Ireland had largely ceased to function.

Brian Faulkner then attempted to water down the impact of the Council of Ireland and retrieve the situation by delaying its executive functions. He announced that there would be a 're-phasing' of the Council's functions until after the next Northern Ireland Assembly elections, which was agreed with the SDLP.[39] But the UWC's power was now indisputable and while Brian Faulkner's executive clung on, the UUUC rejected its 're-phasing' mechanism with Paisley, labelling it Sunningdale 'in two spoonfuls' rather than one.[40] After two weeks of the strike the Executive was forced to resign. On 28 May, Brian Faulkner's Assembly backbenchers told him that he could no longer count on their support, granting the Executive's opponents a majority in the Assembly. In a fortnight the UWC strike had indeed brought Northern Ireland to its knees, humiliated the British government and consigned Sunningdale to history.

The question remained, however, as to why Sunningdale had actually failed and what lessons the UUP could learn from this. First, the power-sharing Executive collapsed primarily due to the fact that a large proportion of the Unionist élite lacked the will to negotiate an inclusive political settlement with Nationalists. Many of them were foolish enough to believe that they could force a return to majority rule goverment at Stormont with political concessions that fell short of a power-sharing administration with an Irish dimension. Second, Sunningdale failed because Anglo–Irish relations were at an elementary phase, the two governments were domestically weak, and Prime Minister Heath did not attempt to find a political balance between the Unionist and Nationalist élites that could be sold as an acceptable formula for government to their constituencies. Third, the Irish government pushed for too much concerning the all-Ireland Council, whereas Faulkner accepted too much. Nationalist leaders could have accepted less and sold a deal to their community. Had Brian Faulkner enjoyed the support of the British government he might have gained more in the negotiations and stood a better chance of selling Sunningdale to Unionism. That, however, would have been no guarantee that Sunningdale would have succeeded as the first two reasons alone were more than enough to ensure its failure.

Sunningdale illustrated that power-sharing with an Irish dimension could not be successfully imposed in Northern Ireland without the consent of the majority of the Unionist population. Sunningdale was, however, a benchmark for future progress on regulating the conflict between the two states. Crucially, the principle of consent first came to be recognized by sections of both governments as the key to any Sunningdale settlement. This power-sharing venture also illustrated the difficulty of fixing a constitutional regulation of the conflict in the absence of ceasefires and through excluding those who resorted to terrorism or unconstitutional methods to further their political goals.

There were many lessons to be learnt from the Sunningdale experiment, and it was the formula the British government returned to in 1998. It illustrated the potential for something to be done within the context of improving Anglo–Irish relations and laid the foundations for any future settlement. Whilst many Unionists were slow to realize it, it was Sunningdale and not the Anglo–Irish Agreement of 1985 that first signalled the British government's willingness to administer Northern Ireland over their heads and create an all-Ireland framework within which to do so.

Brian Faulkner's unusual decision to demand public 'pledging' to his policies left him with a weak mandate for power-sharing and a party split ahead of Assembly elections. He lacked therefore a strong base from which to promote his power-sharing strategy.[41] Having failed to prevent his party from splitting, Brian Faulkner was forced to proceed with a weakened Assembly team, as most of the influential Unionists had declared themselves 'unpledged'.

In the wake of Sunningdale Anglo–Irish relations worsened and the two governments failed to build on the urgency and cordiality that enabled them to broker that deal. Consequently, other than proposals to form a voluntary coalition under the constitutional convention which ended Craig's career,[42] little progress was achieved until British Prime Minister Margaret Thatcher's second term. British policy on Northern Ireland was by then one of military containment. Margaret Thatcher, however, hoped that the Irish government would cooperate with her in order to achieve greater stability in Northern Ireland in return for political concessions regarding its Nationalist community.

On 15 November 1985, Margaret Thatcher and the Irish Prime Minister, Garret FitzGerald, signed the Anglo–Irish Agreement. This committed both states to working closely on Northern Ireland through a joint ministerial council focusing on issues of concern to the Nationalist community.[43] In their attempt to halt the advance of Sinn Féin following the hunger strikes in 1981, the two governments returned to the constitutional issue that had undermined Sunningdale – the Irish dimension. Yet they had not learnt the lesson of the 1974 strike. To Margaret Thatcher's surprise,[44] the Anglo–Irish Agreement (AIA) prompted massive Unionist protest as the government had excluded the entire Unionist élite from the Agreement's negotiation.[45]

Failing to secure a referendum on the AIA, the UUP ended all co-operation with the government. Consequently, 15 Unionist MPs resigned *en masse* prompting a 'mini-referendum' through by-elections in January 1986.[46] Margaret Thatcher had been persuaded by British officials, who had kept in regular contact with their Irish counterparts since Sunningdale, that the only way to advance the security situation in Northern Ireland was to allow the Republic a measure of responsibility for its Nationalist community. She assumed that if Britain conceded a limited role for Dublin in Northern Ireland's affairs, the security situation in the North could be improved through close border co-operation with the Republic.[47] After 1986 it became clear that the AIA had failed. Subsequently, Margaret Thatcher was only interested in the security aspect of the Agreement and damage limitation *vis-à-vis* the Unionists. Where then did this leave Unionism and the UUP's ability to alter the dynamics of politics in Northern

20

Ireland? Unionism had never been in worse shape and the UUP's then leader, James Molyneaux, had entered the cul-de-sac of Ian Paisley's oppositionist politics. The AIA itself failed because Margaret Thatcher viewed it from a minimalist security position and Garret FitzGerald was not going to concede anything on the Republic's territorial claim to Northern Ireland as laid out in Articles Two and Three of the Irish constitution in the absence of serious political reform.[48] From a Unionist perspective opposition to the Agreement had also failed as it left Ulster Unionism isolated within its own country and with nowhere to go politically within Northern Ireland.

In November 1986 Sinn Féin leaders Gerry Adams and Martin McGuinness ended the party's policy of abstention over taking seats in the Irish Parliament.[49] As a result of the political victories Sinn Féin had enjoyed from the hunger strikes, such as the election of Bobby Sands as MP for Fermanagh and South Tyrone, the IRA then employed what became known as 'the Armalite and the ballot box' strategy.[50] SDLP leader John Hume had begun talks with Gerry Adams in order to convince him that the British government no longer held an interest in Ireland and that it was actually IRA violence that impeded the departure of British troops.[51]

By the end of the 1980s both the British and Irish governments were engaged in secret talks with Republicans.[52] Secretary of State for Northern Ireland, Peter Brooke, signalled to the IRA that Britain could not foresee a military solution to the conflict.[53] He stressed that the British government would be 'flexible and imaginative' should Republicans end their campaign of violence.[54] More significantly, he declared that the government he represented had 'no selfish strategic or economic interest in Northern Ireland'.[55]

In 1993 this talks process culminated in the Downing Street Declaration (DSD), which British Prime Minister John Major and Taoiseach Albert Reynolds signed on 15 December of that year. It stated that:

> The achievement of peace must involve a permanent end to the use of, or support for, paramilitary violence ... in these circumstances, democratically mandated parties which establish a commitment to exclusively peaceful methods and which have shown that they abide by the democratic process, are free to

participate fully in democratic politics and to join in dialogue in due course between the Governments and the political parties on the way ahead.[56]

This paved the way for an inclusive political process which Republicans could join if they gave up violence. The DSD marked a turning point in the conflict, and a shift in British policy on Northern Ireland as it opened up the possibility of Republicans being included in a formal talks process at some later date. Whilst Republicans had been moving slowly towards the idea of a ceasefire, a parallel process of dialogue existed between Loyalist paramilitaries and the British and Irish governments, which aimed to achieve the same goals. Community leaders, such as Archbishop Robin Eames, had been meeting Loyalists to reassure them that no secret deal had been done with the IRA behind their backs and that the principle of consent would be central to any deal.[57] Taoiseach Albert Reynolds also personally met with the Combined Loyalist Military Command (CLMC) in Dublin to reassure them of the sincerity of the Irish government's intentions in the process.[58]

Republicans slowly emerged from the cold as Taoiseach Albert Reynolds drew US President Bill Clinton into the process and persuaded him to grant Gerry Adams a visa to visit the US on 29 Janaury 1994.[59] On 31 August that year, the IRA finally announced its ceasefire. British Prime Minister John Major, whose domestic position was weakening in parliament, immediately called for its 'permanence' to be clarified as a pre-condition of Sinn Féin's entry into talks.[60] Senior UUP MP John Taylor (now Lord Kilclooney) indicated a positive response from his party remarking that his 'gut reaction' was that this ceasefire was 'for real'.[61] This was followed six weeks later by the CLMC's own cessation.[62] This body represented the two main Protestant paramilitary groups, the UDA and the UVF. They had come to accept the DSD and signalled their willingness to engage with the political process.[63]

On 22 February 1995, John Major, and Albert Reynolds' successor as Taoiseach, John Bruton, published the Framework Documents. These detailed possible arrangements for a future Northern Ireland Assembly.[64] However, the political process flagged over the next couple of years as John Major's House of Commons majority disappeared and the IRA spectacularly ended its ceasefire on 9 February 1996 with the Canary Wharf bombing in London. The arrival of Tony Blair in Downing Street on 1 May 1997, with a majority of 178 quickly rejuvenated the process. The other significant arrival at the forefront of Anglo–Irish politics was that of Bertie Ahern, who became Taioseach on 6 June. The two governments then appointed former US Senator George Mitchell as Chairman of the plenary talks in Northern Ireland. Assisting him were Canadian General John de Chastelain and the ex-Prime Minister of Finland, Harri Holkerri. The two premiers were not the only new leaders bringing dynamism to Northern Ireland's flagging political process. On 8 September 1995 the UUP had replaced James Molyneaux as its leader with Queen's University Belfast Law lecturer and Upper Bann MP David Trimble.

The New Labour British Prime Minister marked his intention to take ownership of the process begun by Albert Reynolds and John Major. He indicated that an unequivocal ceasefire from the IRA would see Sinn Féin's immediate inclusion in the talks process.[65] Following Tony Blair's assertion that they could join the talks if they signed up to the Mitchell Principles of democracy,[56] the IRA swiftly reinstated its ceasefire from 20 July 1997. Sinn Féin's inclusion days later prompted the DUP and Robert McCartney's United Kingdom Unionist Party (UKUP), to permanently withdraw from the talks. This left the UUP in the unenviable position of either following them out of the door, or going it alone to negotiate a deal with Nationalism on behalf of the Unionist community. It was the defining moment for Unionism in the political process and David Trimble re-entered the talks ignoring the predictable stance of the two right wing Unionist parties. He did so alongside the two smaller Loyalist parties, the Progressive Unionist Party (PUP) and the Ulster Democratic Party (UDP), who represented the UVF and UDA, respectively. Between them the three parties represented the majority of Unionism. David Trimble's actions indicated that the radical and positive change he had brought to Ulster Unionism had taken root. His UUP team were there to cut a deal on behalf of Unionism, with or without the DUP and UKUP.[67] This marked a dramatic shift in Unionist politics.

On 12 January 1998, the two governments presented the 'Propositions on Heads of Agreement' document to the Northern Ireland parties for negotiation.[68] This outlined the key constitutional changes envisaged between the United Kingdom and Ireland regarding the 1920 Ireland Act and Articles 2 and 3 of the Irish Constitution. It sketched out what North–South bodies, an Intergovernmental Conference and a new British–Irish agreement to replace the AIA might look like. Senator Mitchell then gave the parties two weeks to reach agreement over a draft before the Easter holiday weekend.

The draft agreement's Irish dimension was, however, far 'too green'[69] for the UUP and Lord Kilclooney famously announced that he would not touch it 'with a forty-foot barge pole'.[70] The document was then renegotiated when the two premiers rushed to Belfast to deal with the impending crisis – Ahern coming straight from his mother's funeral. Unlike Sunningdale, the Irish government's position over the Irish dimension was renegotiable. They had over-negotiated on strand two and Tony Blair, unlike Edward Heath, backed the Ulster Unionist leader on this issue before a deal was finalized on 10 April 1998. This enabled David Trimble to go to his electorate with a considerable constitutional victory on which to sell the agreement. Ironically, when the DUP leader Ian Paisley turned up to protest outside Stormont against the proposed accord, he was heckled and subdued by the very Loyalists he had rallied and used 25 years earlier to cause the collapse of the Sunningdale Executive. Politics in Northern Ireland had come full circle.

The Agreement itself was shaped into three strands. Strand one addressed the workings of the Northern Ireland Assembly. Strands two and three provided for a North–South Ministerial Council, a British–Irish Council and a British–Irish Intergovernmental Conference. The Agreement also addressed the issues of decommissioning, security, policing, justice and political prisoners. The two governments dealt with the historic constitutional issues that had dominated the debate over Northern Ireland since partition.

The Irish government declared its intent to amend Articles 2 and 3 of its constitution, which made sovereign territorial claims to Northern Ireland. The British repealed the Government of Ireland Act 1920, notwithstanding any previous enactment and provided for referenda to determine whether a future majority for unification existed. As such, the Belfast Agreement signalled the acceptance of an internal political settlement within Northern Ireland by almost all strands of Nationalism and the pursuit of Republican goals by political means alone.

24

David Trimble had been determined to hammer down a strand two section that Unionists could feel comfortable with, guaranteeing them a veto over any all-Ireland decision-making process and leaving accountability and control with the Assembly. This was Unionism's constitutional imperative. Securing it meant David Trimble had been successful in negotiating the constitutional issues that were fundamental to Unionism in any settlement with Irish Nationalism. Crucially for Unionists, both governments recognized that any future change to Northern Ireland's constitutional status had to be 'subject to the agreement and consent of a majority of the people of Northern Ireland'.[71] Northern Ireland remained within the United Kingdom and its status could not be altered without the consent of a majority of its people.

Like Sunningdale, the Agreement provided for a proportionally elected, fully devolved, 108-member Assembly to be elected from the existing Westminster constituencies. Where it differed was in its mechanism for electing the Assembly's executive. The d'Hondt electoral system was employed,[72] whereby ten ministers would be nominated on their party's respective electoral strength and be overseen by a dual premiership of first and deputy ministers. The first ministers had to be elected jointly by at least 50 per cent of both Nationalist and Unionist Assembly members. The Agreement sought to bring Northern Ireland and the Republic's executive representatives together to develop 'consultation, co-operation and action within the island of Ireland' as a whole.[73] But unlike Sunningdale, it tied the decision-making process to the Northern Ireland Assembly and the Irish Parliament, thus providing Unionists with a veto in Northern Ireland on its functions. Furthermore, the list of areas open for discussion in 1998 was considerably smaller than Sunningdale's all-Ireland proposals. To complement that, a British–Irish Council was introduced to help promote harmonious and mutually beneficial development between all parts of the United Kingdom and Ireland.

Of course the Agreement had its drawbacks for both Unionists and Nationalists. Republicans undertook political u-turns by engaging in a process that could not deliver what the Provisional IRA had been fighting for since 1970, that is, the immediate withdrawal of British troops from Northern Ireland and the achievement of a united Ireland. This is a point often unappreciated by the Unionist community when it assesses the Agreement. The issues of decommissioning, prisoner releases and police reform were to David Trimble what the Council of Ireland was to Brian Faulkner. The difference for David Trimble was that the impact of these issues did not seriously damage him before the parties reached agreement.

If the DUP and UKUP had remained in the talks then Sinn Féin could not possibly have gained as much on the security issues as they actually did. Had the anti-Agreement parties in fact negotiated the Belfast Agreement, Unionism's negotiating strength would have almost doubled and either a different agreement would have materialized or indeed no agreement would have been forthcoming. The latter is the more likely of the two outcomes. Unionism had to lose on something symbolic such as policing or prisoners for Sinn Féin to accept an internal settlement. Without this quid pro quo there would have been no agreement at all. It is unlikely this could have been achieved if Unionism had been united. It would also be foolish to assume that Ian Paisley would have supported or accepted a better agreement for Unionism than the one David Trimble negotiated, had it been on offer to him in 1998.

It is ironic that in 1973 the political exclusion of the anti-Agreement Unionists allowed a deal to be brokered by a weakened UUP, yet their self-exclusion in 1998 again enabled their rivals to negotiate a settlement. It also precipitated the crisis within Unionism that followed the accord. On the other hand, while the exclusion of the anti-Agreement Unionists in 1973 aided the UWC strike, the inclusion of the small Loyalist parties in 1998, with their desire to work alongside the UUP, ruled out the prospect of a similar anti-Agreement campaign. Along with the support of the British political establishment, this allowed David Trimble to negotiate a deal.

The ink was not dry on the Agreement before David Trimble's future difficulties were being shaped. His was the very same dilemma that faced any Unionist leader attempting to reach a settlement with Nationalism over Northern Ireland's future. Could a Unionist leader go out in front of his constituency and survive the challenges from those who saw opposition to the Agreement as an opportunity to replace him as the voice of Unionism? The advantage David Trimble had over Brian Faulkner was that he had kept his talks team united throughout the negotiations and had the backing of a large majority in the UUC. However, Brian Faulkner had not been negotiating in a process that included Sinn Féin, and his constituency had not been on the receiving end of 28 years of violence and terror from their military wing. One of David Trimble's chief negotiators saw the weakness of his position and began his opposition campaign on the day of the Agreement. By walking out of the talks, Jeffery Donaldson threw open a rolling challenge to David Trimble's position as UUP leader, which hampered his every move in implementing the accord. Internal division reflected the uneasy position David Trimble held in brokering a deal on behalf of Unionism, while representing just less than half of its electorate in the talks.

David Trimble had negotiated what he thought was the best deal available to his party under the circumstances. Jeffery Donaldson was not alone in his disagreement, as others felt David Trimble should have walked away at the last minute. There were many within the party who felt that David Trimble should not bow to the pressure of 'deadlines' and 'timeframes' which dictated the political process over the future of Northern Ireland at Tony Blair's insistence.[74] It was the old question in Irish politics – whether there would be more or less bread on the table should you leave and return. Jeffery Donaldson thought there would be more, and had John Taylor not supported David Trimble on the day there might well have been no agreement at all. Crucially for David Trimble, the Strangford MP backed his stance on the accord and swung a lot of the UUC with him. David Trimble's chief of staff, David Campbell, suggests that the 'single biggest influence on David going ahead would have been John Taylor. The fact that John supported him made him feel that he had firm support. John is probably the most accurate barometer of Unionist thinking on the ground in many ways. I think his backing gave David the momentum to go forward.'[75] In contrast, Brian Faulkner lacked someone of John Taylor's stature to bolster him at Sunningdale and subsequently sell the deal to the Unionist electorate.

During the negotiations David Trimble did not consider walking out on Tony Blair lightly.[76] The UUP leader had a deep sense of loyalty to the British Prime Minister for the balance he had sought and maintained between Unionism and Nationalism during the negotiations. This was in stark contrast to Edward Heath's treatment of Brian Faulkner 25 years earlier. So, with John Taylor's support, David Trimble announced that he 'didn't think there was anything more to negotiate'.[77] He said he was 'going upstairs' and 'we are going with this'.[78] Fundamentally, David Trimble and John Taylor trusted the British Prime Minister to honour his commitments under the Agreement. They trusted him to force Republicans to follow through on their pledges to decommission before allowing an executive to be formed and this was key to his agreement on Good Friday morning.[79] Tony Blair had written a letter to David Trimble assuring him that Sinn Féin would not be included in government prior to decommissioning shortly before the parties came to agreement.[80] Tony Blair then went to great lengths to consolidate that impression with the Unionist electorate. He made a speech at Coleraine, signing five hand-written pledges which were then distributed across the province as posters. He promised that 'those who use or threaten violence' would be 'excluded from the government of Northern Ireland' and that 'prisoners would be kept in prison unless violence was given up for good'.[81]

Republicans did put weapons beyond use, but not within the timeframe that David Trimble had expected, so he was forced to form an executive with Sinn Féin in the absence of acts of decommissioning. This meant a significant U-turn for David Trimble on the position of 'no guns, no government' that his opponents clung to.[82] Consequently he formed an inclusive executive prior to decommissioning on the premise that Gerry Adams would deliver it in due course. In the event of setting up the executive Tony Blair reneged on his promises to David Trimble and the Unionist community. The UUP Leader agreed to form an executive including Sinn Féin after winning 58 per cent of the UUC. The d'Hondt mechanism was then triggered on 29 November 1999 and an executive was formed, including former IRA commander Martin McGuinness as Education Minister.[83] David Trimble famously declared, 'We've done our bit Mr Adams, it's over to you. We've jumped. You follow.'[84] There was much to be read into that statement thereafter, as the UUP leader became heavily reliant on Republicans keeping their word and equally on Tony Blair holding them to it. Not long into the New Year and it had become apparent that a deal over decommissioning was not forthcoming and the then Secretary of State Peter Mandelson suspended the Assembly on 11 February 2000.[85]

Following an IRA statement on 6 May which indicated its intention to begin a process of 'completely and verifiably' putting arms beyond use,[86] David Trimble won 53 per cent of the UUC in support for plans to re-enter an executive with Sinn Féin at the end of that month.[87] Yet decommissioning from Republicans, complete and verifiable decommissioning that is, was not forthcoming and over the following two years Northern Ireland's political process entered into a phase of almost unending crisis and legislative suspension. This was caused primarily by the inability of Republicans to deliver on their commitment to decommission, or indeed the sort of decommissioning that would have alleviated the pressure on David Trimble, coming from his opponents, that would have enabled him to remain comfortably in an executive that included Sinn Féin.[88] Of course Sinn Féin did not see it like that and felt under no obligation to act in a fashion that would alleviate the Unionist leader's position, even if it would benefit the whole political process.[89]

The implementation phase of the Agreement was marred by the inability of the two governments to square this political circle. David Trimble needed symbolic concessions on the issues of decommissioning and decriminalisation. He also needed a clear sign from the IRA that it intended to stand down if he was to regain the confidence of a majority of his community and go forward with the project. Gerry Adams and Martin McGuinness were certainly not going to deliver decommissioning to the UUP leader's tune, but they had committed themselves to the principle.[90] Their relationship and negotiations with the British government would determine when they did so. The question was open as to whether they were sincere in their commitment to work the Belfast Agreement. David Trimble's position within Unionism in the absence of decommissioning was so precarious in the years that followed the Agreement that for many Republicans it appeared that the UUP leader protested too much. At times Sinn Féin doubted whether his internal difficulties were quite as bad as they appeared.[91]

By October 2003 the Assembly had been suspended since 14 October 2002, following a Police Service of Northern Ireland (PSNI) raid on Sinn Féin's Stormont offices, which was part of an investigation into an alleged Republican intelligence-gathering operation in government.[92] David Trimble then faced what was either his last chance to recover the Belfast Agreement or a political failure that would bring about the demise of his party and mark an end to his attempts to stabilize devolution in Northern Ireland.

Given the prolonged hiatus in the process, Tony Blair had postponed the assembly elections, called on the IRA to make a statement on its intentions, and published the British and Irish governments' proposals for breaking the deadlock between the parties.[93] On 17 June David Trimble again narrowly won a majority in the UUC to go forward with talks to try to implement the Agreement. This dealt Jeffery Donaldson's anti-Agreement movement a crushing blow amidst speculation that he was set to defect to the DUP.[94] David Trimble was battling to maintain his position amidst ever-decreasing circles of support within his own party.[95] The ongoing turmoil in the UUP then culminated when three of David Trimble's MPs – Jeffery Donaldson, David Burnside and the Rev. Martin Smyth – resigned the Party Whip at Westminster.

If a deal was to be reached that would credibly work the Belfast Agreement from the Unionist leader's perspective, decommissioning needed to be on the table up front, verifiable and transparent. These were the symbolic gestures David Trimble needed from the IRA, not just to sell the agreement to the Unionist electorate, but to re-ignite any sense of confidence in that community for an inclusive governmental process with Republicans. UUP negotiator Lady Sylvia Hermon maintains that 'Sinn Féin were in no doubt about what we needed before David could make his statement' in the planned sequencing to restore the institutions.[96] For the UUP, the deal's confidence-building measures were all-important. According to David Trimble, Gerry Adams and Martin McGuinness had agreed that the kind of transparency that he required to create confidence within the Unionist community would be forthcoming from the IRA. This was to occur during the sequencing of events that would revive the political process on the morning of 21 October 2003.[97]

At 7am that morning the British government announced that Assembly elections would be held on 26 November 2003; General de Chastelain declared at a press conference that a third act of IRA decommissioning had occurred. Then the Ulster Unionist leader replied that it lacked the necessary transparency for his party to go forward. David Trimble had put the deal on hold. In a statement the UUP leader said that 'what we needed was a clear, transparent report of major acts of decommissioning of a nature which would have a significant impact on public opinion and demonstrate that we were in a different context. Unfortunately we had not had that; we have not had that at all.'[98] Tony Blair, however, insisted that Assembly elections should go ahead regardless.[99] The British Prime Minister could have halted the process when he saw that General de Chastelain had not delivered the statement that the UUP needed and that David Trimble had been unable to follow up with his prepared statement. The legislative order made under the emergency procedure to call an Assembly election had still to be signed off that evening. The Secretary of State for Northern Ireland, Paul Murphy, accordingly signed that legislation. Lady Sylvia Hermon argues that this 'was a huge error of judgement by Tony Blair because in doing so he relinquished all leverage over the Republican movement to do anything further'.[100]

It was this election date that Sinn Féin had been most concerned with during the sequencing, and having received it from the British Prime Minister they appeared to scupper the deal while the morning's events unravelled. Not only did the act of decommissioning lack the transparency David Trimble needed to proceed, General de Castelain was clearly so physically traumatized by his experience with the IRA that the press conference he held did the very opposite of what the UUP had been hoping for. Lady Sylvia Hermon suspects that Republicans had formed the view that 'Trimble could not deliver the unionist community' so they 'shot it to bits'.[101] It removed any vestige of confidence Unionists had held in the political process and no one in the party felt they could go forward with the deal. Even the most optimistic and progressive member of the UUP's negotiating team felt that the party had been 'led a merry dance and were completely shafted by the Republicans'.[102]

Sinn Féin's intransigence over IRA decommissioning and the British and Irish governments' refusal to punish Republicans for reneging on their commitments under the Belfast Agreement irreparably damaged the UUP in the eyes of the Unionist electorate. Consequently, the UUP and the SDLP lost the Assembly election on 26 November, which left the DUP and Sinn Féin as Northern Ireland's largest and second largest parties, respectively. Jeffery

Donaldson's subsequent defection to Ian Paisley's team on 5 January 2004 further strengthened the DUP's hand.[103] By then, however, anti-Agreement Unionism had little room for manœuvre and Ian Paisley began to drop his oppositionist rhetoric and prepare his party for the quantum leap to pro-Agreement politics.

For me personally the failed sequence of the 2003 UUP–Sinn Féin deal that never was marked the turning-point in David Trimble's political career and the political process as a whole. The moderate centre ground had failed. David Trimble had desperately needed something to deliver to Unionism if he was to survive politically after 2003, whereas Sinn Féin had not. Perhaps they could not resist the opportunity to deliver the blow that undermined modern Unionism's great leader. David Trimble felt he had no option but to try and negotiate a deal regardless of the risks involved, for his whole project was based on the dual premise of political progress and delivering devolution. He simply could not pass up one last chance to make the Agreement work. This was also very much in the nature of the man. The fact that it was David Trimble who put the brakes on that deal was insignificant. The sequence had failed and therefore he had failed. In contrast to the actions of Sinn Féin, David Trimble never publicly went out of his way to make life unbearable within the context of the political process for Republicans or for Tony Blair. He took risks that were necessary to advance the political process and to enable Tony Blair to keep the Belfast Agreement initiative alive.

His Chief of Staff argued that from David Trimble's perspective, 'it was all or nothing at that stage. We had gone so far, we needed one final push to deliver everything – deliver the total decommissioning and total disbandment of the IRA – and only that would change our fortunes electorally.'[104] When I asked David Trimble about this period and the subsequent Assembly election he admitted that 'it was very difficult to run a positive campaign ... particularly coming out of a situation of a failed sequence.' This was the nub of David Trimble's problem within the political process.

I remember sitting in my office one afternoon in April 2001 just before the general election campaign began. David Trimble walked in and told the staff that the election slogan was 'Ulster Unionism Delivering' and to work the campaign around that concept. In my mind this summed up his political leadership in the time I had known him. For the Unionist leader it was always about delivering and what he needed to do within the context of the political process to deliver. That was the Trimble project. He was always attempting to pursue a positive political agenda which did not sit comfortably with the intra-ethnic squabbles of politics in Northern Ireland. The 2003 sequence failed because Republicans had not delivered the transparency that he had hoped for but not necessarily expected. But for David Trimble it wasn't just transparency he was concerned with, for there was also the problem with regard to whether there was going to be a completion to decommissioning. David Trimble admits that he was reliant on 'whether the government was going to do anything during the course of that day that would have provided Unionists with certainty that there would have been completion, both in terms of paramilitary weapons and paramilitarism'. The Unionist leader concluded that 'this was very much an open question and one I very much had my doubts about'.

David Trimble also admitted that while the UUP 'had been pressing the government in the days before that sequence on the issue of completion, we weren't getting a terribly satisfactory response'. He said 'we were simply hoping that things would go right on the day but, of course, they did not go right on the day'. From the perspective of the Trimble project it seems clear that if offered another chance to advance the political process. The Unionist leader was, in his mind at least, obliged to take that chance. The Unionist electorate, however, did not see it that way. David Trimble recalled to me how he encountered one Lurgan voter during the 2003 campaign: 'He told me that he had supported me on previous occasions when we had put Republicans to the test and that we had shown by 2002 that they weren't up to the mark. He then turned to me and said, "so why on earth did you go back again?"'[105]

This was a question many Unionist voters were asking themselves as they went to the polls in the 2003 Assembly election, the 2004 European election and the 2005 general election. The question David Trimble and his supporters were asking themselves was whether they had sufficiently articulated their reasons for doing so and whether that would give Unionists enough cause to continue their support for the Upper Bann MP's efforts to restore devolved government to Northern Ireland. Having been let down by Republicans and the British government, David Trimble had failed to successfully implement the Belfast Agreement and deliver on his 2001 manifesto commitments. It was with these failures in mind that the party went into its 2005 electoral campaign, in its one-hundredth year, to defend its five remaining seats at Westminster and the controversial journey it had taken in transforming Unionism.

2 'Doing the Decent Thing'

Trimble was demonized by the DUP. He was targeted, blamed for everything, and given credit for nothing. People believed the propaganda. Our opposition, which sadly has really been more from the DUP than from Nationalists, totally focused on undermining and destroying Trimble. Sadly, they were assisted by some former Ulster Unionists who instead of promoting the positive achievements of Trimble's time, succumbed to the easy solution. In time, people will recognize what has been achieved. But it's always more difficult to defend decisions that were taken than to oppose them.

Roy Beggs, 8 June 2005

On 8 June 2001, I walked away from the UUP's Belfast headquarters having assisted David Trimble in fighting his second general election campaign as party leader. It had been a politically vicious and physically shattering six weeks and, naively, I left thinking we had suffered a serious defeat. David Trimble himself looks back on it as a 'pretty gruelling' campaign but did not regard the result as a huge setback.[1] The party had lost five of its nine seats and gained two. UUP heavyweights, John Taylor and Ken Maginnis, both stood down before the election. Their seats, Strangford and Fermanagh and South Tyrone, were subsequently lost to the DUP and Sinn Féin, respectively. Three other members of the UUP's old guard fought and lost their seats in that election. Cecil Walker was humiliated by the DUP's Nigel Dodds in North Belfast, William Ross beaten by their East Londonderry candidate, Gregory Campbell, and William Thompson, who had won West Tyrone against the odds in 1997 as a result of a split Nationalist vote, lost to Sinn Féin's Pat Doherty. The UUP did, however, gain two new MPs in that election: Lady Sylvia Hermon convincingly defeated UKUP leader Robert McCartney in North Down; and David Burnside topped the poll in South Antrim, having lost to the Rev. William McCrea the previous year in a by-election caused by the death of Ulster Unionist Clifford Forsythe. This left the party with six seats in the House of Commons after David Trimble, Roy Beggs, the Rev. Martin Smyth and Jeffery Donaldson were returned.

Fast forward four years. We have lost Jeffery Donaldson to the DUP after he quit the party on 18 December 2003,[2] and I am returning to our new HQ at Cunningham House on Belfast's Holywood Road to take my place in the campaign team to defend our remaining five seats. As I boarded my Belfast flight a host of questions were running through my mind. What has the UUP done since 2001 to prepare itself for the titanic battle it faces for the heart and soul of Unionism? What has the party learnt from the 2001 general election campaign? Is 2005 simply the election the UUP has to lose? Or is there something that can be done, even at this late stage, to halt Ian Paisley's DUP in its tracks?

There were certainly those within the UUP who were not expecting any success. David Burnside, for one, thought that the party was seriously under-equipped for the task it faced. He did not think 'the party had learnt anything from 2001', nor did he think its leadership had learnt anything from his South Antrim by-election defeat in 2000,[3] or the 2003 Assembly election defeat. Burnside blamed his party's situation in 2005 on 'head in the sand, out of touch leadership'. Leadership, he argued, which 'on every occasion when there were problems, divided the party rather than uniting it'.[4]

The UUP had received a stark warning that they needed to pull up their socks before 5 May from a *Belfast Telegraph* public opinion poll published on 10 March 2005.[5] The poll's findings sent shockwaves through the UUP. The joke in Cunningham House was that those with their heads in the sand could only feel them from the neck down. But register on the Richter Scale it did, putting the party's Province-wide support at just 16 per cent, the lowest in its hundred year history. In contrast, the DUP had polled their highest ever with 28 per cent, while the SDLP and Sinn Féin were evenly matched with 20 per cent each. This was a 3 per cent mark up for the SDLP and a 3.5 per cent drop for Sinn Féin from the parties' 2003 Assembly election results. With the image problems Republicans had been encountering over recent months it was probably fair to assume that they had lost some support, while another significant section of the Nationalist electorate were too embarrassed to admit they intended to vote for them. The IRA had been blamed for carrying out the largest bank robbery in UK history at Belfast's Northern Bank on 20 December 2004[6] and subsequently for the brutal murder of Robert McCartney at Magennis' Bar in Belfast on 30 January 2005.[7] The *Belfast Telegraph* poll indicated, however, that only 32 per cent of Catholics thought the IRA were responsible for that robbery, while 65 per cent of Catholics said they felt satisfied with Sinn Féin's response to Robert McCartney's murder. This was a finding as shocking to those inside Cunningham House as was the UUP's predicted electoral disaster. While Republicans had actually made the best of a bad situation, by inviting McCartney's grieving relatives to its Ard-Fheis, the IRA made a mockery of Sinn Féin's diplomacy by volunteering to assassinate Robert McCartney's killers.[8]

Ironically, these incidents seemed to have hurt the UUP more than Sinn Féin, as Unionist opposition hardened towards the idea of going into government with those accused of recent criminal and paramilitary activities. The allegations of robbery and murder failed to halt the advance of Sinn Féin's vote in the Republic. It actually increased by three per cent in a county by-election in Meath.[9] For Ulster Unionists there seemed little to be optimistic about as the *Belfast Telegraph*'s prediction was lower than the party's 2004 European parliamentary election performance, where Jim Nicholson's seat was retained with just 16.6 per cent of the vote.[10] The *Belfast Newsletter*'s headline illustrated the growing 'media consensus' as to where Ulster Unionism was electorally.[11] It read 'Nicholson is swept home on DUP wave.'[12]

It was with these thoughts and fears that I set out for Cunningham House on 30 March 2005. The party had sold its claustrophobic, Victorian pile at Glengall Street in central Belfast back in 2003 and I had never visited the new headquarters before. The Glengall Street offices had been squeezed between Belfast's Europa Hotel and the Royal Opera House. Having survived multiple IRA bombing campaigns it had since been peacefully reduced to a car park. On arrival I found Cunningham House to be a modern, if architecturally unattractive, functional two-storey office building on the edge of East Belfast. Unionist heartland.

On my first night back in Belfast, on what was the first page of my 2005 campaign diary, I reflected on the UUP pre-election gathering at the Mandarin Chinese restaurant on the Newtownards Road. Present were Campaign Chief Tim Lemon, Policy Officers Dr Brian Crowe and Alison Laird, Westminster Officer Claire Kirk, Website Manager David Christopher and myself.

30 March 2005

The atmosphere this evening is pessimistic and the discussion black. Everyone mulls over the *Belfast Telegraph* poll and whether we can significantly increase on that over the coming weeks.

'Sixteen per cent syndrome' has firmly taken root. Regardless of whether the prediction accurately reflects public opinion or not, its effect on staff morale has been devastating. Brian, the party's policy supremo, is the most pessimistic.

I had first met him in Serbia where we were training local councillors on how to run constituency offices and canvass potential voters for support. As we set off from Heathrow we joked that perhaps we ought to try the same thing in Northern Ireland some time.

When we arrived in the Vojvodina province of Northern Serbia, the girl at the hotel desk smiled at Brian and said 'How are you sir?' Brian smiled back, leaned across the counter and said, 'I'm an economic, social and constitutional conservative.' I headed for the bar before she started on me.

Brian and I differed in our political outlook on almost everything, so there was a lot to argue about over a weekend in the Balkans. The joke in HQ was that he was so right wing he made Genghis Khan look like a Marxist. As I quickly discovered, these sentiments were well founded. I suggested to him one afternoon, in jest of course, that once he had saved the union he should go east and free Palestine, of its Palestinians. Before he laughed I'd swear I saw a 'now there's an idea' look on his face. Tim Lemon joked that if we lost the election

George Bush would have a space waiting for him in the militant wing of the Jewish lobby.

Brian Crowe's analysis is that the *Belfast Telegraph* poll showed how irrelevant it would be to run a 'centrist' campaign in 2005 – not least because it revealed that a majority of Roman Catholics did not believe the IRA committed the Northern Bank robbery. How on earth, he argues, was a 'shared future' possible with the minority community refusing to face facts concerning the IRA? Therefore, for people like Crowe, the idea of the 'centre' is a complete myth. He argues that the party's top brass seemed to have simply ignored the poll and that any attempt to raise the issue for discussion has been swept aside as irrelevant. Yet there are senior dissenting voices.

Lord Kilclooney had warned David Trimble and the UUP's Peers of the poll's accuracy during a private dinner at Crockfords Casino in London, on 23 March, which was hosted by the former deputy treasurer of the Conservative Party, Lord Steinberg. Kilclooney told his colleagues that the party was on a 'downward spiral' and, if it did not take 'drastic action', was facing a severe defeat. Kilclooney's remarks were not well received by the UUP leader and he later remarked that Lord Laird was the only member of the parliamentary party present who seemed to be taking the poll seriously.[13]

Yet the leadership itself has been deeply shocked by the poll's findings. Party Vice-Chairman David Campbell, or 'The Undertaker' as he is affectionately known in HQ, tells me how personally disappointed he is by them. Campbell is called 'the undertaker' because he glides through a room, ashen-faced and dressed in black, without ever saying a word. He nods gently while picking up a paper or setting down a bag and then glides out again in silence. He has been David Trimble's negotiator, aide, right-hand man and trouble-shooter throughout the post-Agreement period.

But no one in HQ ever seems to have any idea what it is he actually does. What they are sure of though, is that he does it in complete silence. He is one of those people who is aware of everything that is going on, yet possesses the ability to tell no one anything about it.

Something which is a very rare quality in the minefield of gossip that is Irish politics.

I first came across Campbell in 2000 at Westminster but I had heard of him before from Nationalists who had been negotiating the Belfast Agreement. One former SDLP Minister told me that Campbell was a person who would sit in meetings or negotiations listening and saying very little. But when he did speak everybody would sit up and take notice. And so did I, as one of the first things I noticed when I met him was just how analytically bright he was compared to many of his peers. He is also a very personable man when you got to know him but, I guess, not a lot of people know that.

He tells me he is very disappointed by the poll and gutted by its impact, as we had had a really fantastic centenary weekend just before it was published. Everyone was on a high and the morale of the party had been boosted.

He tells me that when he met with David Trimble that week in London DT was also extremely shocked. Campbell said, 'we heard about it and our hearts stopped because really all the good of that weekend had been undone in one fell swoop. It was hard to comprehend.'

I knew what he was talking about as I had handed David Trimble the poll results at Westminster as they came through on the *Belfast Telegraph*'s website. I had been sorely tempted to knock, slide them under his door and duck for cover.

But it wasn't just that the party was on a high because of the centenary weekend. HQ had been running what seemed to be a very successful leaflet-dropping campaign across the Province. Website Manager, David Christopher, the party's eccentric computer whizz-kid from Galway, tells me that before the poll came out they were coming to the close of that campaign, having distributed over 1.2 million leaflets on 6 different topics across the Province.

David, or Dr Who as Trimble's police escorts called him on account of his unusual dress sense, tells me about the 'positive feedback' coming in and that people are beginning to feel 'quite optimistic' about the election on the back of it. He says when the 16 per cent poll figure hit the front pages it was a 'real kick in the teeth'. It brought home 'the magnitude of the challenge we are facing'.

What the party leadership has missed is that the Unionist electorate have moved into a completely negative position as far as Republicans are concerned. As one unsympathetic Belfast journalist puts it to me, 'you can't jump first twice you know. It just doesn't make sense. And if you try it you'll either trip up in front of everybody or fall backwards trying to steady yourself.'

I've only been back in Northern Ireland 12 hours and I am already tiring of Irish humour.

Election Chief Tim Lemon seems nervous. Well he is nervous. He is, after all, the UUP's elections chief. I had met Tim in 2001 during the previous campaign where he was running against Peter Robinson in East Belfast on a 'the future's bright, the future's Lemon' ticket, mimicking the mobile phone advert for Orange. For this, naturally, Tim remained the butt of many jokes, but the slogan summed him up as he is a positive, optimistic and likeable character and while definitely Lemon, not half as bitter as the man who beat him in that election. I actually stole his idea and gave it to some young Yushchenko supporters in Ukraine last year as their revolutionary colour was orange. They seemed to like it too.

One thing is for sure, the troops have yet to be rallied, they are hungry for a good policy, and the DUP clearly have one – get rid of us. The one we have, Trimble's call to scrap d'Hondt, sounds like a Free Presbyterian ban on posh Belgian beers. We'd be lucky if the political anoraks, who spend their Friday nights mulling over the minutiae of electoral systems and wondering how they might find their way out of Belfast's Linen Hall Library without a map, pay it any heed.

As we leave I notice Secretary of State Paul Murphy at the next table enjoying what might possibly be his last supper in Belfast. He is well respected within the Party – he would be missed if Blair shuffled him off to Whitehall.

41

April Fool's Day

'Joker hijacks website domain before Allister can register it'[14]

Round one to the UUP!

A Young Unionist member (who wishes to remain anonymous) today put egg on the DUP's bib at the beginning of a month's electioneering.

DUP MEP Jim Allister had unwisely installed a huge sign on the front of his East Belfast office – **WWW.JIMALLISTER.COM** – without actually buying the domain name.

DUP hackers got a shock when they logged on to find Jim had put his web sign up but forgotten to buy a website. The domain name had not been purchased by anyone nor the site properly installed. In the meantime he was gazumped by the Young Unionist hacker. The site now reads: **'TOO SLOW JIM!'** with a link redirecting cyber-squatters to the Ulster Unionist's official webpage.

Responding to this cunning trick the DUP's Jim Allister said:
'The Young Unionists' puerile stunt in relation to my website [sorry Jim, I'll have to stop you there – its clearly **not** your website] only succeeds in drawing attention to Mr Nicholson's lack, after 15 years in Europe, of not just a website [you still haven't got it Jim – you don't have one, you only have a sign] but, more importantly, a High Street constituency office.'[15]

Like, yeh, Jim, that's just exactly what it drew my attention to – cyberspace-cadet.

The UUP's 2001 Westminster election campaign had been about delivering the Trimble project. Failing that, its 2003 Assembly election campaign should have been about going back into government with Sinn Féin after a substantive act of transparent IRA decommissioning.

In five weeks' time, what will the 2005 Westminster election be remembered for? Had events transpired as the two governments intended, by April 2005 the DUP would have been well on their way to setting up a power-sharing administration with Sinn Féin. Ian Paisley's DUP had accepted the British and Irish governments' proposals for a comprehensive agreement in December of 2004.[16] When it became apparent that no transparent decommissioning would be forthcoming, the DUP leader began arguing that the IRA needed 'to be humiliated' and that they should publicly wear 'sack cloth and ashes' for their crimes.[17] This killed off all hopes of a pre-Christmas deal and the DUP were very lucky to have walked away when they did, as the IRA were subsequently blamed for carrying out the Northern Bank robbery and the McCartney murder in the following two months. UUP Chief Whip Roy Beggs said they were 'one grubby Polaroid away from sharing power with the biggest bank robbers in European history'.[18]

So what were the issues the UUP would fight its 2005 campaign on, and what were its core policies? In my mind the UUP faced the same dilemma as the Conservative Party on mainland Britain. There were no cataclysmic election issues for David Trimble's party to get its teeth into. Every good policy initiative the Conservatives had come up with over the last year had been stolen by the Labour Party, polished, and spun out the front door of 10 Downing Street. The DUP had done the same thing to the Ulster Unionists.

The UUP's new policy on Sinn Féin was that the IRA must 'disarm, disband and desist' before they would be fit to go back into government with.[19] At the UUP's Annual General Meeting on 5 March 2005, David Trimble argued that they should 'release politics from the d'Hondt straight-jacket' as it granted the 'IRA a veto on political progress'.[20] The DUP were also scrapping d'Hondt and calling for greater local accountability to be vested in the legislative process in the absence of devolved government.[21] Moreover, they were demanding a voluntary coalition with the SDLP as a panacea to all Northern Ireland's ailments.[22]

The UUP needed a message, a policy and, a media strategy and it needed them fast. During the first Cunningham House war room brain-storming sessions the obvious political factors rose to the surface. The comprehensive proposals had been sold by the DUP as something resembling the 'fair deal' they promised Unionists in their

2003 Assembly election manifesto.[23] As David Trimble put it, they had been trying to give the public the 'impression that they could achieve political progress without any of the awkward bits'.[24] This 'fair deal' manifesto provided the reassurances that many Unionist voters wanted to hear:

> *I don't want four more years of Trimble's concessions*

> *I don't want an amnesty for on-the-run terrorists*

> *I don't want [Sinn Féin's] Gerry Kelly as Minister for Policing and Justice*[25]

The DUP argued in their 'fair deal' document that it was in fact IRA concessions David Trimble was in the business of delivering and that he had more to offer the unrepentant Republican Movement. They then gave Unionists a choice. They quoted former Stormont Minister and UUP candidate for South Belfast Michael McGimpsey as saying, 'we are not talking about changing the [Belfast] Agreement'.[26] The DUP response to this was what many Unionists wanted to hear – a firm commitment to change that agreement. The DUP were talking about scrapping the Belfast Agreement and replacing it with something that was better for Unionism. The UUP's immediate task was to unravel what the DUP were really offering in December 2004, and why they had backed away from their last-minute deal with Sinn Féin. The party had to explain to Unionists what this 'fair deal' amounted to and point out what was obvious to Northern Ireland's political élite – the comprehensive proposals did not represent a significant re-negotiation of the Belfast Agreement.[27]

Regardless of what swung Ian Paisley against the deal at the last minute, the 2004 comprehensive proposals failed to put an end to the thorny issue of decommissioning in December 2004. The DUP were in a situation where all the other political issues had been negotiated and agreed. The remaining issue to be addressed was how transparent decommissioning would come about. From David Trimble's perspective:

Paisley had been manoeuvred into accepting sharing power with Republicans and the only other thing outstanding was the modalities of decommissioning. At the time I thought Republicans were bound to deliver that to the government's satisfaction and once that happened Paisley was trapped. I think he realized at the last minute that if he went with this he would be hugely vulnerable and that is where the business about sack cloth and ashes came. And then it turned out that Republicans did not deliver what the government wanted in terms of the modalities of decommissioning.[28]

What is interesting here is this issue of transparency. The text of the comprehensive proposals did not actually mention any photographic record of decommissioning. It simply mentioned photographs of the weapons to be decommissioned. It read: 'The IRA representative has told us that the IRA will have photographs of the weapons and the material involved taken by the IICD [Independent International Commission on Decommissioning].'[29] David Trimble therefore argued that 'the government's requirements would have been satisfied by photographs taken of the weapons that the IRA intended to decommission. There would not necessarily be any photographic record of the actual decommissioning event or the weapons being decommissioned.'[30] What the government was looking for was so little that it was surprising that Republicans failed to deliver it. More so if you take the view that their failure to deliver it meant that the deal collapsed in circumstances where blame could not solely be put on the DUP. Why then did Sinn Féin not deliver? It seemed to me that there were three possibilities. Sinn Féin could not deliver the IRA decommissioning, Sinn Féin could not get the IRA to give up criminality or Sinn Féin could not bring themselves to do a deal with the DUP. Photographic evidence was not the problem. The fact that the IRA decommissioned in the first place bears out this argument. As for the DUP members that were aware of what their leadership was getting itself into in their negotiations with Sinn Féin, they most likely put their lucky escape down to divine intervention.

The UUP had to remind the public that at its core the DUP remained a *sectarian* party. We had to ask people how a divisive oppositionist party could possibly be expected either to further the interests of the union or to deliver devolved government on the basis of sharing power with Nationalists. The problem the UUP faced was that it was increasingly clear in 2005 that most Unionists had become opposed to the idea of power-sharing with Nationalists because Republicans were now that community's dominant voice. Given a choice, the vast majority of Unionists would have opted for direct rule over any form of power-sharing with Sinn Féin.

The DUP's record at Westminster was extremely weak. Having never fully engaged as a political party in the House of Commons – not to mention its tea rooms and bars – Westminster remained a foreign country to Ian Paisley's MPs. Moreover, they remained foreigners to all those who inhabited its corridors of power. The UUP had to highlight the glaring contradiction between the DUP's profession to be the 'party of the union' and the fact that their attendance rate and contribution to UK political life in the nation's parliament was scarcely better than that of the SDLP. With the suspension of the Northern Ireland Assembly on 14 October 2002, following a Police Service of Northern Ireland (PSNI) raid on Sinn Féin's offices over spying allegations, the only legislative scrutiny on issues affecting Northern Ireland took place in parliamentary committees at Westminster. These are made up of MPs from all the UK parties except for Sinn Féin, who abstained from taking their seats in the House of Commons. Of the UUP members, Sylvia Hermon alone participated in 38 of the 98 committees on Northern Ireland legislation in her first parliament. In contrast, the DUP collectively only managed 18 appearances in the same parliament.[31] This was an appalling statistic that summed up an appalling record. But would it cost them votes in Northern Ireland?

3 April

'Voters will decide who has a record of achievement' – Jeffery Donaldson[32]

In the back of everyone's minds in Cunningham House, the 16 per cent rating of the *Belfast Telegraph* poll was gnawing away, yet we have a job to do and an election to fight. Despite the mammoth task facing us, people knuckle down to work in the first week of April and Cunningham House is awash with enthusiasm and ideas.

There is little time, however, to find a campaign slogan as the material has to be with the designers in just days. At least there is broad agreement from the campaign strategy team and staff that we need to put clear blue water between ourselves and the DUP.

We are certain the majority of Unionists do not feel that Paisley represents them. As junior UUP press officer Peter Munce puts it, the DUP represent the 'religious fundamentalists and sectarian bigots' that have given Unionism a bad name on the mainland and blackened Northern Ireland's image worldwide.

We have to remind Unionists that while the DUP talks tough on terrorism, it was Paisley who is reported to have told the RUC at Stormont on 24 June 1986, 'don't come crying to me if your homes are attacked',[33] and who had, in 1981, promoted a 'third force', or Protestant militia, to protect Loyalists.[34]

This was that man Enoch Powell once described as 'a greater threat to the Union than the Foreign Office and the Provisional IRA rolled into one'.[35]

We have to point this up, not just to the Unionist electorate, but to all the decent people who want Northern Ireland to work, be they Protestant, Catholic or dissenter.

The party somehow has to explain that even though the implementation of the Belfast Agreement had failed, a return to the rejectionist politics of the 1980s will be damaging to Unionism. For many Unionists, however, the years since the Belfast Agreement was negotiated are memorable for one thing only – the rise of Sinn Féin despite its failure to honour its commitments under that accord. Tony Blair too had broken his promises to the Unionist community and this had not gone unnoticed. As for David Trimble, many Unionists blamed him for the Republican's failure to deliver and for Tony Blair's failure to punish them for it.

The problem David Trimble faced was that the DUP, despite having accepted the parameters of the Belfast Agreement, had never progressed from playing short-term politics with the electorate. They had knocked on Unionist doors across Northern Ireland telling people what they wanted to hear in their hearts and minds. Ian Paisley was ruling out power-sharing with Sinn Féin for a generation. In doing so, the DUP were consolidating the perception that David Trimble represented everything that was wrong with the Belfast Agreement. The UUP knew the majority of Unionists had moved away from the idea of sharing power with Nationalism. Their task was to point out to the electorate that the alternative to that shared future was a return to the political and social conflict they had experienced in the past. The party had to warn voters that it would be more difficult to achieve any sort of peaceful co-existence with Nationalism on the basis of devolved government with Sinn Féin and the DUP as Northern Ireland's two largest parties. In my mind we had to tell people that the relative peace and stability Northern Ireland had been experiencing over the last decade should not be taken for granted.

4 April

'The defining moment ... or another false dawn?'[36]

Tonight we brain-storm over possible election slogans along the theme of the UUP representing a 'non-sectarian' alternative to the DUP. It is a painful process.

The buzzword from above is 'decency'. Ulster Unionists are decent people. Can anyone argue with that?

War-torn UUP Communications Director and Zionist hard-liner in his spare time, Alex Benjamin, suggests 'Ulster Unionists ... speaking your language'. Not bad. Infers that Paisley doesn't speak for you unless you are a Free Presbyterian of course. There are many, many famous Paisley quotes, but remarks such as Paisley's comment following the death of Pope John XXIII: 'This Romanish man of sin is now in hell', do not sit lightly with the average Unionist, or anyone for that matter.[37]

After all, this was the international dinosaur of Unionism who had, on 11 October 1988, nearly caused a riot by calling Pope John Paul II 'Christ's enemy and anti-Christ' when he addressed the European Parliament.[38]

Alex crawls out of his first-floor bunker to go to a meeting with the billboard designers and East Belfast candidate, Sir Reg Empey. Alex smokes so much that when he emerges from his room smoke percolates into the air from the fabric of his clothing, giving onlookers the impression that he has just staggered out of a bomb blast. He also looks fairly like someone who has actually just staggered out of a bomb blast. It is as if the look of shock that comes across his face when he has to call DT with bad political tidings had become his permanent expression.

Alex and I had both been hoping to run a poster campaign that was imaginative *and* hard hitting. My idea for a National Lottery 'scratch card' poster had been binned despite the designers coming back with some very interesting variations.

The first one is a scratch card with a hand rubbing a coin across it. Underneath there are 'three Paisley's heads' – like a fruit machine – or you could get three Paisley heads and three Adams' heads if you're really lucky. The caption beneath reads:

'Better Luck Next Time ... Vote Ulster Unionist.'

Next is a roulette wheel with the heads of all the Sinn Féin and DUP leadership where the numbers are supposed to be.

The caption beneath reads:

'Don't Gamble on your Future ... Vote Ulster Unionist.'

The best of the three is a poster representing a five-card poker draw with four aces dealt: Ian Paisley, Gerry Adams, Peter Robinson, Martin McGuinness, and then a joker – Sammy Wilson.

On 6 April the general election campaign began in earnest and Cunningham House was buzzing with activity. Northern Ireland's MPs set off for Westminster for the last ever Prime Minister's Questions of the parliament and, for some, what may be their last appearance in the House of Commons. Former SDLP Leader and Foyle MP John Hume rose and spoke, for what was his last time in the chamber. He bowed out of British politics by calling on Tony Blair to press for a special department in the European Union (EU) to engage in worldwide conflict resolution.[39] His fellow Nobel Peace Prize winner, Upper Bann MP David Trimble, was not called by the speaker of the House of Commons.

Back in Belfast, Sinn Féin President Gerry Adams captured the news headlines by calling for the IRA to 'consider' its position and move towards standing down.[40] A clever tactical ploy to ensure the question of the IRA's future did not dominate the election agenda over the coming weeks. It would also rally wavering SDLP voters, ever hungry for political progress, to back Sinn Féin's peace strategy one more time. UUP parliamentary party leader Roy Beggs quipped that 'Adams was talking to himself'.[41]

In South Belfast the DUP selected a retired Royal Ulster Constabulary (RUC) man, Jimmy Spratt, to run against Michael McGimpsey. This seemed a rather strange choice for the DUP. As acting Chairman of the Police Federation, Jimmy Spratt had not been overly critical of the Patten Report on police reform in Northern Ireland.[42] He said that while 'there is much in this report that we [the RUC] are happy with ... Patten has made 175 recommendations, a majority of those have our support; some need further considerations by my federation, and a few ... we reject.'[43] This was a far cry from the DUP's line on Patten.

7 April

'Decent people ... vote Ulster Unionists'

This is the message, this is the slogan, and we will run with it. It's nobody's first choice but it could be worse. It seems to grow on everyone during the day. There is no real discussion as to why ... we are just going with it and that is that. It's unclear though why it is 'Ulster Unionists' and not 'Ulster Unionist'.

I think most of us like it because it is less boring than our previous slogans. It is certainly better than the last one – 'Simply British' – which came with its own 'fish and chips' icon attached. This message was so appalling that when asked, most UUP staff members flatly denied that it was the party's slogan at all, pretending instead that it was some sort of wind up.

For me, what made the 'Simply British' slogan so cringe worthy was that it made me think of Johnny Adair's Loyalist paramilitary gang's drinking anthem: Tina Turner's pop song 'Simply the Best'. Shocking. We might as well have had a cardboard cut-out of Michael Caine standing behind DT at our press conferences.

But the 'decent people' idea certainly was going to attract media attention and rub a few people up the wrong way. Is it offensive? I don't think so. Mind you, they do say an Ulsterman will drive one hundred miles out of his way to be insulted ...

What is crystal clear is that it is bound to grab the headlines; it's a bit cheeky. Decent people do vote Ulster Unionist – don't they? Well ... perhaps, just not very many of them.

After the first week of the campaign it seems clear to me that if we are to significantly increase on the *Belfast Telegraph* poll rating of 16 per cent then we have to do something radically different.

But what could it be?

The media are taking the poll as gospel, the DUP are acting like the election is already won and the public seem totally disinterested. If the party simply goes through the electoral hoops then it is finished. We know our backs are to the wall but there is a growing determination to turn the tide.

There were three target groups the UUP could focus on if it was to poll close to its 24.7 per cent 2003 Assembly election first preference vote. First, there were the traditional Ulster Unionist voters who had lent

51

their support to the DUP in the previous two elections. Second, the lazy 'garden centre Prod' or 'stay-at-home' voter, as they were known,[44] the people who had apparently lost all interest in politics due to the unpleasant sectarian nature of political life in Northern Ireland. Third, those Alliance voters who in the past had been prepared to lend their vote to the UUP in order to halt the DUP/Sinn Féin advance. The party faced serious problems in attracting votes from all three of these groups. However, on the basis of the *Belfast Telegraph* poll, if the UUP could attract 2 per cent from each of them then it would win 22 per cent of the overall vote. Such a result would give the party a fighting chance of holding a majority of its Westminster seats and be received as a considerable success internally.

7 April

'Real battle is against voter apathy'[45]

Why had traditional Ulster Unionist voters gone over to the DUP or simply just stayed away? Could the party address the issues that had caused its supporters to vote DUP and find the initiative to win them back? Could those voters be wooed over the next month with little more than threats and breast beating?

To me that section of the electorate had forsaken the UUP because the party leadership no longer listened to, nor represented, what they were saying. When it did listen, it failed to act, and when it did act, those actions had proved painfully ineffective.

Equally damming was the fact that Trimble's love-hate relationship with the public, and the party, had become all too one-dimensional. So how could he attract some of these voters back over the next few weeks?

By appealing to their British sensibilities? By suggesting that they had gone beyond the pale by voting DUP?

The fact that many Ulster Unionists had crossed over to the DUP in the first place suggests that the party needs to offer something radically different in order to entice them back. In an election without key issues and one that looks set to be dominated by the legacy of Trimble and the Belfast Agreement, this seems virtually impossible. As for the lazy 'garden Prod' – why did these people not vote for the centre-ground parties? Who exactly are they? Do they exist at all? It's true that the number of people in Northern Ireland that are turned off by the political process has steadily risen. And the only time this gardening voter has put his head above the grass in recent years was during the 1998 referendum on the Belfast Agreement – when over 81 per cent of people voted.[46]

With that Agreement's failure to rapidly transform Northern Ireland's political life into something close to normal British constitutional politics, the garden Prod slumped back into his deckchair, with a Pimms and lemonade in one hand and an *Ulster Tatler* in the other (though perhaps these days it's more likely to be a copy of the *Sun* and a bottle of Stella). Disinterested and disaffected by a political process stagnating around him, yet not dismayed or disgruntled enough to ever do anything about it.

This 2 per cent 'garden vote' seems to me like the most unlikely of groups from which we might gain votes.

On the one hand, our aim is to frighten him into voting to halt the two extremist parties from dominating Northern Irish politics for the foreseeable future, yet at the same time, our relentless battle with the DUP for the heart and soul of Unionism has meant we are not distancing ourselves from the political war that apparently turns him off.

The fact is that we are bunkered down in the trenches of the front line. Perhaps the UUP's best hope is that when confronted with the terror-vision of a DUP/Sinn Féin carve-up in Northern Ireland, Alliance voters will reel back from the edge and come to our rescue. The Alliance Party's *raison d'être* was, after all, to create a non-sectarian political centre ground.

Having themselves failed over three decades to make any headway on that political project perhaps they might come to their senses. Surely for an Alliance voter it would be like cutting off one's nose to spite one's face not to support the two main centre-ground parties with Northern Ireland so clearly on the brink of polarization?

Refusing to do so would ensure the dominance of the two extremist parties in Northern Ireland for the foreseeable future.

Are the Alliance Party and the UUP not singing from the same secular hymn sheet anyway? In my mind, at least, the answer is yes.

But, as to the question of forging the kind of electoral pact between the centre parties which helped Hermon unseat McCartney in North Down in 2001, it seems to be no.

Trimble's speech writer, Steven King, or drstevenking@hotmail.com to his friends, has been arguing that this is a battle for survival therefore we should be concentrating solely on the four or five seats we can win. This seems logical but it's not something that is happening.

We had a meeting this morning with the party's new Chief Executive, Will Corry, and thrashed out our ideas. It was the first formal meeting with Will who has just been parachuted in from the private sector. He has taken everybody by surprise and been a real breath of fresh air for the party. Imagine bringing concepts such as planning, structure and co-ordination to a political party. 'He'll not last long here', joked Alex as we left the meeting.

Will has been drafted in partly to replace the party's longest-serving and longest-suffering officer Jack Allen. Jack was one of the best-liked party men amongst his peers and, as the Honorary Treasurer of the UUP, has ensured that none of the party's funds are ever spent on anything. Over the years he had built up a very solid reputation for fiscal prudence. The joke in Cunningham House was that you could always tell Jack was in the building as the lights in the gents had been switched off.

54

At the meeting Steven says we should not waste energy on candidates who have no chance of winning. He said he brought this up with DT and complained about energy being wasted on no-hope candidates and he was 'Oh, like who, like who?' And when he mentioned someone, DT said 'Oh, they're not no-hope candidates.' If DT doesn't think they are no hope candidates then the candidates themselves are hardly likely to take a different view. I have a feeling we'll be relying on spin for this one.

As soon as the election campaign began the Alliance Party came out fighting. Their North Down candidate, David Alderdice, publicly claimed that the UUP had taken a 'lurch to the extreme',[47] while North Belfast hopeful, Tom Campbell, accused the UUP of attempting to 'mirror and copy' their Unionist rivals.[48] The Alliance Party launched a hard-hitting poster campaign with slogans such as 'Sharing Works; Sectarianism Costs' and 'Alliance Works; Tribal Politics Costs'.[49] In other words, in terms of rhetoric, there was little to separate the Alliance from the UUP or the SDLP. The crux of their argument was, however, that despite the opportunities afforded to the two centre-ground parties under the Belfast Agreement and its Single Transferable Vote (STV) electoral system, they had both completely failed to build on that centre ground. Arguably, had the moderate Unionist and Nationalist parties been doing their jobs properly, or had the Belfast Agreement in fact worked, the Alliance Party should have ceased to exist after the November 2003 Assembly election. So, with UUP/SDLP's failure very much in mind, the Alliance Party was on the one hand fighting for its electoral life, given that it barely managed to retain all six of its seats in that Assembly election, while dropping 2.8 per cent of their vote.[50] On the other hand, it sought to take advantage of the weakness of its moderate rivals, regardless of whether it benefited Sinn Féin or the DUP.

So no agreement between the moderate parties materialized before the election campaign began. Alliance leader David Ford ended speculation over a deal between the two parties when he publicly accused David Trimble of offering him a peerage if his party stood aside in four constituencies, including Upper Bann.[51] But at the start of the campaign, Ford had reminded voters that there were two elections on 5 May, highlighting that it was 'realistic' for his party to focus on the council elections that day.[52] But there was to be no alliance between the UUP and Ford's party over this point. The gloves were off and the Alliance Party were determined to hold on to what they had.

Friday, 8 April

End of Week One
'Beware Balkanisation – Mallon'[53]

UUP Party Election Broadcast (PEB) comes out. It has a nice tone and Trimble lays it on the line:

Northern Ireland faces a 'shared future or a divided society'.
Are you listening David Ford?

I like it ... it's nicely balanced between the elder statesmen of the party and the new boys, namely, Basil McCrea, Rodney McCune and Gareth McGimpsey. It's positive, forward looking and has a tough message from the leader – 'Let's not go back.'

All we need now is the policy to follow it up ...

So where are we a week into the campaign? We began on a very low ebb, yet, by Friday, the campaign team has gelled, clicked into gear and developed the positive mentality and motivation to fight this campaign. Self-esteem couldn't be higher. The new Chief Executive, Will Corry, has made a great impact on the war room staff and we are working solidly as a team.

The UUP's long-serving education spokesman, Roy Beggs, has secured extra funding from NIO Minister Barry Gardiner for school dinners starting from September.

We are hoping to feed this issue into his campaign. My colleague from Westminster, Claire Kirk, came up with the idea of running a Jamie Oliver-style campaign in Northern Ireland a few weeks ago and got Beggs to promote the 'Feed me Better' campaign among backbenchers in the House of Commons. He tabled a parliamentary motion to help raise the profile of Oliver's campaign, gaining the support of 159 MPs from across the parties. Claire thought it would be a good idea to do it at home. We are just waiting for the go-ahead from Oliver's people and, of course, Northern Ireland's TV chefs.

South Belfast is looking better – Michael McGimpsey is confident and the DUP have selected a political nobody 'Splitter Spratt'.

Upper Bann is a worry ... DT not very focused in his constituency, obviously, doing everything else under the sun but he seems reasonably happy all the same, although perhaps not worried enough about himself.

No one is expecting the positive blast we are going to give this campaign ... but can it work? The difference is that after a week we believe it can!

Sunday, 10 April

'Splitter Splatter: which will matter?' – McGimpsey[54]

Gatwick Airport 4.36pm – text message from a reliable London source telling me we are in for a 'seismic shock from the DUP tomorrow'.

I reply, asking 'Who, what and where?'

The next text simply states what many of us had already feared.

'Smyth/Molyneaux.'

Is it all about to go badly wrong?

The DUP have been very quiet. We have been expecting a dirty tricks campaign from them but what exactly have they got?

On Monday 11 April former Ulster Unionist leader Lord Molyneaux and out-going South Belfast MP, the Rev. Martin Smyth, appear in the local papers photographed with DUP candidate Jimmy Spratt. The press took this to mean an endorsement of the DUP candidate by the two UUP representatives. David Trimble and Michael McGimpsey were quick to argue that it was nothing of the sort, taking the view that a photo is merely a photo. Michael McGimpsey warned Unionists that Jimmy Spratt's actions would do nothing 'other than increase the likelihood of a Nationalist taking the seat by dividing the Unionist people'.[55] Something of this nature had been expected in Cunningham House but, perhaps at least, not so explicitly from Lord Molyneaux. As it turned out, he also appeared on the literature of the DUP's Lagan Valley candidate, Jeffery Donaldson, and there was also a picture in their manifesto of the former UUP leader with Ian Paisley at the Cenotaph in London.

The two Ulster Unionists had let it be known in the most public fashion that they preferred an unknown DUP candidate to the man selected by their own party. If the unfolding crisis in the UUP's campaign could be caught in 'one grubby polaroid', then Jimmy Spratt's was it.[56] It appeared that the party's outgoing MP was willing to throw away a huge UUP majority and risk the possibility of losing South Belfast to a Nationalist candidate simply to ensure Michael McGimpsey was not elected. Martin Smyth, however, denied giving his consent for his photo to be used in the DUP's election literature. He shared David Trimble's view that a photo was just a photo. He said 'people take pictures of me and they turn up in different places. I didn't sign any form, I didn't go out canvassing, but I was out canvassing with the only two Unionist candidates who asked me' [David Burnside in South Antrim and Rodney McCune in North Antrim].[57]

Martin Smyth had failed to get his own anti-Trimble candidate Colin Montgomery selected, therefore endorsing Jimmy Spratt as the next most effective means of attack. Smyth argued that 'McGimpsey would never have won South Belfast anyway', because of his 'baggage' and 'self interest'.[58] He added that had he supported him, or had a deal been done with the DUP to keep South Belfast Ulster Unionist, he doubted whether 'either party could necessarily sell it on the ground' as people would have emerged to 'run as independents anyway' in order to prevent Michael McGimpsey gaining the seat.[59] Lord Molyneaux was also acting in a fashion that would maximize the damage to the party he had served his entire political career. It was his 'Geoffrey Howe moment' against David Trimble but, ironically, the main beneficiary of his actions was his life-long political rival, Ian Paisley. A man who had labelled the former Ulster Unionist leader a 'Judas Iscariot' during a press conference in Belfast on 30 May 1994.[60]

The Molyneaux/Smyth photo opportunity highlighted the weakness of the UUP's position having failed to agree a deal with the DUP over South Belfast and Fermanagh and South Tyrone. Even in the absence of agreement, the DUP seemed confident enough to challenge the UUP over South Belfast and unperturbed about the possibility of the SDLP holding the seat for the next parliament. If that were to happen they seemed convinced the UUP would not be able to stand again in that constituency should Michael McGimpsey lose. In other words, even though the UUP held the seat before the election, the DUP intended to blame David Trimble should it fall into Nationalist hands as a result of their decision to split the Unionist vote. With the outgoing UUP MP supporting the DUP candidate it was obvious that this argument would be credible with Unionists. For the party leadership, however, Smyth's failure to publicly endorse the candidate which 'the association that had selected him time and time again and who then selected Michael McGimpsey', was 'an act of gross treachery' derived from 'ten years of bitterness'.[61] As for Lord Molyneaux, David Burnside said that 'pictures were used very cleverly by the DUP' and 'there was no doubt that there was bad feeling'.[62] Those in Cunningham House were horrified by the Unionist peer's actions. One insider described his treachery as 'despicable' from 'a man who got to where he is because of the Ulster Unionist Party'.[63]

The problem for David Trimble was that he had been in no position to negotiate over these two seats. He could not have handed South Belfast to his Unionist rivals. Michael McGimpsey was a long-standing Trimble ally who was viewed by some as the UUP's 'leader in waiting'.[64] He had also just won a selection contest against Martin Smyth's candidate to defend the UUP seat. Had David Trimble attempted to concede South Belfast he would have opened up another front of internal dissent and indicated he had no faith in his party holding the UUP seat with the largest majority. Abandoning Fermanagh and South Tyrone would have been equally problematic for David Trimble. This was Ulster Unionism's last outpost west of the Bann, and the party's candidate, Tom Elliott, was one of its best electoral newcomers.

Lord Kilclooney, however, had been arguing since the beginning of 2005 that South Belfast was already lost and that the party would be wise to accept Fermanagh and South Tyrone, where they would at least be guaranteed one seat.[65] David Burnside made the same case, suggesting that David Trimble should have dropped Michael McGimpsey in South Belfast. He argued that had he been leader he would have traded and 'kept Fermanagh because of the splits it would create in South Belfast so, on balance, Tom Elliott is the more likely candidate to unite Unionists in Fermanagh than Michael is in South Belfast'.[66] The problem with these arguments, as North Down candidate Sylvia Hermon put it, was that 'the party leader doesn't really have very much power under the party's constitution'.[67]

When defining what the crisis in the UUP amounted to over the Molyneaux/Smyth photo, the legacy of disloyalty and indiscipline within the party was at the root of the problem. The UUP had become 'a laughing stock'[68] within British politics and a liability to Downing Street with its inability to end the infighting that plagued David Trimble's leadership. The now famous Talkback incident during the 2003 elections, when Jeffery Donaldson called into a live radio programme to publicly castigate his party leader 'illustrated just how bad relations within the party had become'.[69] By 2005 the leadership's long-term failure to foster any semblance of unity around the UUP's key policies had irreparably tarnished its image and brand name with the Unionist electorate. Sylvia Hermon took the view that 'when it came to senior party members there was a nervousness about dealing properly with them'. As for David Trimble, he was just 'too tolerant of disloyal and disruptive behaviour'.[70]

After Jeffery Donaldson defected from the UUP, internal division appeared less obvious to the outside world. In the absence of his anti-Agreement leadership campaign, division amongst Ulster Unionists quickly resurfaced over personalities. Lord Molyneaux and Martin Smyth were not out to destroy the UUP. It was the Trimble project they wished to bring an end to, and if the UUP got bruised in the process, well that was politics. Consequently, the paranoia within the party over indiscipline and splits had led to a leadership where power was concentrated among the select few. This only served to increase the disconnection between the party and the electorate and compound the increasingly deep-rooted suspicion between party members and its leadership. It was a vicious circle that, without the mask of the policy issues that anti-Agreement Unionism clung to, became all the more damaging to the party.

12 April

'**BOMBSHELL: UUP heavyweights backing DUP in two election battles**'[71]

War Room on a major low after the Molyneaux/Smyth bombshell. HQ has denied it was an endorsement by the UUP men but the whole episode is just farcical.

Imagine Margaret Thatcher coming out a couple of weeks before polling day and endorsing one of Robert Kilroy-Silk's candidates.

They may be yesterday's men but it seems that if they had only one breath left between them, they would expend it by calling for DT's head.

It's a terrible blow to the campaign ... never thought I'd put pen to paper and say it, especially not in the second week of the campaign, but Trimble is finished. I can't believe I just wrote that, but surely it's all over.

But not to worry ... the public have little to fear from Trimble's demise. The DUP are about to come to the emotional rescue of the downtrodden Prod. They are going to stand up to the two governments. They are going to smash the legacy of the failure that has been David Trimble, smash his UUP, then smash Sinn Féin, and banish the IRA to a quarter century of servitude for their crimes. Right?

3 Flogging a Dead Horse

Trimble put it in the manifesto: 'We'll drop D'Hondt; we no longer want D'Hondt.' But an inclusive executive was an essential bit of the Belfast Agreement. He couldn't say: 'The agreement has failed.' He was still battering on saying: 'There's no other show but the Belfast Agreement.' But when we were actually in the general election he said we do not support an inclusive executive which is an essential ingredient of the Agreement. It's the policy of 'keep flogging a dead agreement'.

David Burnside, London, 25 May 2005

On 12 April the DUP screened their first party election broadcast of the campaign. It focused almost entirely on David Trimble's attempts to implement the Belfast Agreement. In it the DUP accused him of letting Sinn Féin get away without decommissioning and for delivering 'a concession a day to the IRA'.[1] It summed up the DUP's electoral strategy – one more push and the UUP would be gone forever. They had spent their 2001 campaign demonizing David Trimble. They then spent the next four years reinforcing the public's perception that the Belfast Agreement had failed them and that Trimble could never deliver a 'fair deal' for Unionism. Their message to the public in 2005 was that the bad old days were over and that the UUP would finally be replaced by a party that could be trusted to exclude Sinn Féin. The 2005 battle between the UUP and DUP was all about which party was the most likely to exclude Sinn Féin from government. Having got off the hook at the end of 2005, the DUP were clearly the party with the best track record of giving Republicans no leeway in the political process. As David Trimble's speech writer Steven King put it, 'even if we had written pledges in our own blood that we wouldn't go into government with Sinn Féin no-one was going to believe us. It was about Sinn Féin in government and we aren't going to win that argument.'[2]

If that was the case, was Peter Robinson simply flogging a dead horse by 2005? Was there to be no election campaign based on any political issues or policies from the DUP? Would the Unionist electorate not demand to know where the political process was going before it handed Ian Paisley a mandate to end power-sharing? Was the UUP so out of touch that its opponents needed nothing other than David Trimble's track record to defeat him? The media's attitude to the Ulster Unionists gave an early indication of where the answers to these questions lay. By and large they showed little interest and to my mind had become disenchanted with the political process itself, or at least the dishonesty of the parties at the centre of it. The only thing that seemed to be getting Northern Ireland's journalists out of bed in the morning was the possibility of a big upset in David Trimble's Upper Bann and, of course, Foyle, where the SDLP leader Mark Durkan was fighting for his political life against Sinn Féin's Chairman Mitchell McLaughlin. This was in stark contrast to 2001, where the press followed David Trimble across the Province as he carried out a diary crammed with political, electoral and social engagements.

12 April

'No Ulster Unionist seat is Safe' – Paisley[3]

David Trimble (or DT as he was known to everyone in politics) joined the war room staff for this morning's meeting. Everyone feeling a bit freaked out by the DUP's electoral broadcast. It gave me goose pimples in my own living-room. DT hadn't seen it and it was rather difficult to explain to him what it was like.

It began with scenes of thunder and lightning breaking open a black, cloudy sky. This was followed by a doom-laden message from Robinson who is actually standing outside Cunningham House, reminding people of how bad Northern Ireland was under the UUP.

It had the feel of a 1970s Hollywood 'B horror movie'. And if anyone in London was watching they would think we were living in the Dark Ages. The special effects – thunder and lightning at the beginning, followed by a shot of Robinson sporting a Gerry Kelly/Elvis Presley-style quiff in a Martin Bell suit – are truly surreal. Gold Stars for DUP P.R. Inc. – they should go global.

The BBC's Louise Duffy confirmed to Alex that the Beeb knocked it back for failing to adhere to PEB regulations and they had to re-shoot. I'd hate to see the first draft!

In spite of this, it was business as usual for the UUP leader, who continued to focus on the politics regardless of the media's disinterest. On 13 April he unveiled his party's controversial poster billboard at a photo shoot in Belfast. It read *Decent People ... vote Ulster Unionists.*'4 Media interest on this occasion was high but, tellingly, none of the other Ulster Unionist parliamentary candidates were present and it was not long before some of them were furious over replica posters being erected in their constituencies. South Antrim candidate David Burnside, who is usually a fairly thick-skinned character, was among the first to be hit by this offence from Cunningham House. He described the poster campaign as 'a joke'. He said they 'turned people against us, made people laugh and joke at us, and make snide comments. I said "keep it out of my constituency" when I became aware of it, and I had my own workers cutting down the posters at the Sandyknowles roundabout.'5

The idea behind the poster was obviously to send out a rallying cry to all decent people to get behind the party. This was very much against the backdrop of the bank robbery, the McCartney murder and the sectarianism of the DUP. Yet if the message is not obvious and if we have to start unravelling it for people, then perhaps it was not such a good idea. The campaign slogan – 'Decent People ... Vote Ulster Unionists' – first emerged from a UUP HQ/Stormont Staff Communications Group in late 2004 as an expression of a core Ulster Unionist value. A campaign seminar for the Party Executive in March 2005 found that 'decent' was widely supported as a summary of the Party's values.

An internal memo on the campaign message read:

```
The intention behind the slogan is to rally 'decent
people' to the Ulster Unionist Party: in other words, it
```

recognizes that there are decent people throughout the
community, voting for a variety of parties. Our Party is
seeking to reach those who have voted DUP, Alliance or who
haven't voted, as well as core Ulster Unionist voters.

We are reaching out to people who share our values —
hardworking, law-abiding citizens ... who seek a
peaceful and tolerant Northern Ireland.

We entirely respect the judgment of voters who
disagree with us — but our firm conviction is that
Ulster Unionism is the surest and safest political home
for the values of decent people. There is, of course, an
implication in the slogan that other parties espouse
different values.

Recent events have borne this out. Joe O'Donnell of SF
this morning refused to condemn the intimidation of the
McCartney family: this inability or unwillingness to
condemn mob-rule speaks volumes about the values SF
stands for.

The DUP's Party Election Broadcast — with its
untruths, divisiveness, fear-mongering, entirely
negative tone, and deliberate omission of any reference
to the DUP's deal with SF in December 2004 — is a
different example of a political party employing values
contrary to Ulster Unionist values.

Previous party election slogans have been criticized
for being bland.

The press attention surrounding this slogan, while
perhaps initially uncomfortable, nevertheless provides
an opportunity for the Party to draw attention to our
campaign and values — and our desire to reach out to
those who share our values.

The campaign slogan — 'Decent People ... Vote Ulster
Unionists' — is a call to those who share our values to
vote Ulster Unionist.

Dr. Brian Crowe
Policy Officer
13 April 2005

The following day David Trimble ran a full-page advertisement in the *Belfast Newsletter* detailing a series of quotes from Mitchel McLaughlin. There were extracts from his analysis of what the DUP had conceded to Nationalism in the comprehensive proposals.[6] The concept behind the advertisement was to create a media debate over the glaring contradictions between what the DUP were telling the public the comprehensive proposals contained, and what they actually entailed for the political process and Unionism. Had it not been for the lack of transparent decommissioning in December 2004 and had the DUP/Sinn Féin deal been agreed, then Ian Paisley would have signed up to an agreement that actually put a timeframe on when policing and justice matters would be devolved to Northern Ireland. This meant the distinct possibility of Sinn Féin taking on a ministerial role in this department under a new Assembly. Furthermore, it was understood by the UUP that the deal granted observer status to Northern Ireland's elected representatives in the Irish Parliament.[7] In other words, Nationalists elected in the UK would be able to sit in the Dail.

The comprehensive proposals did not alter the fundamentals of the Belfast Agreement in any significant way. They were an aside to that agreement. However, Mitchell McLaughlin's analysis highlighted the unwritten additions the DUP had agreed to in principle. Few of these amendments would be welcomed by the DUP's electoral constituency and went further than David Trimble had been prepared to go on the issue of policing and justice. Trimble argued that 'whatever gains the DUP had made in terms of what they called a decontamination period they had paid for by committing to intensive negotiations on the devolution of policing and justice and agreeing to settle all those issues before the devolution of power to the Assembly.'[8]

In 2004 the DUP had, in fact, experienced a Trimblesque escape. Had they completed a deal with Sinn Féin that preceded the Northern Bank robbery and the McCartney murder, then the focus of the election campaign and the media's interest in the Comprehensive Proposals would have been different. David Trimble, however, had spent the last decade explaining the fine print of the Belfast Agreement to journalists, the technicalities of the negotiations to his party, and the minutiae of its implementation to the public. At the same time he had skilfully out-manoeuvred his rivals and maintained his position. But by 2005, the UUP man had ground to a halt politically and the media, the public and large sections of his own party had stopped listening to him. It did not actually matter whether David Trimble was right or wrong over what the comprehensive proposals entailed for the political process. The DUP had the ear of the Unionist electorate and as David Burnside put it, 'any deal Paisley could offer, always had to be a better deal than Trimble's. That's why this constant clever criticism about "oh you've got a deal ... only for a couple of Polaroids you'd have been in government". That's bad politics.'[9]

For me this illustrated a fundamental problem with David Trimble's leadership and handling of the Belfast Agreement. He was not always able to explain what he was doing politically, why he was doing it and where it would take Unionism, in language ordinary people understood. That, however, could be deemed unfair as Lord Kilclooney (formerly John Taylor) quipped that 'a good car salesman would have had difficulty selling the Belfast Agreement and David Trimble's not even a car salesman!'[10] In UUP Communications Director Alex Benjamin's view, 'you can articulate an argument, you can rationalize this, that and the other, but if you're not in touch with what people are thinking on the ground and you're trying to explain your rationale in an overly convoluted way, then you're going to lose people. People just want it in black and white and Trimble was always looking at the grey area.'[11]

13 April

'Grumpy old men Unionism has shocked many voters'[12]

Very poor turnout at the 'Decent People ... ' poster launch today but it sure got plenty of attention. If the candidates won't stand by it then what will the public make of it?

Donaldson said he was outraged and that the electorate would be offended. Let's hope so! They should get out more too.
But will the penny drop?

Phones have been ringing off the hook with unemployed DUP people ringing in to complain about the Decent People posters, or at least that is the official line we are spreading among ourselves.

Discussions today and much enthusiasm at last over what we are going to attack the DUP with.

It would appear that we are down to the bald grass in terms of policy and direction ... or maybe not ...

We'll do what we always do when under pressure ... attack the DUP. It's like a bad habit you just can't shake, but hey, what the hell ...

> Bad day at work ... attack the DUP!
> Spill mustard on your tie ... attack the DUP!
> Your son has turned out gay ... attack the DUP!
> DUP have attacked us!!! COUNTER-ATTACK THE DUP!

The public hate it. The media are bored of it. It gets us absolutely nowhere yet ... we can't quite resist the temptation.
The DUP are also of course self-confessed junkies of the Unionist civil war. Well after all, they started it. Didn't they?

While attacking the DUP remains one of our core pastimes, their campaign is solely based around destroying the UUP in its centenary year. They don't even disguise it, just look at their website, there is nothing else on it. It is almost pornographic Trimble-bashing.

Surely the Northern Ireland electorate cannot vote for a party whose only policy is to break David Trimble?

Wake up man, of course they can!

But we do have the comprehensive proposals to bat with.

Aside from the fact that we have been arguing that the DUP have failed to change one sentence of the Belfast Agreement and the government have publicly stated that that is the case, we are actually arguing that the comprehensive proposals add some rather unpleasant amendments to the Belfast Agreement.

So ...

How do we do it this time? Well, it's pretty similar to the Belfast Agreement actually, which went along these lines:
1) Nobody will read the Agreement, so we sell the public our interpretation of it.
2) Nobody trusts us, so we seek third party endorsement on it.
3) The British Government publicly agree with every word of our interpretation.
4) We run with it and as soon as we get going the Government shaft us by implementing an entirely different accord ...

Oh dear ... so what do we do this time?

Well, the electorate won't believe or listen to what we say the comprehensive proposals are. They will believe the DUP's assurance that they are, in fact, a 'fair deal'. While the facts may well be on our side, the public is going to treat us like the boy who cried wolf again on this one.

In the referendum campaign we had the whole British political establishment and the media, by and large, endorsing our interpretation of the Belfast Agreement.

Now we are on our own.

So what can we do?

Well, if they won't trust us, we'll just have to get a Shinner to do the talking for us.

Mitchell McLaughlin will do, he's pretty bright.

We'll take out a whole page ad in the paper and Mitchell can explain to the Unionist electorate on our behalf just exactly how the DUP have conned them.

Genius!

14 April

'Trimble goes for low-key poster launch.'[13]

Media failed to pick up on the fact that none of the candidates turned up for the poster launch.

They do however point out that the smiling youthful people on the poster look like they should be in a toothpaste ad and couldn't vote UUP even if they were decent enough to do so – they are unmistakably North American!

Today it was third time lucky for Molyneaux. The former UUP leader finally got it right backing David Burnside in South Antrim. Having gone over to the Dark Side twice in the last week – photographed with Splitter Sprat (DUP) and appearing in his former researcher Jeffery Donaldson's election literature – (Yes, hard to believe it, I know, DUP as well), the UUP man comes up trumps to back a candidate from his own party! David Burnside (UUP).

Sighs of relief all around Cunningham House.

It is still three strikes and you're out in here, isn't it?

What Molyneaux actually said today on Talkback was our line. He seemed to be rowing backwards from what he had done.

Alex had been telling the press that the Spratt photo was just a snap taken at a police federation event.

Molyneaux said he had been in hundreds of photos and they could not all be taken to be endorsements of this or that.

He actually used our line, but naturally, time has been called on the story, the damage done, and the media largely ignored it.

15 April

'Trimble tried to bribe me' – Ford[14]

Today we feel the campaign has really begun. DT is very unhappy about the impact we are making in the media and the lack of direction after being knocked off course by Molyneaux/Smyth. This, however, is a good thing – we need to step up a gear.

Step it up a gear is exactly what Ford has done. He has accused DT of trying to bribe him with a seat in the Lords in return for the APNI standing down in certain constituences. I didn't realise DT had any favours left to give. Like the Duppers, the only thing that seems to be capable of getting Ford's party front page news is Trimble.

Roy Beggs is photographed in the *Newsletter* with his Celebrity Chefs – Paul Rankin, Robbie Millar, Jonathan Alden and Nick Price. Looks like his campaign to kick-start Jamie Oliver's 'Feed me Better' campaign might be on the cards.

Office is being bombarded with calls over 'decency' – someone said it must be a DUP dirty trick. Those sneaky Duppers.

3.30PM

News breaks that Michael Copeland has had his offices and home searched by PSNI over alleged links to a money-laundering investigation involving a Belfast Estate Agent.

DISASTER! THIS DOESN'T LOOK TOO DECENT!

Back to crisis management and fire-fighting already (how long had it been – 6 hours?).

If there is a silver lining on today's black cloud it is Molyneaux's endorsement of Trimble on today's 'Talkback' programme. Well, it was an accident, but an endorsement's an endorsement, right? – especially during an election.

When asked whether he was supporting UUP candidate (Burnside) or DUP candidates (Splitter Sprat and Donaldson) Jim said he was only supporting one candidate and that was 'David Trimble ... aaahhh ... I mean David Burnside'.

Thank you Freud.

The UUP was set to launch its manifesto on Monday 13 April and step up its campaign on a positive note. This meant following Monday up with a series of mini-manifesto launches to spell out new policies on issues such as education, water rates, health and agriculture. But the launch was publicly postponed shortly after East Belfast MLA Michael Copeland's offices were searched the previous Friday, as the party began to manage the unfolding media crisis.[15] Michael Copeland, who shares an office with Sir Reg Empey in East Belfast, also had his home searched by police who – having removed a computer, bank statements, credit cards and mobile phones – said the seizures were 'part of a probe into money-laundering.'[16] Michael Copeland's response was to deny any wrongdoing, and issue a press statement arguing that he had done 'nothing illegal', that the incident had the 'whiff of a dirty tricks campaign' about it, and that he felt that it was a 'crude attempt to smear' his reputation and that of his party colleagues 'in the run-up to a general election'.[17]

On Monday morning, having put back the manifesto launch until Wednesday, David Trimble backed Michael Copeland stating that having had discussions with him over the weekend he was quite sure that he had 'not been engaged in any corrupt activity'.[18] Over the same weekend, David Trimble spelt out his 'centrist' vision regarding a way forward with the SDLP. But in the wake of the Copeland incident the only person who seemed to be listening, diplomatic as ever, was the BBC's David Frost. Trimble called for a 'cross-community administration based on the UUP and the SDLP'.[19] He argued that a power-sharing administration 'that brings in every party isn't going to work under the present circumstances'. He said voters could either opt for the UUP/SDLP model or 'endorse the extremes and reinforce stalemate'.[20] It seemed highly ironic that these were the ideals so many Protestants and Catholics had taken a step towards establishing as a political settlement for Northern Ireland in 1998, yet by 2005 many of those very same voters looked set to reject them by voting for parties that fundamentally opposed the ethos of such pluralist sentiments.

18 April

'Dirty Tricks rumours a "hellish lie"' – Paisley[21]

9AM

Campaign team on a major low today – more calls from the public regarding our 'Decent People ... ' ad, and they aren't people ringing in to congratulate us on another bright idea.

Copeland incident has totally knocked us for six. Fire-fighting the whole weekend instead of getting on with our positive campaigning.

Tim Lemon and Will Corry came in heavy at this morning's meeting to try and lift the spirits of some of the younger members of the War Room team. You could cut the sarcasm in the air with a knife.

Tim gave his single transferable speech about how people outside would give their right arm to be inside Cunningham House fighting this campaign for DT, and standing firm on the great progress we had made in Northern Ireland. He said people would be queuing up to do that job.

I had averted my eyes from Alex Benjamin's gaze for as long as I could and when I finally made eye contact with him we both erupted into fits of laughter. 'Queuing up outside they are!' exclaimed Alex, 'and they'll be hammering the bloody doors down soon if we don't get back to work!'

1PM

Paisley comes out spitting fire at lunchtime. He tells journalists that any talk of 'dirty tricks' regarding the Copeland incident were a 'hellish lie'.[22]

But who accused him and how does he know?

Not us any way. We didn't get round to it.

The DUP leader's old rallying slogan: 'If you throw a stone into a pack of dogs, the one that yelps is the one that's hit' rings true.

Manifesto launch put back until Wednesday. Alex comes clean about admitting to the press that we had actually cancelled our manifesto launch and got it in the neck a bit. I don't think he feels it there anymore though.

We do, however, seem to be doing OK in North Down and South Belfast. Upper Bann still a worry but DT is getting a very good response on the doorsteps, as are most of our candidates.

6PM

We shut up shop early tonight and head into town for a few desperately needed pints at McHugh's Bar.

Terrible atmosphere, almost comical, the enthusiasm is running out of everyone. People are asking themselves what can possibly go wrong next?

Someone upstairs must have been listening in and not feeling in any way inclined to show mercy.

DISASTER STRIKES BEFORE WE HAVE FINISHED OUR FIRST PINT!

6.45PM

Alex takes a call from the *Newsletter*'s Political Editor, Stephen Dempster, who informs him they are running a story on UUP Lisburn Councillor David Archer in tomorrow's paper. David has apparently been involved in a 'late night drinking incident' with a mate at Lisburn's council offices.

7PM

I call DT, who sounds like he didn't even hear what I was saying. He responded with 'Oh, OK, fine', before hanging up. Guess he has his bad news deflector-shield switched on full beam!

Alex deals with the media gazing out of the dusty window of McHugh's smoking at least two cigarettes at once.

7.30PM

I finally manage to get Archer on the phone and thankfully he is not too far away. He agrees to come and sort things out.

8.30PM

By the time he arrives we have all moved upstairs to deal with some of the pints we had been addressing before Dempster interrupted us. Archer calls to say he is downstairs. I rush down to meet him and buy him a double Bacardi and Coke. He needs it.

He looks shattered. We chat for a while and then he calms down. He then turns to me in all seriousness and says, 'Is it just you here, Mike, yeh?'

Poor David fails to see the funny side of it when I tell him the whole campaign team is upstairs waiting for his version of events!

Anyway, after much pandemonium we eventually get things sorted out and David explains to the *Newsletter* that he had had quite a few drinks with a friend and then foolishly used Lisburn's Council Office facilities to have a few more in the middle of the night. Good timing! Everyone sees the funny side of it but it's going to look awful in the papers.

I'm pretty sure he'll have to, well ... do the decent thing ... and ... fall on his sword. Alex suggests that the rest of us follow suit.

On 19 April, as it emerged that North Down's council offices had also been raided by the PSNI,[23] David Trimble warned his party to 'cut back the paranoia' over dirty tricks relating to Michael Copeland, and get on with running the general election campaign.[24] The following day, with the UUP manifesto launch set to take place, the papers report that David Archer Junior has quit the election race amidst an inquiry taking place into an alleged incident in Lisburn's council offices. The Council's Chief Executive had written to Archer stating that he was investigating a 'late night incident' in the Council's Members' Room, which had been logged by a security firm.[25]

The same morning, *Daily Ireland* reported that the UUP's South Belfast Willowfield branch was disbanding as its 15 members intended to support the DUP's Jimmy Spratt.[26] This was quickly dismissed by Michael McGimpsey as 'another one of the DUP's dirty tricks'.[27] It seemed that no matter which way the party turned, there was to be no escaping it – scandal had poisoned the political atmosphere in Cunningham House and drowned out the party's message ahead of its delayed manifesto launch.[28]

19 April

'Raid stalls UUP manifesto launch'[29]

Atmosphere shocking in HQ today – Alex says he's 'demob happy!'

Geoff suggests forming an orderly queue outside DT's office to collect our machetes and directions for the leader's paranoia cull.

Archer is not in the papers but after it became apparent that an 'incident' is under investigation, he issued a statement saying he intends to resign from the electoral race and pursue business interests in London. None of us have any doubt he'll be back ... having done the decent thing and resigned ... I know ... but there's still mileage in it ... right?

In our morning meeting I make the suggestion that we should perhaps take the huge 'Decent People ... Vote Ulster Unionists' banner off the side of HQ? Nobody laughs! Well it would be pretty funny, right, and we'd get a lot of media coverage for it, and they do say that all publicity is good publicity ...

They do still say that, don't they?

But seriously, the Copeland/Archer stuff has totally killed us off in what is supposed to be the beginning of our campaigning in earnest. Instead, it's turned into a blow-by-blow nightmare. The DUP couldn't write the script.
Geoff McGimpsey looked at me in disbelief this morning, and said, 'Can you imagine two more weeks of this?'

'Yes,' I replied, 'Indeed I can.'

20 April

'UUP man quits election race and council'[30]

8AM

Bad press today as the Archer 'incident' makes front page of the *Newsletter*'s country edition.

9AM

Panic stations at dawn. DT bursts into the war room screaming at us that Burnside will not turn up for the manifesto launch unless al the 'Decent People' posters are scrapped from the launch. That is not a problem at the launch but it certainly is in terms of getting the candidates there.

None of our candidates know that the big red Westminster bus we have hired has 'Decent People ... Vote Ulster Unionists' plastered all over it!!!

9.20AM

Campaign diary co-ordinator and bus expert, Barbara Knox, calls the bus people and tells them to scrape all the 'decency' stickers off the bus – ASAP. That will do rightly, no one will know any different.

10AM

Call comes in from the bus driver that they have successfully sand blasted all the stickers off, along with about five coats of paint! The bus is totally unusable.

War room is in complete pandemonium.

10.07AM

Joke doing the rounds that DT was seen going into his office at nine-thirty with a shotgun in one hand and a bottle of vodka in the other. Half an hour later he staggers out completely drunk and shoots Alex Benjamin.

10.15AM

The girls come up with a novel idea – blow up lots of helium balloons and tie them onto the bus. This will cover up the huge gaping patches where the 'decency' stickers have been sand blasted off.

At this stage no one would be surprised if Basil Fawlty walked into the building with a fire extinguisher in one hand and a can of red paint in the other.

We simply can't ditch the bus – the media are expecting it, as are all the candidates.

Barbara calls the driver and tells him to bring the bus anyway.

10.30AM

Burnside walks in the back door to find Brian Crowe, Alison Laird and myself manically pumping up helium balloons. 'Someone having a party?' he quips, smiles, and walks on.

10.40AM

As the candidates begin to arrive, most of the balloons have been tied onto the bus, with ribbons and sellotape affixing them through the windows.

Geoff's dad, West Belfast candidate Chris McGimpsey, turns up, has one look at the balloons and says to me, 'Whose bloody idea was that?'

'Geoff's,' I replied.

4 Is This Bus Going To Westminster?

Even the day the general election was called we seemed to be on the back foot. There was an enormous sense of anti-climax. We'd been waiting and waiting and suddenly the election was called. I flew home that afternoon and went straight to party headquarters in the expectation, given we knew the election was coming, that everything would be ready to roll, the party would kick into action, the manifesto would be out, and my candidate material would be ready to go. All I would have to do would be to stand there, look pretty and get my photograph taken. I remember going to headquarters at about five minutes to five and there was hardly anyone else there. I shouted: 'A general election has been called. Where on earth is everybody?'

Sylvia Hermon, 7 July 2005

On 20 April the UUP finally launched its manifesto after arriving at Stormont Hotel in a vintage Route Master London Bus – destination Westminster.[1] All 18 parliamentary candidates descended from their battlebus into a hotel foyer packed with local press. The mood was good, the party was united around its latest policy document and the media were responsive. There was little though, in terms of style rather than substance, to deflect Peter Robinson's comment that the UUP's double-decker was a 'clapped out' vehicle offering a 'second class ticket to a united Ireland'.[2]

David Trimble spelt out his party's proposals for a way forward. Northern Ireland needed a voluntary coalition comprising the UUP and the SDLP to form a cross-community administration at Stormont that excluded Sinn Féin.[3] If nothing else, it marked a departure from the UUP Leader's 'inclusive' stance over recent years. This was, however, something which Mark Durkan had firmly ruled out the previous day at the launch of his own party's manifesto.[4] This position illustrated the gulf that existed between the UUP and SDLP. David Trimble could not include Sinn Féin in government at any price whereas excluding Sinn Féin, regardless of what they did, was a price the SDLP could not afford to pay. Trimble said the Unionist electorate 'would not support or tolerate now, or in the foreseeable future, the formation of an executive that would include Sinn Féin'.[5] When questioned on how he thought the UUP would perform on 5 May, the Unionist leader told journalists that his party was 'coming back strongly' and that he was quite sure that it would be returned to Westminster 'with more than five members'.[6] The Unionist leader's optimism reflected his indefatigable spirit and the fact that the majority of his candidates were getting a very good response on the doorsteps despite the bad press that had beset the party from the outset of its campaign.

Having ruled out voluntary coalition, the SDLP set out its 'better way to a better Ireland' agenda. Moderate Nationalists were going to pressure Sinn Féin to accept peace within the parameters of the Belfast Agreement.[7] Durkan reminded voters that it was his party that had put 'inclusion into the agreement' and that he had 'stood strong against every trick and tactic to take it out'.[8] This was in stark contrast to the message being sent out to Sinn Féin by the Irish government. In the wake of the McCartney murder and the Northern Bank robbery, Taoiseach Bertie Ahern had been hinting towards the possibility of excluding Sinn Féin for some time – but had stopped short of actually saying it. The Irish government stated that there would be 'no fudge' and 'no budge' on IRA criminality, telling Gerry Adams to 'go away and think about it'.[9] Irish Minister for Justice, Michael McDowell, had described the provisional movement as the 'embodiment of all that is anti-Republican'.[10] In a press statement issued before the McCartney killing he said, 'there is and can be no room in representative politics or in governmental institutions anywhere on this island for any political party allied to any group which supports the use or threatened use of force or violence'.[11]

While endorsing Durkan's electoral stance in Northern Ireland, the implicit message from Dublin was that Sinn Féin could be excluded, for until they ceased paramilitary and criminal activity in Northern Ireland, direct rule would remain the norm.[12] But while both the SDLP and the UUP had been warning their own constituencies about the dangers of voting for the extremists, there was no joint centre-ground message wavering moderates could relate to.

20 April

'Trimble puts on brave face despite SDLP rejection'[13]

In spite of everything our manifesto launch goes off well and is received in good spirit by the media. The candidates all have fun travelling on the bus, despite half the balloons detaching themselves and floating off into the horizon from the Holywood Road. We have to take the long way to Stormont via the Newtownards Road, which doesn't help minimize the balloon losses. The driver informs us that 'she doesn't do speed bumps'.

I nearly have a heart attack when a message comes through on my mobile from Roy Beggs shouting: 'Mike, where the hell's the bus?'

As my stomach churns furiously I have visions of him standing alone outside Cunningham House, balloons clinging to the branches of the trees above his head, wondering where everyone is.
As I race to the lower deck to ask if anyone has seen him I catch sight of him standing impatiently at Stormont's gates waiting for us. We are running fifteen minutes late.

It all turns out to be a lot of fun. The media make very little of the bus' somewhat unfortunate features and the lack of UUP paraphernalia. One of the young Robinsons is lurking in the background with a digital camera snapping frantically before being ushered away by DT's bodyguards.

The actual conference itself is OK until Eamon Mallie reaches for his questions and DT reaches for his gun. It certainly gives everyone a lift but the distinct lack of policy, given Durkan's rejection of our core proposals, makes it little more than a good photo-shoot.

82

Everyone is breathing huge sighs of relief for having finally got it over and done with.

The following day the DUP followed suit, launching its manifesto at Edenmore Golf Club, Magheralin, in the heart of David Trimble's Upper Bann constituency. Ian Paisley declared the Belfast Agreement dead and buried, before telling Bertie Ahern, 'keep your dirty hands off the internal affairs of Northern Ireland'.[14] Using his predictable firebrand rhetoric, he spoke of a final victory over Republicans and a new dawn in Northern Ireland's history. He told the flock of journalists that this election was a 'battle between victory and defeat for the IRA and the salvation of the union'. Ian Paisley also warned Unionists that 'only by retaining the DUP as the biggest party in Northern Ireland, could the IRA be defeated'.[15] Peter Robinson went on to demand a voluntary coalition with the SDLP, but the message of their electoral campaign was loud and clear – unity in strength around the hard men of Unionism was the only way to stand up to Sinn Féin.

Northern Ireland's bookmakers did not share David Trimble's optimism over the likely outcome of the election. Eastwoods were predicting his party would return to parliament with just one seat. When their book opened on 22 April the DUP were firm favourites to take nine of the eighteen seats, Sinn Féin six, the SDLP two and David Trimble's UUP just one.[16] The good news for his party, if it could be seen as such, was that while Sylvia Hermon's seat was safe in the eyes of the gambling man, only Roy Beggs' was definitely lost. The odds did, in fact, give the UUP a fighting chance of maintaining its position at Westminster. The future, if the bookmakers were to be believed, was in the Ulster Unionist's hands – they could make it or break it over the next fortnight.

In Upper Bann the UUP leader was valued at 5/4 behind his DUP challenger, David Simpson, at 4/7; favourite in South Antrim was William McCrea at 4/5 with UUP hard-liner, David Burnside, at evens; South Belfast was a three-horse race between the UUP, DUP and SDLP, with Michael McGimpsey at 2/1, Jimmy Spratt 7/4, and Alasdair McDonnell coming up the middle for the Nationalists at 6/4; Sylvia Hermon was plain-sailing over DUP rival, Peter Weir, in North Down at 2/7 and 9/4, respectively; and Sammy Wilson was now the bookies' clear favourite to unseat Roy Beggs in East Antrim at 1/4 over the Larne man's 5/2 odds.

21 April

'DUP Rottweiler snaps at the wheels of Trimble's election bus'[17]

DUP manifesto launch today.

Paisley leads the press conference which turns out to be little more than an anti-Trimble tirade and an ultimatum to the SDLP that they must enter a voluntary coalition with the DUP, or face being put to the wall by the tide of triumphant Unionism that is set to sweep Northern Ireland.

Is there something about 'voluntary' that the DUP doesn't understand? Never mind.

Paisley talks of a 'final victory' and a new dawn in Northern Irish politics. It's a bit unclear whether the final victory is over the UUP or Sinn Féin. My guess is he means the UUP and wants voters to think it is Sinn Féin.

Paisley argues that the IRA have been defeated and that the only way for them to recover from that defeat is for Sinn Féin to become Northern Ireland's largest party.

It is traditional ranting stuff, no holds barred from the DUP leader, and ... probably exactly what many Unionists want to hear. Smash Sinn Féin – Ditch UUP.

When Donaldson defected he gave the DUP middle class respectability. Many Ulster Unionists thought 'if Paisley is OK for our Jeffery he must be OK for me'. Jeffery helped them smooth over some of their sectarian rough edges. He gave the DUP the middle-of-the-road political legitimacy they had always craved.

Perhaps Jeffery has taken the decent people with him ... if he has, then we are sunk.

The DUP don't need to hide Paisley any more. They are still ashamed of the demon doc but the days of damage limitation

84

when he opens his mouth are over. Traditional Ulster Unionists are not listening to the nasty remarks any more. It's not him they are voting for, nor do they suddenly feel that the DUP's core values are something that they can relate to.

It's a vote to reject the failed implementation of the agreement and the party that failed to implement it in the way in which it promised it would be implemented.

22 April

'Trimble woos Portuguese'[18]

Having been written off by the bookies yesterday DT has written to Portuguese voters in his constituency – in their own language – urging them to vote on 5 May.

Steven King has assured everyone that DT's letter was been translated correctly into Portuguese before being posted.

'How do you know?' someone asks.

'Well you'll find out in tomorrow's papers then smart-arse, won't you,' responds King.

There is also much talk of a Northern Ireland Office poll putting McGimpsey a few hundred votes ahead in South Belfast. Whether this is a recent poll or not is unclear.

Similar stuff appearing on blogging site, Slugger O'Toole, with reports of recent NIO polls putting the UUP ahead in South Belfast with the SDLP second and DUP third. No facts or figures though – just conjecture.

If McGimpsey is ignoring the bookies' predictions then Burnside certainly isn't. Rumour has it that he has been going into bookmakers in South Antrim shouting 'Place yer last bets lads, there'll be no more of this come 6 May if McCrea gets his way!'

Burnside is in a very odd position in that he is a hard-line Unionist yet he is up against one of the most far-right candidates in Europe, fundamentalist Free Presbyterian preacher, William McCrea. Burnside, however, is one of the only Ulster Unionists to have won back a seat his party had lost to the DUP having beaten McCrea in 2001. The only other time this had occurred was when the UUP's John Carson retired from North Belfast in 1979 and former UUP MP for Woodvale John McQuade, who had since joined the DUP, won the seat due to a split Unionist vote. He did not contest it in 1983 and North Belfast was regained by the UUP's Cecil Walker who held it until 2001.

The problem for Burnside in South Antrim was that he does not have a lot of room for political manoeuvre. He cannot outdo McCrea as a hard-line Unionist and common wisdom suggests that those who want a hard-liner will vote for the real thing in the DUP man. David is, however, unlikely to attract a lot of soft Unionists or Alliance voters as he is seen as a divisive figure who flipped and flopped over the Agreement when it suited him.

Burnside has not settled well in parliament in his first term and having fallen out with Trimble has become his most prominent critic since Donaldson joined Paisley's team.

I get the impression that he doesn't like being an MP all that much or at least that he is very frustrated by the limited influence members of small political parties have in the House of Commons.

I have noticed this with quite a few MPs from different parties over the years – being an MP perhaps isn't quite what they expected it to be or at least isn't what they hoped it might be. In actual fact, being a member of Parliament can be a very lonely job and a rather thankless task at times. I have no doubt there are many members from all parties who become thoroughly disillusioned with their role.

Today we run a press conference in HQ spilling the beans on a privately-funded trip the DUP have recently taken to the Republic of

Ireland, visiting senior Irish business figures. They snuck out from Belfast City Airport and dined with the southerners before heading back. The purpose of the press conference is to highlight the hypocrisy of the DUP as they covertly entered into a dinner dialogue in the beautiful south.

The media look like they are pretty disgusted at having been dragged all the way to Cunningham House to hear such a pathetic news item. Telling tales on people only works a) if there is an audience to listen, and b) if the person you are telling on has something to be frightened of.

'Pity it wasn't the Bermuda Triangle', remarks one of the journalists on the way out of Cunningham House.

'Or The Vatican', laughs another, 'then you'd have a story.'

Well before the outset of the campaign the DUP had it engrained in the Unionist electorate's mind that they were not just ruling out power-sharing with Sinn Féin, but ruling it out for a generation. They had flipped and flopped over this question before their manifesto launch, yet their message was clear enough to me. The public could trust Ian Paisley to exclude Sinn Féin. What helped consolidate this perception was that UKUP leader Robert McCartney, who always sought to outflank Ian Paisley on the far right, publicly accepted the DUP's private assurances that Sinn Féin would not be in government until they had fully disarmed and reformed their criminal network.

After a private meeting with the DUP leadership, McCartney announced he would be standing aside in North Down, giving the DUP's Peter Weir a free run at unseating Sylvia Hermon.[19] McCartney claimed he had received assurances from the DUP that they were ruling out power-sharing with Sinn Féin for a generation.[20] Regardless of the wording that was used, or the true intentions of the DUP leadership, the impact of this went a long way towards consolidating the electorate's trust in the DUP. There was much speculation that McCartney would be joining whoever else the DUP hand-picked for the House of Lords after the election.[21] This was the same McCartney who once described Paisley as 'a fascist' who was more interested in an independent Ulster – a mini Geneva run by a fifth-rate Calvin – 'than Union with Britain'.[22]

As the DUP's campaign got underway its position over if, when and under what circumstances they would share power with Sinn Féin became confused. By the second week, the DUP had moved away from the McCartney view but, towards the end of the campaign, Ian Paisley had brought his party back to that original position. On 14 April, during an interview with the BBC's Noel Thompson, Peter Robinson stated that he expected to be in talks with the two governments 'immediately after the elections' and denied telling McCartney that the DUP were ruling out power-sharing with Sinn Féin for a generation. He went on to point out that his party had 'no difficulty in terms of asking people to go forward on the basis of complete and verifiable decommissioning'.[23]

A week later, on Monday 25 April, Ian Paisley declared that 'all this talk' that the DUP were eventually going to sit on the other side of the table with Sinn Féin/IRA is 'nonsense'. He then caused a storm by suggesting that David Trimble was counting the days until 'the electric chair and the rope'.[24] When questioned on 'Good Morning Ulster' three days later, the DUP leader further distanced himself from his deputy, confirming that there would be no power-sharing deal with Sinn Féin. In a rather odd turn of phrase, he claimed that he had personally ensured that this policy, his policy, 'would be the DUP line' long after he was dead.[25] This remark was in stark contrast to Jeffery Donaldson's statement on RTE's Vincent Browne Show the previous Thursday, that the DUP had 'moved beyond Paisleyism'.[26] Reg Empey's subsequent call for the DUP leader to 'clarify his party's confused and muddled approach' on where they really stood on 'returning to the so-called comprehensive agreement of last December' was met with silence.[27] This seemed to be a clear signal that the DUP leader was back in charge and Peter Robinson's voice was being drowned out.

23 April

'Contradiction in DUP claims regarding Sinn Féin – Empey[28]

Frustration is the name of the game today – DUP policy shifts are making no impact in the media.

In different times this would have been a media story that ran for weeks, but not in April 2005.

The public and the press have stopped listening to what we are saying, regardless of whether it's the truth or not.

The press are, of course, churning it out all right.

The Newsletter, according to its Political Editor Steven Dempster, are doing a two-way propaganda split on photos and stories between the DUP and the UUP.

The joke is that we will get 100 per cent coverage if that is the case, as writing about anything other than us seems to be well beyond the capacity of the DUP's press office.

The media, like many of the politicians, seem to be staggering blindly through the electoral motions. Political inertia has gripped Northern Ireland and there is nothing we can do about it.

24 April

'Robinson launches DUP campaign to oust Trimble'[29]

So what does ruling out power-sharing with Sinn Féin for a generation actually mean? If the DUP are so convinced that it will take Sinn Féin/IRA twenty-five years to disentangle itself from the terror and criminality that underpins their movement, then why were they on the verge of a deal to implement the Belfast Agreement with them five months ago?

Which policy is the leadership's policy and who is defining the DUP's policy? In December 2003, with Paisley's health seemingly fading, Robinson determined the DUP agenda and pushed hard to re-establish the Assembly – with Republicans. Had it worked, the DUP would have gone into the Westminster election seeking a mandate to share power with Republicans. In the absence of that deal and with the Northern Bank robbery and the McCartney murder making international headlines, the DUP had to misinform the electorate on what they actually intended to do after the election and seriously risk splitting the party if and when they did undertake a huge policy U-turn.

Yet as the DUP's election campaign unfolded, instead of hiding Paisley from the media spotlight, the DUP leader has increasingly taken on a more visible front-line role.

This is in stark contrast to 2001. The DUP's spin doctors hid Paisley from the cameras for fear his commentary would damage their electoral fortunes. Compared to winter 2004, Paisley seems to have firmly re-established control over his party. Paisley's position on sharing power with Sinn Féin is the dominant message emanating from DUP headquarters. To make matters worse our campaign is actually reinforcing what the DUP were saying. Our statements keep referring to how a vote for the DUP will create stalemate. We stop short of saying what is implicit in these comments, that this stalemate will come about because the DUP will not deal with Republicans. But that is exactly what Unionists want to hear. As our Stormont Press Officer Geoffrey McGimpsey put it, 'whenever we were guffawing at Robinson for saying no power-sharing for a generation, the electorate were nodding at his honest sagacity'.[30]

On the one hand we were issuing statements warning people that Northern Ireland is facing Balkanization with Empey's 'Bantu'-style Paisley/Adams carve-up on the cards, yet on the other we are repeatedly telling the public that the DUP are definitely going to do a deal with Sinn Féin after the election.

On 25 April Roy Beggs launched his Celebrity Chef's Challenge at Belfast High School as part of his campaign to deliver more government funding to improve school meals in Northern Ireland. Roy Beggs had been in touch with Jamie Oliver over bringing his campaign to Northern Ireland, and helped politicize the school dinners issues in England by gathering the support of over 150 MPs[31] for Oliver's 'Feed me Better' campaign.[32] Having secured funding from NIO Minister Barry Gardiner, to commence in September 2005, Roy Beggs then put together a team of 'Northern Ireland's celebrity chefs' to take the message of nutrition and healthy eating to children in school canteens and home economics classrooms in his constituency. Beggs' celebrity chefs – Paul Rankin, Jenny Bristow, Nick Price and the late Robbie Millar – each took on a different theme during the week to raise awareness of how children's meals could be made more nutritious in Northern Ireland's schools.

For a politician the bookkeepers had long since written off as the UUP's least likely candidate to hold his seat, Roy Beggs was running a campaign that ignored the deficit of the *Belfast Telegraph* poll and simply stuck to the bread-and-butter issues affecting his constituents on the ground. If nothing else, it was a positive diversion from the monotonous drivel concerning 'dirty tricks' and 'scandal' that had marred the UUP's campaign to date, and a welcome one at that. While the world was crumbling around Cunningham House, Roy Beggs' celebrity chefs were visiting state, catholic and integrated schools across his constituency with Ulster Television screening a nightly 'dinner diary' on their evening news.

25 April

'Challenge gets chefs ready, steady, cooking'[33]

Beggs' dinner test got off to a cracking start today at Belfast High School – all the hard work has paid off. Our press conference was packed out with journalists, cameramen and children. Claire and I were a bundle of nerves but it worked a treat. Fruit and Veg guru, Brian Chapman, set up a marvellous display so Beggs and Co were up to their eyes in cabbages and strawberries.

As Roy donned his kitchen apron and fielded questions from the youngsters, somebody's mobile kept going off in the background. TV chef Paul Rankin, much to the children's delight, answered it and let on that it was Jamie Oliver calling in to see how the launch was going.

What wasn't to the teachers' delight, however, was the Downtown Radio man who, when Rankin answered the phone, tripped over the pile of cameras and wires while trying to record what Paul was saying, letting off a string of four-letter expletives in front of the kids, before tumbling to the ground. There's always one.

After the press conference we all headed upstairs to the home economics classroom where Nick Price made chicken nuggets, chicken risotto, coleslaw and rhubarb crumble. Doing a taste test, Nick compared his recipe to Sainsbury's own nuggets. The difference was amazing and it was clean plates all round. Nick was so impressed with the kids that he promised to come back every year to do something with one of Belfast High School's home economics classes.

The whole thing is turning into a real success – just what the campaign needed.

The following day Ian Paisley was rebuked by Mark Durkan for his comments about David Trimble facing execution at the hands of the electorate. Mark Durkan commented that it was 'appalling' that on the one hand, 'Sinn Féin were covering up murder', while on the other Ian Paisley was 'bragging about death'. He warned voters over the potential future 'these parties offer the people of the north'.[34]

Travelling from town to town across Northern Ireland in the DUP's red, white and blue battlebus the DUP leader, who seemed oblivious to all this criticism, declared that David Trimble's political career was coming to a close. Ian Paisley was looking more energetic than he had done in years, was sounding more like his old self and was attracting more media attention to his party than any of Northern Ireland's other political leaders. The sign on his bus read 'Leadership That's Working', and in terms of feet on the ground they certainly appeared to be.

26 April

'Trimble's goose is cooked' – Paisley[35]

Claire and I rush out to get the papers to see how Beggs' Celebrity Challenge has gone down with the media.

Belfast Telegraph's front page headline reads 'Ex-UUP man in pitch invasion'. (This refers to a riot that followed a Linfield–Glentoran football cup final).[36] Interesting variation on a theme, but not really what I am looking for.

Inside we score a hat-trick in the big three papers with colour photos of Beggs and his chefs, plus the front page of the *Daily Ireland*.

They printed a glossy photo of Beggs with the chefs whipping up some food – only the headline reads '**Trimble's Goose is Cooked**' above a pre-election political obituary of the UUP.
   It only takes one good apple to spoil the basket – right? Not as far as the Irish media are concerned.

Hazel Legge, the party's Head of Administration, brings in a leaflet that's been delivered through her door from a concerned Unionist group which looks set to cause a bit of a storm.

On 26 April Alliance Party Leader David Ford produced a leaflet used for canvassing on UTV's election special programme, accusing Roy Beggs and the UUP's campaign team of running 'a dirty tricks' propaganda effort to undermine the Alliance Party's electoral prospects.[37] The leaflet in question asked Alliance voters to '*vote with your heart, and then vote with your head*', (i.e. for Alliance voters to support their party at the local council elections and then to lend their vote to the UUP in the Westminster poll in order to save the seat from the DUP). David Ford was doubly incensed as the leaflets, distributed by a 'Concerned Unionist' grouping registered in Belfast, used the Alliance Party's colours – giving voters the impression that it was indeed Alliance literature.[38] On the same show, Roy Beggs and Sammy Wilson clashed over the Comprehensive Proposals. Wilson clung to the DUP line that there will be no power-sharing with Sinn Féin, while standing beside Sinn Féin's Mitchell McLaughlin, who argued the very opposite.

26 April

'Wizard Beggs hopes his spell works'[39]

Beggs is in Whitehead Primary School today with Robbie Millar, owner of Shanks' Restaurant at Clandeboye and former Whitehead pupil himself, cooking up his own special kind of oriental fishcakes. He thinks it will be a challenge to get the children to eat fish. It is also Robbie's birthday today, so the kids give him birthday wishes before he gets them to try his fish.

We are then joined by UTV's Pamela Ballentine for the dinner taste test and yet again it is thumbs up. It is working well. None of the local papers have bothered turning up so far, no interest from them whatsoever.

As soon as we finish off at Whitehead Claire and I rush back to HQ to prepare for tonight's TV showdown in Larne.

One nerve-racking evening coming up with Roy Beggs taking the stand on UTV's first election special. Also starring on tonight's show is the SDLP's ('teddy boy') Alban Maginness, Sinn Féin's ('never fired a shot in anger') Mitchell McLaughlin, the DUP's ('easy rider') Sammy Wilson, and Alliance Party Leader ('no, I'm the only non-sectarian one here, honest') David Ford.

Roy has been put through his paces in HQ by Brian and Geoff, in what I can only imagine as a good cop, bad cop routine and when I arrive he seems brimming with confidence and ready for his big night.

When we get into the television studio at Larne leisure centre there are only about 35 people in the audience and as TV shows go, it is the least daunting of any I've been to over the years. Well ... that's easy for me to say.

I sneak backstage as the audience are rehearsing the start of the show with UTV's Fearghal McKinney. I find Roy in the make-up room and do my best to bolster his confidence as we walk towards the stage.

At the beginning, the politicians all read off a script to introduce themselves, except Roy, who speaks about his record as East Antrim's MP over the last 22 years.

All the politicians are very, very nervous before the show. Nobody wants a repeat of the 'Cecil Walker moment', when the UUP man appeared on the 2001 UTV 'Election Insight', on 15 May, without his hearing-aid switched on.

The Walker incident marked an absolutely appalling start to our campaign, but while it was painfully embarrassing it was by no means the only comic TV moment of 2001. During that election the DUP were still refusing to be seen publicly talking to or sitting beside Sinn Féin candidates despite the fact that they worked with them in local councils across the Province.

This tactic was to give the Unionist electorate the impression that excluding Sinn Féin from the political process was something that could be achieved and would be achieved should they back the DUP.

I had the wonderful experience of attending UTV's 'Election Special' in Cookstown. It was a priceless show and Geoffrey McGimpsey, now the party's Stormont press officer, and I were very excited to have a ring-side seat that evening. On the stage they had set up a TV screen to replace the DUP's East Londonderry candidate Gregory Campbell, who refused to go on stage. Instead he appeared live on a television from the next room. For those readers not from Northern Ireland, this is what could be described as our provincial sense of humour.

Trimble's then communications chief, David Kerr, had driven us to the show and sent us into the audience armed with nasty questions for the unsuspecting panellists.

When it came to my turn I almost burst out laughing in front of the cameras. Just when I was about to ask Sinn Féin's Pat Doherty why, since Republicans were accepting the same deal that was on offer to the SDLP in 1973, have we had to endure 30 years of murder and terrorism, I heard Geoff whispering in my ear:
  'Ask Mike Nesbitt to turn that TV down!'

I didn't get much response but was very glad to have it off my chest.

A few days earlier Gregory Campbell had been on the BBC's lunch-time radio show, 'Talkback', and I had ducked out of the Glengall Street office to find an anonymous telephone on which to ring in and give him stick for running away from negotiating a settlement with Nationalism in 1998. I was in full flow when DT apparently walked into the war room, heard me on the radio and asked David Kerr, 'Where on earth is he?'

Kerr pulled back the blinds and quickly spotted me in a phone box in Oxford Street bus station arguing away with whoever had just cut me off. 'Oxford Street bus station', said Kerr as the UUP leader left the room shaking his head.

When I came back everyone was in fits of laughter. But it is little moments like that which really lift people's spirits during a long and gruelling campaign and that get you through the day.

But there was no stage-fright for Roy Beggs in Larne this evening. He comes across clearly and calmly as the party's elder statesman, compared to Sammy Wilson, who gets the bit between his teeth and seems pretty excited. Sammy also takes a lot of flak from the panel of journalists, who, to be fair to them, are very good. Overall, probably a score draw between the UUP and DUP.

These electoral spots, however, are all about not looking bad and I am very happy with Roy's performance.

Ford goes off on a rage about the pseudo-Alliance leaflet that's been doing the rounds. It makes good TV for about thirty seconds.

Beggs, who knew nothing about it, vehemently denies that the UUP campaign team – of which he is a member – has any knowledge of it. If nothing else, it gives Northern Ireland's battalion of conspiracy theorists something to chew over. Ford does have a point, to be fair, but the fallout from the leaflet will be hard to measure in electoral terms.

Either way, it's good publicity for Alliance, as they have been struggling to make any impact in the media this week. Now they have a scandal all of their own – well not quite their own.

27 April

'Alliance in dirty tricks row'[40]

Ford is on the attack again in today's papers and HQ denies any involvement in publishing the leaflet in question. It emerges that the 'Concerned Citizens' group has not been registered with the Electoral Commission. Our North Antrim candidate, Rodney McCune, makes the papers with his 'Ring Rodney Day' idea, asking voters to call him for a chat about electoral issues. Paisley has yet to call.

With a week to go before polling day the UUP leader hit Ian Paisley with a broadside, arguing that a vote for the DUP would send 'the nasty face of politics' to represent Unionism at Westminster.[41] He then launched a scathing attack on the DUP's electoral strategy which, he claimed, aimed to maximize the party's total vote at the expense of keeping Fermanagh and South Tyrone Unionist. It was clear that the DUP agenda was to crush their Unionist rivals and if seats were lost to Nationalist candidates in the process, then that was a secondary issue.

As the Northern Ireland parties began their last week of campaigning the Ulster Unionists seemed to be over the worst of the bad press that had dogged their efforts in the first fortnight. By way of contrast, the DUP leader was looking evermore like a man on the brink, albeit in his eightieth year, of the biggest victory of his long political career. As for the SDLP, and constitutional Nationalism as a whole, they felt so threatened by Sinn Féin that Fianna Fáil members had begun openly supporting the SDLP in Northern Ireland. Gerry Adams formally complained to the Irish government about their 'interference' in the election after Irish Foreign Minister Dermot Ahern canvassed South Down with its outgoing MP Eddie McGrady.[42]

27 April

'Jeffery Valley reflects changes in Unionism'[43]

One week to go

If the papers are to be believed the result remains a foregone conclusion and the campaign to date has only served to solidify that view among political commentators. Yet if the moderates are to be taken at their word Northern Ireland is undergoing a stocktake on the political process, after which the electorate will pull back from the brink and reject the Sinn Féin–DUP stalemate.

The atmosphere in this morning's meeting is fantastic. Everyone is working hard and ready for the grand finale.

DT comes in and nips that firmly in the bud. He is very unhappy about how the campaign is going, both internally and externally. General feeling at HQ, however, is that even if everything had been done differently, the media would still have been full of the same bad news stories regarding the scandals, dirty tricks, vote splitting, as well as the perception that we are a dead horse in the stocks taking a pounding from all who fancy a pot-shot.

No one really has an answer to the 'what else can we do?' question. Plenty of people are asking it though. Plenty of people are saying this or that is wrong with the campaign. But not one of them, unfortunately, is calling up saying, 'Look guys, here's a good alternative to that, run with it.'

It's not just that the body is willing and the mind is weak, it simply isn't possible to turn water into wine, especially when you haven't even got water to work with. Bad press is bad press.

So where are we with a week of normal campaigning left to go?

It's all gone so quickly that there hasn't been time to stand back and get a broad view of what is going on.

We feel totally written off that is for sure, yet, ... somehow, there are still the last vestiges of enthusiasm to be found among the team, and come 8am, everyone is always raring to go.

People are running on nervous energy and holding out for one last push. We need to do something big to finish with, to remove the sour taste this campaign has left in most people's mouths before they go to the polls. But where will it take us? What form will it take?

There are still some UUP believers out there, albeit not very many, jamming the blogging waves on journo-chat site www.sluggerotoole. com. While most observers seem to think the UUP will be soundly beaten in South Belfast, someone with the handle of 'Hansolo' claims to have seen NIO polls that put the SDLP ahead of Michael McGimpsey by hundreds of votes with Spratt trailing way behind. And there have actually been a number of letters in the main papers recently suggesting that Sinn Féin supporters are switching to SDLP to snatch the seat, so, ...

Anyway, one irate – presumably DUP supporter – has dubbed 'Hansolo' the UUP's 'Comical Ali' after Saddam Hussein's loyal lieutenant, who, in 2003, famously spoke on live TV of an Iraqi victory as US troops were running around firing off weapons on the camera shot in the background. I guess Ali didn't believe in the force either.

Forty-five-year-old, Lagan Valley candidate, Basil McCrea, has been the TV star of the UUP over the last 10 days with his 'think big' campaign to oust the sitting MP, Jeffery Donaldson.

He has run a bright and high profile campaign. One of his key policies seems to be his opposition to water rates. He has had a large trailer displaying a 'Stop the Drip' sign across his constituency.

That seat will be a litmus test for Unionism. If Donaldson increases his majority then that is where Unionism lies.

John Taylor was always known as the 'Unionist barometer' for his fox-like instinct for feeling which way the current was running within Unionism. Now, for very different reasons, our barometer is the man who has been a long-term thorn in Unionist leaders' sides. If he is to have the last laugh in the Trimble–Donaldson saga, then the re-alignment within Unionism will be a seismic shift.

5 Spun Out

Trimble's people power was lacking. Where he was seen initially as being courageous in having taken the Ulster Unionists to the fore, the follow-up aspect in terms of getting out and explaining the message in detail to people just wasn't there. The problem with communications is that you've got to send out a message. If it's a good message you send it out again and again and again. We never did that. A bit like Paisley used to be. In terms of dealing with your problem, Paisley didn't really resolve your problem. What he did was screech 'this is dreadful what's happening to this man'. He then got huge press coverage about how he was going to tear some poor government minister's head off and then it went away because the next week he was championing someone else's cause.

Ken Maginnis, 21 July 2005

When the 2005 general election entered its last week, a sense of inevitability had crept into the UUP's campaign. From the perspective of those at Cunningham House, it had been a campaign that had never really got off the ground, following the catalogue of scandals, dirty tricks and self-destruction. The message Ulster Unionist candidates were receiving on their constituency doorsteps, however, seemed to indicate the very opposite. From across Northern Ireland UUP candidates, young and old, were returning to Cunningham House with tales of 'a fantastic response on the doorstep' and 'a great deal of people pledging their support'.[1]

Seasoned campaigners such as Roy Beggs remarked that they had no reason to believe the *Belfast Telegraph* poll was likely to come true. Beggs commented that he was having, 'the most enjoyable election campaign' of his entire parliamentary career. He said the reception he was receiving on the doorsteps in all boroughs of his constituency was 'very positive'.[2] Outgoing MP for South Antrim, David Burnside, commented he had 'never fought a better campaign' in his political career.[3] David Trimble himself was also picking up good feedback on the ground in Upper Bann. This was in stark contrast to the scenes of violence at Banbridge in 2001, when the Unionist leader and his wife, Daphne, were 'punched and kicked, both inside and outside the count, by DUP supporters'.[4] These images were viewed worldwide and portrayed Unionism at its very worst. This was how Ian Paisley's supporters treated Nobel Laureates in Northern Ireland.

So why was the UUP receiving a good response on the doorsteps when the media and the bookmakers had the party written off? Would these public pledges of support for the UUP transfer into votes come 5 May, or were they simply empty promises? Were the candidates merely experiencing a different mood from the Unionist electorate compared to the outright hostility they faced in 2001 over issues such as police reform, prisoner releases and Sinn Féin in government? Had the UUP's 2005 campaign actually influenced the electorate to the extent that it would enable them to maintain a significant position at Westminster in the next parliament? The electorate was certainly calm compared to the unpleasantness of 2001 and 2003. The UUP's canvassing teams, however, had become fearful of knocking on doors given their experience in the previous two elections.

These were the questions the party was asking itself in those key constituencies where the struggle between the two main Unionist parties was reaching a climax. South Belfast was the hardest of these seats to call. On 28 April, Michael McGimpsey claimed he was well ahead of Jimmy Spratt in the battle to replace Rev. Martin Smyth. His analysis was based on private polling, which he said put him a few hundred votes ahead of SDLP South Belfast candidate Alasdair McDonnell.[5] Aside from all the spin in the newspapers, it was apparent by the weekend before the election that the result was too close to call in South Belfast, South Antrim, Foyle and Upper Bann. These were the seats where the 2005 election would be won or lost for Northern Ireland's four main parties. Should John Hume's seat fall to Sinn Féin in Foyle, then both his protégé's leadership and their party's fortunes would be irreparably damaged. As for the UUP, if Ian Paisley breached Upper Bann then both the Unionist leader, and his party, would be facing the greatest electoral shock in its one-hundred-year history.

28 April

'Close-run South Belfast heading for a photo finish'[6]

The media has closed in on South Belfast, Foyle and Upper Bann as we prepare for the final showdown. For the SDLP and ourselves, turn out will be crucial.

The DUP and Sinn Féin will get their vote out. They always do. If the trend of voter apathy continues we will be the party most affected. If our voters stay away, as many of them did in 2003 and 2004, then we will be decimated.

As for the SDLP, they will likely need UUP votes to hold significant majorities in South Down and Foyle.

We need to do something big next week to grab the headlines and enable us to go out with a bang. Over the past few days the DUP and Sinn Féin have been very quiet indeed – too quiet.

At least we are enjoying a week with no scandal – thank God for small mercies.

It certainly doesn't give us much time to come out with our positive message, whatever that might be.

Looking back on the campaign so far, we never actually began to achieve our initial goal which was to hit the DUP with negative campaigning and then follow that up with a big positive message/campaign. We never had a chance with all the bad press. It seems that this was all it took to smother our campaign before it even got off the ground.

In the last week of electioneering there was to be no let-up in the rift between David Ford and the UUP. It emerged that the 'dirty trick leaflet' in question had been designed by a company the UUP had previously used. David Ford called for an immediate investigation and Cunningham House again protested its innocence. David Trimble accused Ford of engaging in electoral 'stunts'[7] and UUP Communications Director, Alex Benjamin, described the coincidence as 'bizarre'.[8] On the same day, UKUP leader Robert McCartney repeated his call for voters to back the DUP at the polls, claiming an 'overwhelming majority' of Unionists had lost all confidence in the UUP.[9] Yet an unusual source of support for David Trimble came when his old political adversary, Séamus Mallon, stated that while the SDLP had an 'excellent candidate in Upper Bann', he was in no doubt that there would be people in that constituency 'who will make their judgements as they see the best way of using their vote'.[10]

This was similar to how Cunningham House privately viewed the Nationalist contests in South Down and Foyle. While the party clearly wanted its candidates, Dermot Nesbitt and Earl Storey, to hold up the UUP vote, it was hopeful that Ulster Unionist voters would lend enough support to the SDLP to keep Sinn Féin at bay in those constituencies. This was in stark contrast to the DUP's attitude that they must defeat the UUP regardless of whether that defeat was to the benefit of Sinn Féin. So outflanked were the two moderate parties that Mallon's remarks were as far as either could go in terms of publicly reaching out to each other. To say they would work together in the future, however, was something they both agreed on, but as to how they would do it was another matter entirely. During the election the SDLP could not call for Sinn Féin to be excluded from any post-election government, whereas the UUP could offer nothing other than a belated promise to do just that.

The two moderate centre-ground parties both had similar messages regarding their view of the political process, but they were too weak either to say so or to offer moderate voters a message they could relate to. At best, they sent out mixed messages to their own communities. David Trimble and Mark Durkan had their hands tied, for had they moved closer to each other during the election campaign, both leaders would have opened up a new line of attack for the DUP and Sinn Féin. As such, the impact of their call to the electorate in Northern Ireland to avoid a Sinn Féin-DUP Balkanization scenario fell totally flat. As one party insider put it, the UUP does not have a message apart from 'we're nice and they're not. The problem is that everybody in Northern Ireland knows that. People know that the DUP are unpleasant to others but the issue is whether they are going to keep Sinn Féin out of government or not.'[11]

30 April

'Still clinging to the middle of the road, no matter how narrow the path'[12]

It's the end of a reasonably good week – Beggs' school dinner campaign went very well indeed, with Paul Rankin visiting Ulidia Integrated College in Carrickfergus, and Jenny Bristow wrapping things up at St Comgalls in Larne.

For Roy, win or lose, the Celebrity Chef's challenge had been the icing on the cake of his campaign and a lot of fun. He told me how satisfying it was to have built on Jamie Oliver's idea and to have been able to do so in our own way through the state, Catholic and integrated schools. I hadn't thought about it like that and it was indeed something special in the sense that this was just the sort of politics unimaginable in Northern Ireland only ten years ago.

It made me smile when the TV cameras picked up 'Roy Beggs' on the back of the children's T-shirts. I had spent the whole weekend hand-printing them at an old friend's shop in Belfast. On the front of the shirts was the blue 'Celebrity Chef Challenge' logo and on the back Roy's name and that of all the different sponsors.

It was good politics. We were seriously addressing the needs of the people and what was best for the future of our children. We also got a lot of great press from the initiative and it's been the icing on the cake for what has been a really good campaign in East Antrim. But it is not over yet.

Claire and I join Roy and Wilma Beggs with their team in Whitehead and Island Magee. We receive a quiet response in Whitehead and a very bad one on the Island. There is little enthusiasm for either the UUP or the campaign in general. I have a few fleas in my ear by the time we head back to Belfast at dusk.

This is the first canvassing I have done in 2005. It is a completely different experience compared to 2001. Hitting the doorsteps in Strangford and East Belfast four years ago I received a baptism of fire from the Unionist electorate. Every third or fourth call ended up in a long wrangle over police or prisoners. These issues were huge barriers to most Unionists. There is one thing you can be sure about when it comes to Ulster folk, if they have something bad to say to you, they sure aren't half quick about saying it.

Today the anger over the Belfast Agreement's painful issues has gone. Unionism does in fact seem to have swallowed those bitter pills. But that doesn't mean there is to be no more payback for those who administered them. There is certainly some animosity towards DT himself. Some people say they are against him and not the party.

Many people are taking our literature but not stopping for a chat. It is noticeably difficult to engage people about the election or the process. The only person I really got chatting to is a man whose daughter was in the home economics class at Belfast High School when we visited. We had a real laugh as he told me that his daughter asked Roy who she should vote for and Roy told her that when she was eighteen she should back the UUP.

Her dad said she was definitely not voting for Mr Beggs as she was already eighteen and had taken grave offence that the outgoing MP had failed to recognize this!

Some of our candidates seem to be taking this docile atmosphere as a good sign, but on the basis of today things do not look good.

News comes in at teatime that the DUP are to be rocked by a major

106

sex scandal in tomorrow's tabloids. Something about a DUP Westminster candidate, a male masseur and a Belfast hotel room. It's from a most reliable source, but still, I'll believe it when I see it.

The DUP and Sinn Féin were not having it all their own way. On 1 May the *Sunday World* reported details of how their Free Presbyterian gospel-singing candidate for Newry and South Armagh, Paul Berry, had allegedly been caught in a honey-trap by a disgruntled member of the gay community. According to the tabloid newspaper he had met Berry through an internet chat-room before they arranged to meet.[13] Berry, who had driven to meet the man in a Belfast hotel room, denied anything other than a massage had taken place, which was required for an old 'sports injury'.[14] DUP HQ quickly put a lid on this affair and refused to answer questions on the subject, other than to say that the matter was being dealt with by Paul Berry's lawyers.[15]

On 28 April, PSNI Chief Constable Hugh Orde made a statement indicating that the IRA were still actively recruiting volunteers, and targeting potential victims in Northern Ireland. Sinn Féin reacted furiously to these remarks, with Gerry Adams accusing Orde of having directed his comments in order to make a 'political intervention' during an election campaign.[16] Following that, the SDLP came out fighting as John Hume entered a scathing war of words with the Sinn Féin president. The outgoing Foyle MP attacked Gerry Adams for suggesting his party had abandoned the Hume–Adams initiative and said that his comments were an 'insult' to the electorate.[17]

2 May

'Voters look to safety at the two extremes'[18]

War room staff absolutely shattered this morning. The odd joke about Paul Berry's groin strain barely lifts anyone's spirits.

Orangemen hold a mini-May Day rally in support of Fermanagh and

South Tyrone MLA Tom Elliott at Stormont, which is a nice boost.

Plans are being drawn up for a spectacular press conference tomorrow at Belfast's Waterfront Hall or the Odyssey. We'll have lots of young Unionists and people standing outside with DT doing a walkabout for the cameras, spelling out his vision for the future.

DT cancels it at 9.30. We have to come up with something else – pronto.

Anyone got any bright ideas?

Everyone is very depressed. It's not clear what we can do to finish on a high note. Geoff suggests closing Cunningham House for a couple of days!

Tim and Will rally the troops for one last push. Tomorrow is the last day of election coverage in the papers, so we pull together a few 'round-up' press releases, and prepare victory speeches for our candidates!

DT is beginning to really look as if he is at a loose end. I have never seen him before in a situation where he doesn't know what to do or where he is not two or three paces ahead of everyone else.

It's very odd. We've been sitting here waiting for him to show us the direction we should be going in, but it's pretty clear he does not know himself. How could he? Such is the impossibility of the situation he faces. The most telling thing is that there is no sense of urgency coming from him. He's been looking at the campaign diary and it's half full. Four years ago he had options galore. Today we are cancelling press conferences because we know the media won't bother to turn up.

On the Tuesday before polling day David Trimble ran a Tony Blair style letter advertisement in the *Belfast Telegraph*, spelling out where his party was coming from in negotiating the Belfast Agreement, how a victory for the DUP and Sinn Féin could set Northern Ireland back years, and what the alternative to this would be:

Ulster Unionists take their responsibilities seriously. If there was the chance of an agreement that secured our position in the UK, I had to explore that option. Others failed in their duties.

I always believed that people with a past could have a future. But they had to change.

We gave them the opportunity. They failed the test.

I forced suspension of the Assembly in the teeth of fierce opposition. Why did we succeed? Because it was clear we had gone the extra mile for peace.

Our opponents said they wanted to smash the Agreement. Then they wanted a new Agreement.

Last December, but for a couple of photographs, Sinn Fein would have been in government with the IRA still intact. In 2005, that's not good enough.

Ulster Unionists don't pretend there are simple solutions. We don't offer false hope. But I know this: voting for the worst of both worlds will leave us with the worst of all worlds.

I don't want a generation of bitterness and no-hope politics. Let's give Northern Ireland the best possible chance of a democratic, peaceful future. Do it on the 5th of May. By voting Ulster Unionist.

David Trimble

3 May

'No surprise that odds stacked up against Trimble'[19]

Nerves are frazzled at HQ today. It's got to the stage where there is very little left to do and not much we can do to influence things.

Press conference planned for Stormont tomorrow with DT and the big hitters. After that, we split up and join the teams around the Province for their last-minute efforts.

I'm really looking forward to getting out there and knocking on some doors. Last week felt like pulling teeth – a waste of time, churning out the same old garbage we have been harping on about for weeks. The only way our candidates can have an impact in this election is through the work they have been doing on the ground. It will be won or lost on the doorsteps.

The media war has been a tit-for-tat affair getting us nowhere. If we rounded up all the candidates nursing shrapnel wounds and dislocated egos we'd need a field hospital at Cunningham House car park to cope with them. At least in football they send you off the pitch if you get a bloody nose ... but then again, football is not a blood sport, is it?

Claire and I head up to Larne at last with East Antrim MLA Roy Beggs Junior. We get a much better response on the estates today with a lot of promises of support and a good deal of positivity. Totally the opposite from the weekend, people are stopping to chat with us and Roy is having fun getting out there with the locals.

On one estate I get surrounded by a lot of schoolchildren asking me what I am doing. As I give them Roy's cards he comes walking around the corner. Five minutes later, having signed their cards, he's chatting to one of the girl's parents on her mobile phone, telling them how he's won over the new generation but he still hopes he can count on the older ones' votes too. All good fun.

Do we think we can win East Antrim? No. But it's all about going out with our heads held high and putting up a good fight. It is beginning to look like that in most constituencies.

The penny is finally dropping with some people at Cunningham House that we will most likely lose all our Westminster seats. Sylvia looks to be the only one with a reasonably good chance. Yet, in spite of everything, the message from South Belfast and Upper Bann remains good. But is it all talk? Are the politicians simply going through the motions? The answer to that is definitely NO. There is too much at stake.

Fair enough, we have run out of ideas and there has been no strong message throughout this campaign, but our main candidates all still feel they can squeeze through on a good day with a high turn out. A high turn out is imperative.

Are they in denial? I don't know. It has, for sure, been an appalling campaign. Right from the outset it's hard to think of anything that has gone according to plan. And it hasn't been because people have been making huge mistakes at HQ or that everyone hasn't been putting in the blood, sweat and tears. Events have conspired against us, while many within the party have conspired against us, too, in order to create some of those very events.

The truth is that, days before the poll, no one really has the faintest idea as to where we stand in the key constituencies. The only thing we are rock solid positive about is that it isn't a good position to be standing in. While some commentators are predicting a wipe-out, others are saying it's too close to call.

But there is also definitely an element of 'fence sitting' stemming from the fact that DT has 'pulled it off' so many times in the past when he has looked doomed.

No one wants to call time on David Trimble and get it wrong.

On the eve of polling day, Northern Ireland's political parties set out their platforms for the last time. The DUP's final message urged the electorate to end the reign of David Trimble as a representative of Unionism in Northern Ireland. Very much in keeping with a campaign that had largely focused on the man they had worked tirelessly to demonize and tarnish over the previous decade. In case anyone remained confused as to where Ian Paisley's party stood on the political process before polling day, the DUP leader spelt it out loud and clear.

> If the parties which have entered into government in the past with the terrorist IRA/Sinn Féin win it, then the momentum to surrender to Dublin dictatorship will prevail, and those Unionists who in the past surrendered will continue their false-hoods and treacheries ...
>
> Let me make it unequivocally clear that the DUP will never enter government with IRA/Sinn Féin.
>
> Note carefully – this is free from any ifs or buts or turnings.
>
> To enter into Government with the terrorists of IRA/Sinn Féin would be treason. Of that we will never be guilty.[20]

There had been much debate during the campaign as to whether the DUP were really ruling out power-sharing with Sinn Féin for a generation and if Ian Paisley was to be taken at his last word of the campaign then had returned to his old policy on power-sharing – rule it out on principle.

In contrast, the UUP leader reminded the electorate of his achievements as the voice of Unionism over the previous decade and told voters that Northern Ireland's best hope for the future was a coalition of the moderates. David Trimble defended the decisions he had taken, decisions he argued had left Northern Ireland a far better place than in 1998 and 'unambiguously in the United Kingdom'. He argued that under his leadership Unionism had grown 'stronger', and for the first time in decades become 'respected'. David Trimble castigated the British Prime Minister for his 'untrustworthiness', and his repeated failure to live up to his promises to the people of Northern Ireland regarding Sinn Féin's entry into an Executive prior to decommissioning. Trimble said the best way for his party 'to achieve progress' was to rebuild 'a moderate coalition' with the

SDLP.[21] The question remained as to whether the Unionist electorate viewed this pledge to piece back together the broken UUP–SDLP pact, or Ian Paisley's commitment to permanently exclude Sinn Féin from Northern Ireland's political process, as the more attractive option.

The SDLP leader did his moderate counterpart no favours, sending out a warning that the DUP's agenda was to ensure Sinn Féin became Northern Ireland's largest party so that Ian Paisley could then declare the Belfast Agreement dead.[22] The UUP's problem there was that most Unionists already believed the Agreement had failed them and that one of the DUP's key election slogans was that the only way Unionists could prevent the 'nightmare scenario' of Sinn Féin as Northern Ireland's largest party was to vote DUP.[23] According to Mark Durkan, all this talk was just 'Sinn Féin and the DUP trying to pump each other up'.[24] The big problem for his party and the UUP was that it seemed to be working.

For Sinn Féin's part, Gerry Adams warned that violence would fill Northern Ireland's political vacuum if progress was not speedily achieved after the election. He voiced his concern that 'the peace process' was on 'a downward spiral'.[25] In West Tyrone, his colleague Pat Doherty increased the tension by claiming that, according to Sinn Féin's returns, 'in terms of popular support' they could become Northern Ireland's largest party. The West Tyrone candidate added that a strong Nationalist vote would serve as a 'reality check' for those Unionists who had not come to realize 'that the days of domination and second-class citizenship were over' and that a 'process of change' was irreversible.[26]

The DUP and Sinn Féin were speaking the same tongue to different congregations. Gerry Adams was warning Nationalists that the only way Sinn Féin's recent achievements could be built upon was by backing his party. His was the movement that would not give an inch to the backlash occurring within Unionism as a result of those achievements. In the same vein, having demonized David Trimble and downplayed the huge constitutional gains his party secured under the Belfast Agreement, the DUP were telling Unionists that the only way to halt the rising tide of Nationalism was to back their candidates.

The two parties had similar electoral strategies regarding their Unionist and Nationalist rivals. The objective was to squeeze the moderate vote. The method was fear and sectarian triumphalism. Fear within each community of the perceived threat of the growth and domination of one nationalist identity over the other. Triumphalism in that there was a sense of security in consolidating under the wing of extreme Unionism and Nationalism, given the failure of the centre-ground parties who brokered the Belfast Agreement. The result, they hoped, would be Reg Empey's sectarian 'carve up'.[27] This election had been a timely reminder that the DUP needed the IRA as much as its Unionist bogey man, David Trimble, in order to run their double-edged fear campaign within the Unionist community.

4 May

'PAISLEY v TRIMBLE'[28]

Eve of Poll

Last day in the office, no pun intended, as we gear up for polling day.

The optimists, well Dr King at any rate, think we'll finish on three seats. The pessimists, Dr Crowe at any rate, one or none. What about me? Well, I think we'll convincingly win in North Down, and then hold either South Belfast, South Antrim or Upper Bann in that order of likelihood. One, maybe two seats.

Let's hope we're all wrong.

King spotted that Irish bookmakers, Paddy Power, are offering an accumulator on the amount of seats the UUP will win, with odds of 10/1 on the party to take three seats or more. Quite a few bets have gone down on this over the last 24 hours.

Gambling aside, no one has any handle on where we are or what will happen tomorrow. Most of us haven't seen the outside of Cunningham House for a month. There is a certain detachment from reality that creeps in when fighting a general election campaign.

One of the candidates came into Cunningham House yesterday and told us that the DUP had pulled out of South Belfast and were reinforcing their troops in Lagan Valley. I simply didn't have the heart to tell him that I had made that up several days ago.

Someone once said 'Don't believe everything you read,' but in politics, a healthier slogan would be: 'Don't believe everything you write' (or 'anything' if you work in the DUP press office).

Every good spin doctor suffers from a bit of 'washing-machine syndrome' now and again, but sometimes, over the last week or so, I've felt like we've been spun out. Tomorrow is 5 May, so no doubt, one way or another, there is a reality check heading our way.

It's like waiting for your exam results; only the electoral oddity is that you don't get high marks for hard work or answering the questions correctly. I do remember making a lot of stuff up in my exams but...

In the absence of yesterday's spectacular press conference we held a low key event in Belfast to round off the campaign. It was a bit of a tetchy affair on the street just outside the gates of City Hall and Mallie did his usual paper-clip in the works act. We stood around watching with the security guards for any troublemakers from the DUP. The funny thing was that the only passers-by who stopped to observe were tourists. An Austrialian man of Irish Catholic descent stopped and asked me what was going on and who was speaking. He said, 'Oh, David Trimble! He is a great man indeed. Everyone thinks very highly of him in Austrialia, what he's done for Northern Ireland and that.' I thanked him, and Alison Laird gave his smiling children some UUP boiled sweets to suck on. It was a sign of the times that at our last press conference of the campaign, not a single local person, on a bright sunny morning in the city centre of Belfast, stopped to hear what Trimble was saying. They just ignored him.

In 2001, we would have thought twice about having a conference there. We would have had security everywhere, cars stopping, DUP hecklers working doubletime shouting 'Traitor Trimble' and the like. But not in 2005.

I asked UTV's Ken Reid how he thought tomorrow might pan out. Maybe he didn't want to rub it in, but he said he wasn't 100 per cent sure. 'It has been a very weird campaign,' he remarked, and 'one that will be won or lost on the doorstep.' I suspect he is right.

Claire, Geoff and I go for one last spin on the merry-go-round in Carrickfergus. We cover a lot of ground and get a fairly good response. It is a gorgeous day and I wish we could turn back the clock a few weeks and spend every day of the campaign like this. There is something irresistibly satisfying about going door-to-door, chatting to people and finding out what is going on. It's a fantastic buzz. It's what politics is all about.

We are not, however, provoking a great deal of interest. People are happy to stop and chat, and no one has much to complain about, but mention the election – what election?

As we are leaving the main street, I shout across the road at a couple of young women:

'Are you going to vote for Roy Beggs tomorrow?'

'We're not from round here,' they reply.

'Neither's Sammy Wilson,' I retort, but they don't seem to hear me.

6 The Man Who Fell to Earth

The *Belfast Telegraph* poll reflected what I was hearing on the ground, in talking to people. I got the feeling that we were in for a trouncing. I won't just complain about the leader being out of touch. I think the entire leadership of the party was out of touch, especially the officers who are vested, constitutionally, with the responsibility of policy-making in the absence of decisions taken by the UUC. It seemed to me in the last number of years, especially since our significant defeat in the 2003 Assembly elections, that they were being unrealistic. They were not accepting that the DUP were now bigger than we were. In fact, they were acting as if nothing had happened. Unfortunately it had happened, it was bound to get worse and they were not in touch with that reality.

Lord Kilclooney, 13 July 2005

On 5 May voters went to the polls to decide which of Northern Ireland's main political parties would be the dominant voices of Unionism and Nationalism during the next parliament. There had been a sense of *déjà-vu* about this election, as if history was about to repeat itself. Back in the early 1970s, British Prime Minister Edward Heath had attempted to break the Unionist mould by creating a centre ground in Northern Irish politics through the Sunningdale Agreement, having prorogued Stormont and returned security powers to Westminster.[1] When that power-sharing agreement faced the searing test of a general election in 1974, SDLP leader Gerry Fitt was the only pro-Agreement candidate returned to Parliament.

Twenty-five years later, Tony Blair had attempted the same thing, only his deal was based upon the premise of inclusivity, that the door to the political process was open to everyone in 1998. In contrast, Sunningdale excluded the anti-Agreement opposition and the Republican movement. Both ventures had failed and the predicted outcome of the 2005 election was that the Unionist mould would in fact be recast in the form that successive British governments had worked to avoid. In fact, one of the reasons that the British government actually dissolved Stormont back in 1972 was for fear that Ian Paisley might one day become Northern Ireland's Prime Minister. This was something Downing Street had not been prepared to contemplate.[2] Like Brian Faulkner, David Trimble looked set to be crushed by the gathering forces of anti-Agreement Unionism. Both men had undergone radical conversions in their political careers, taking on the idea of power-sharing in Northern Ireland and made it their own. David Trimble, especially, as he had been at the forefront of William Craig's Vanguard movement, which helped break Sunningdale.

Against all the odds, both Ulster Unionist leaders had gone out in front of their own communities and brokered a deal with Nationalism that many of their colleagues and constituents were psychologically unprepared for. David Trimble's venture, however, was ultimately the more successful of the two. The UUP leader had played a major role in changing Northern Ireland from a war-torn burden on the British State into a potentially prosperous region of it. Equally important was David Trimble's contribution to Unionism. He had radically transformed how his community was perceived internationally. Under him, Unionism also became respected and accepted within UK politics, where it had been an embarrassment to its own government for decades. Yet if the pundits were to be believed, the Unionist electorate was set to reject David Trimble despite these achievements. Nationalism was also billed to undergo a seismic shift of equal proportions. The SDLP were apparently facing the same treatment from their electorate as the UUP. Very few of those commentators were voicing the fears of the moderate parties with any great sense of urgency. In fact, no one except the UUP or the SDLP seemed particularly worried that Northern Ireland was going to the extremes. A new strand of short-term thinking had emerged from the Northern Ireland Office, giving the current setback in Northern Ireland's administration a rather glossy sheen. It was not a setback at all. The argument went that it would most likely be easier to broker a deal between the right-wing parties, as everyone knew where they stood.[3] The question they were not asking was what sort of deal would it be?

As I woke up with a splitting headache on polling day I wondered what, if anything, the UUP had achieved over the past five weeks. On reflection, the last four years had been the party's opportunity to work the 1998 Agreement. This had been without success. Should the UUP win this election was there anywhere else it could take the political process on the back of that failure? Was David Trimble's party in fact the right vehicle to carry the Belfast Agreement forwards into its next phase, or had it run out of steam? How could agreement be reached by the DUP and Sinn Féin if they emerged with strong mandates that had little or no relation to the ideals of the Belfast Agreement? Does Northern Ireland need four or five years of polarization for it to carry out a stocktake on the Belfast Agreement and what it truly entailed? Will Unionists – politicians and constituents alike – ever look beyond their own backyards in Northern Ireland? The answers to these questions seemed fairly obvious on polling day, but in politics that is no reason not to get out of bed and fight for what you believe in.

5 May

'Trimble fights for survival as Province turns to extremes'[4]

Polling Day

Slept in at last today before Geoff McGimpsey picked me up at noon to go and cast my vote at Newtownards Model School. UUP stalwart Myrtle Cook was outside in the rain handing out Gareth McGimpsey's literature. It struck me there was a sense of desperation creeping into our campaign if one McGimpsey has to pick me up to vote for his own cousin three hundred yards from my house. (Maybe he doesn't trust me after all these years). It was just as well that he did as when we arrived I discovered that I had forgotten my passport! Really feeling the heat today, I'm totally exhausted.

Geoff and I head to Dundonald to spend the afternoon canvassing outside a polling station there. As we arrive the DUP's Strangford candidate, Iris Robinson, is already there chatting to passing voters.

As we approach she croaks, 'Are you boys going to vote?'

'We already have,' I reply.

'I hope you did the right thing,' she says, smiling as we walk past to find a spot outside the gates of the station to pitch our tent.

'The Decent Thing', Geoff shouts back at her and she laughs.

One thing is for sure, come tomorrow, she will be having the last laugh in my constituency. Her majority is bound to be considerably increased. It's a miserable afternoon and the voters trickle in and out. All in all we get a poor response from most of them. A lot of people wouldn't even take our leaflets.

At teatime Geoff goes to the next polling station and Claire joins me. A few minutes later a canvasser from the PUP comes along. When he sees we are Ulster Unionist he smiles and says politely,

'Don't mind if I join you, do you?'

'Not at all', we reply.

'Don't fancy setting up stall down there', he says smiling and pointing to the end of the street where the DUP team are handing out their glossy leaflets.

It's always the same when you meet people who are linked to, or represent, the Loyalist paramilitaries. They've never a good word to say about the DUP. I guess they have been used and abused by them so many times over the years.

He talks to me about working-class issues and how there is a need to address the problems local people face in their own communities. He said the bounce the PUP and UDP got from the Agreement has gone and that there is a massive lack of leadership in his area and connection with the rest of society. Drugs are a big problem.

What about the UVF drug dealers I ask nervously. He says the PUP are totally against drugs and drug dealers but powerless to do anything about it. In his opinion, the only way to solve the problem is to make those who are part of the problem part of the solution. The longer they are ignored the worse it will get.

Quite a few of the locals seem to know him and he is well received. It was nice to have met him, but also a bit embarrassing. All I am armed with is a hollow message and I haven't recognized a soul here all day. The disconnection that exists between us and the electorate is stark. If I had a pound for every time someone had said to me that they might have voted for us if someone had bothered canvassing their area ...

By 6.30 we have run out of flyers and run out of steam. Claire and I head down to the Moat Inn on the Newtownards Road for a quick pint to revive our spirits.

I've barely disturbed the cream on the top of my Guinness before Strangford MLA David McNarry bursts in shouting 'How did I know I'd find you in here?'

An hour or so later, local council hopeful Hazel Legge arrives with her literature and we head off with Tim Lemon to Belfast for a night out with the team.

The mood, surprisingly, is fantastic. This, however, is more to do with the fact that we can wash our hands of the campaign and sit and wait for the results. Our work is done. Unlike the rest of the UK, we will not know our fate until Friday morning, as counting does not start in Northern Ireland until the day after the vote.

Well before polling stations have closed we have put it all to the back of our minds and are enjoying a well-deserved escape from Cunningham House.

121

By 6 May Northern Ireland's electorate had spoken and the fate of its politicians was sealed in the ballot boxes lying unopened across the Province's schools and leisure centres. It had been, if nothing else, a campaign that would most likely be remembered for the big political scalps that were predicted to be taken when the counting was done. There had been no clear message from any of the parties; there had been no policies to catch the eye; and there had been no interest in anything other than whether David Trimble or Mark Durkan could fend off what had become personal challenges from their rivals in Sinn Féin and, more so, the DUP.

The BBC had travelled the Province offering members of the public sweets from jars labelled with the different political issues of the campaign.[5] At the end, the jar representing 'water rates' was less full than that of the 'orange/green divide', yet no one was in any doubt that this election, above all in recent years, would turn out to be a sectarian head count in the rawest sense. The *Daily Telegraph* argued that 'Unionist disillusion' with David Trimble's handling of the Belfast Agreement, and the rise of Sinn Féin, 'had allowed the DUP to capture the centre ground'.[6] If the UUP were to shed more votes than they had in the 2003 Assembly election, then it would be the bulk of those voters who had begrudgingly given the agenda of the 1998 centre ground one last chance at that election that went to the DUP.

With the lack of any grandstanding on policy before polling day, all eyes were on the key seats as the beauty contest got under way. The *Belfast Telegraph* had its predictions laid out on the first page with the bookmakers' favourites making all the running.[7] The main parties were neck-and-neck in so many constituencies that recounts were predicted in almost a dozen seats, with at least a third of the eighteen expected to change hands. In the final analysis, it predicted that both the UUP and the SDLP would be reduced to just one seat each at Westminster, with David Trimble and Mark Durkan losing their positions in the cull. Sylvia Hermon and Eddie McGrady were the only moderates worth betting on. Even then, the North Down candidate represented the liberal wing of the UUP in what was Northern Ireland's most unorthodox constituency, while McGrady's fight in South Down would almost certainly be his last. Such a forecast meant polarization of Northern Ireland's political landscape and decimation for the architects of the Belfast Agreement. Yet the media, the public and the British government did not seem at all perturbed by this likely outcome. Mark Durkan was rated at evens with Mitchell McLaughlin set to take the seat at 4/7. The situation had not improved for his Unionist counterpart in Upper Bann, valued at 2/1 to retain his seat, against his gospel-singing opponent who remained the favourite at 2/7. It was against those odds that Northern Ireland's great tactician, and some would say great gambler, faced his third and perhaps last general election as leader of the Ulster Unionists.

6 May

'If it's goodbye to the UUP, then it's good riddance'[8]

The Count

9AM
After three hours of sleep at Geoff's house, having sat up until four watching my old university professor, Tony King, adjudicate over what looks set to be a blow to Blair on the mainland, we head for Strangford to grab a fry at my house and then drop Geoff off at the count at Ards leisure centre.

10AM
No sooner are the sausages sizzling than our cellphones start ringing – we are very late and everyone is in HQ waiting for the results to come in.

11AM
When we arrive at the war room we are met with the ashen faces of the dishevelled team. They all look like they haven't slept in days. I don't make it to the white board, where Brian is doing his Peter Snow impression without the smiles, before someone tells me East Antrim is gone and everywhere else is looking decisively shaky. Dr Ken Bishop, Roy Beggs' speech writer in Larne, is perched on the end of the table looking shattered.

I call Roy Junior on the mobile and he tells me they are not even bothering to count the vote tallies anymore. It's finally over for Roy.

11.30AM

News comes in that DT's vote is holding up in Upper Bann, Burnside's in trouble in South Antrim and our vote has collapsed in Strangford and East Londonderry. It's not even midday and it is already obvious that we are facing meltdown.

The party is in a state of shock. People are walking around in circles bumping into each other looking for something to do, like wound up clocks that have enough spring in them to move, but not enough to keep time. We had all been expecting bad news but we seem to be facing a wipe out across the board. Is it possible that we are going to lose everywhere except Upper Bann?

David Campbell and Lord Rogan have been in and out but they are as speechless as everyone else. Denis Rogan is not as badly off as some, however. He had heard that Paddy Power were offering odds of 10-1 for the UUP to win 3 or more seats. Denis wondered if he could better that and went to Eastwoods to discover that they were offering 4-1 for the same bet. Convinced the party would win at least three seats he asked Steven King to place the bet for him over the internet. He bet the maximum of £75. Jack Allen did the same, as did party chairman James Cooper, David Campbell and Ken Maginnis.

As it turned out, Rogan's bet didn't work out. Steven had entered the wrong name on his credit card, Denis Rogan, instead of Lord Rogan. When he went to use his card again it had been stopped and he couldn't understand why. The credit card company informed him it had been blocked after the bookies had found a discrepancy on the card. The election still hadn't taken place at this stage and Rogan was furious that his bet had not gone through and Steven was in the doghouse. So everyone's now walking around with a long face, except Denis who is £75 up!

12PM

No word from Sylvia, but Geoff says things are looking good for her. They are at the same count. Derek Hussey has lost in West Tyrone and Fermanagh and South Tyrone is a landslide. The same can be said for Gareth McGimpsey and David McClarty in Strangford and East Londonderry. East Belfast is looking safe for Robinson as well.

In 2001 I had been in Strangford with David McNarry who was our candidate there and Sylvia, who was challenging Robert McCartney in the constituency next door in North Down. David lost to Iris Robinson but Sylvia came through on the day. It was the first time I met her and she was so thrilled to have won the seat. McCartney famously beat her to the podium and prevented her from making her acceptance speech which was shocking bad manners but she went on to build up a really good reputation in her first four years at Westminster. When she was doing committee work the ministers would arrive well briefed by their civil servants as they knew they would receive a proper cross-examination from the North Down MP.

She had other admirers too and one memorable afternoon she had the House of Commons in fits of laughter. She rose to speak after the then Home Secretary, David Blunkett, who had been away. Sylvia remarked how nice it was to see the Home Secretary back in the House, commenting on how well he was looking before making her point in the debate. When Blunkett rose, he thanked the honourable member for North Down and remarked how she was looking very well herself, much to the delight of the Labour backbenchers who roared with laughter. Sylvia was always very nervous when going to speak in the Commons but she always got her point across well and her legal training made her stand out amongst the opposition MPs.

In the war room Alex Benjamin seems shell-shocked and Tim has hardly said a word since I got here. There is almost a sense of amazement among the team – how could it be looking this bad after all the hard work everyone put in? Our campaign has made no impact at all. In fact, given the circumstances and the chain of events, it has possibly made it worse!

1PM
Roy Junior confirms East Antrim is definitely lost and probably by a long margin. By the sound of things that looks like the pattern across

the whole province. Everyone in the party knew that if we were to stand any chance of holding seats we would be heavily reliant on a good turn out.

3PM
Everyone is feeling the heat and Paisley's prediction about the 'rope' and the 'chair' now seems off the mark only in terms of common decency.

Crowe has scored out East Antrim, South Antrim and South Belfast from his electoral results map, all gone for sure. The only two remaining are Upper Bann and North Down.

It looks like the SDLP have come through the middle in South Belfast after all. McGimpsey is trailing Spratt in third place but it's unclear by how much. My prediction that the Shinners would back the SDLP looks correct. Our last bastion in Belfast is gone. Devastating.

Good news in Foyle coming through, Durkan holding up well against McLaughlin. Likewise in South Down.

Conflicting reports still coming in from Upper Bann. SF tallies make it sound like DT is holding on. They are usually correct, but it would seem so unlikely given all the other results, unless a lot of SDLP voters transferred.

Why do we not have our own tallies? It seems incredible to me that we are sitting biting our nails over the UUP leader's future and all we have to go on is SF tallies. It's crazy!

4PM
News in that Burnside has lost heavily in South Antrim. There will be no recount. If Burnside has lost to Willie McCrea then how can Trimble have won?

David McNarry is the first out of the stalls – he's been on UTV calling for DT to resign and expects the UUP leader to have taken this decision within '48 hours'.

126

Burnside appears on the BBC at the count being ridiculed by Noel Thompson, whose Christmases all seem to have come at once. He does, however, sound very measured, Burnside that is, as if he was expecting it at any rate.

I had spoken to Burnside before the campaign about how he rated his chances and he was certainly the most open and realistic of the sitting MPs regarding how bad things were. He reminded me that East Antrim MP William Ross had lost to Gregory Campbell in 2001 on an anti-Agreement/anti-Trimble ticket so he was taking absolutely nothing for granted.

Burnside can't answer Thompson's questions, because there is a crossed line with another interview going on in Burnside's headphones. Not that Thompson is giving him much of a chance.

4.30PM
Next up is Paisley, who looks set to have increased his huge majority. Thompson gives him hell about his blue-eyed boy's trip to the Ramada Hotel. Sorry Noel, all is forgiven. He does a Jeremy Paxman and asks him the same question about six times before Paisley drowns him out with a clap of thunder and storms off.

4.45PM
Burnside concedes on the BBC that he has lost. Lord Kilclooney appears on Thompson's TV panel with the DUP's Jim Allister, Sinn Féin's Bairbre De Brun and the SDLP's Brid Rogers.

Kilclooney declares it an unprecedented defeat for the UUP and calls for all the Party Officers to resign. He dodges the question as to whether DT should join them. Thompson then asks him, if he was the party leader and had suffered such a defeat, 'would you resign?' Kilclooney admitted that he would do so.

5PM
No certain word yet from Upper Bann, but Sylvia looks to have done very well. We will have at least one seat at Westminster after all!

Roy has lost by about 7,500 votes. Unbelievable.

Sammy Wilson makes his acceptance speech as East Antrim's new MP. He looks very relieved and tells an unintelligible joke about electoral fraud which passes over my head. Oh well, he certainly isn't the worst person in the DUP to lose your seat to, I guess. He has an innately human side to him that most of his colleagues either lack or keep well hidden.

Roy Beggs appears on the BBC shortly afterwards and is very dignified in defeat. He pays tribute to David Trimble for having left Northern Ireland a far better place than he had found it.

When asked who is to blame for the loss of his seat, Beggs replies that as the sitting MP it is entirely his responsibility, but expresses his disappointment at the many broken promises of support he had received on the doorsteps. He praises his team for their work during the campaign and said it has been a great privilege to have served as East Antrim's MP for 22 years.

I wondered how he could be so graceful at a time like this. While those around him were losing their heads, Roy's was squarely on his shoulders.

It was a sad moment in a long, varied and ultimately successful career. They say all political careers end in failure but Roy should never have won in 2001. He did so because he had always put in the work at constituency level. That made the difference compared to the Ulster Unionist seats that had been taken for granted and neglected by the party over the years.

Michael McGimpsey appears at HQ shortly after he is soundly beaten by both Spratt and McDowell, the first SDLP candidate ever to win South Belfast. He looks shattered and deflated, a ghost of the man he was yesterday.

David Campbell walks in, saying nothing, before lifting up a copy of *The Times* and walking out gazing at its crossword page.

'Batteries on his solitaire machine must have run out,' quips Geoff. It is the first time I've heard laughter in hours. Alex said he'd phoned the *Belfast Newsletter* and found an answering machine telling him that all the hacks have been given the day off. Apparently they wrote the UUP's obituary months ago.

No surprise really, but the big shock of the afternoon is still to come and it isn't that Paisley has forgotten the words to the national anthem.

5.45PM
All attention now shifts to Upper Bann. The DUP leader has been spotted travelling towards the Banbridge count to join his colleague, David Simpson.

David Trimble, Nobel Peace Prize Winner, former First Minister of Northern Ireland, Leader of the UUP since 1995, and MP for Upper Bann since the death of Harold McCusker in 1990, is about to be defeated by the DUP.

Deathly silence falls over the war room.

Only the TV buzzes with background noise and unscripted chatter as the tension builds. We can see pictures of the hall where the count will take place and the candidates are lined up at the back of its stage.

DT is there, stony-faced and downward-looking as he endures what must be the most painful moment of his political life. The wait before the electoral officer reaches the stage to read out the verdict on his Upper Bann career. It is the fifth time he has been in this position and it looks certain to be the last. There has been no recount so we assume that he has been convincingly beaten.

There is a rabble outside baying for this man's blood. We have heard already that they taunted him and Daphne as they walked the gauntlet from their car to the count centre. Rumour has it that the DUP have been working hard on the ground to extract the poison

129

from their foot soldier's teeth for fear of a repeat of the shocking scenes of violence that followed Trimble's 2001 victory.

This time the DUP seem more media-conscious than ever. Many have even accused DT of having provoked the 2001 assault himself by giving the hungry crowd the thumbs up as he left the count four years earlier. A clear case of man bites dog if ever there was one.

It seems hard to believe that Trimble is about to come crashing down to earth this wet miserable afternoon. I guess from the neutral spectator's viewpoint, this is the beauty of democracy.

Has DT foreseen such a defeat? If he has it is not evident from his demeanour over the last weeks or in fact as he stood there alone on the stage. Although, at times, over recent months, he had seemed uncertain, lacking the drive and dynamism that makes him so distinctive from his peers. One thing was for sure, he has been misinformed as to the expected outcome and that is written all over his face this afternoon.

'David Simpson, DUP, 16,679'.
The jeers went up around the hall. At long last, the DUP had achieved their greatest ever victory. The one thing in politics they prized above all else. They had destroyed the UUP leader in Upper Bann.

'David Trimble, UUP, 11,381'.
'I declare David Simpson the new Member of Parliament for Upper Bann.'

Trimble, a man whom I know has huge inner reserves of confidence and nerves of steel, looks utterly shattered as the numbers echo around the hall. He has lost by over five thousand votes, shedding almost six thousand in total from his 2001 result.

Simpson then walks forward to make his short acceptance speech, but does not look like he is fully able to enjoy his moment. How could he? The world's eyes are on the man standing right behind him, red-raced, twitching nervously and fixing his glasses in that way he fixes his glasses.

At Cunningham House there is silence.

King stands beside me writing down the figures as if he does not trust his own ears over what he has just heard. '5,000 votes', he says, '5,000 votes. Even Trimble's Catholics have deserted him', he murmurs.

Everyone here knows Trimble to be one of the bravest politicians Northern Ireland has ever had, yet none of us have ever seen him face a political test like this one. We all know what matters most to Trimble and that is the honour and privilege of representing Upper Bann and Northern Ireland at Westminster. This is the thing he enjoyed most about being a politician and it was also, to my mind, the thing he does the best.

As he walks towards the front of the stage it is clear from his mannerisms just how difficult a moment this is for him. When he finally speaks he is on the edge of his emotions and once or twice it seems that he is about to lose them.

He doesn't and in steadying his nerves and speaking sincerely about what a great privilege it has been to represent his constituents at Westminster over the past fifteen years, he denies the sweetness in victory his enemies crave.

Trimble admits defeat and says that today has 'obviously been a considerable success for the DUP, but, they will know that with that success comes responsibility'.[9] For the first time in his political career, the great man of Unionism leaves the stage and departs through the back door.

As the TV commentators begin to digest the impact of Trimble's collapse Cunningham House is shell-shocked. We have just witnessed an historic moment, and, as Alex puts it, the end of the Trimble Project.

131

An hour later I am travelling to the Stormont Hotel with Tim Lemon when the car phone rings and it is Trimble. He sounds solemn and shocked, and as humble as I have ever heard him in the years I have worked for him.

He instructs Tim to tell all the staff that it is not their fault and not to feel too down-hearted about the defeat. He says that the electorate have 'politely dumped us on the doorstep'.

Just for a moment, Trimble sounds not at all like himself and then I realize that, in defeat, I am seeing yet another side to the complex and contradictory character that he is.

Before I leave for home, I see Sylvia making her acceptance speech in North Down. At least we have Sylvia. It is a little ironic though that she is the only candidate to win; North Down is so distinct from all of the other East of the Bann constituencies and Sylvia from the rest of the UUP candidates. She has laid her critics to rest and while it is small consolation for the party that she is the only sitting MP to hold her seat, it ensured that we would at least have a presence in the House of Commons. Given her excellent track record over the previous four years this is something to build on. More importantly, Sylvia's approach to constituency work sets both a high standard and an excellent example for her colleagues to follow.

It has been a truly devastating day for the UUP. I have thought many times that it is an election we had to lose for a number of reasons, but that doesn't make the defeat any easier. Everyone working on the campaign is devastated and some personally upset. They all seem glad, however, that it has been a clean sweep. Such a defeat clears the way for a true process of rebuilding and reform.

I sit later that evening with my brother and I wonder why no one in Cunningham House saw the scale of the defeat coming. I remembered that when I had been out canvassing in East Belfast after work some weeks ago the people on the doorsteps had been very quiet and difficult to engage.

But when pressed one woman in her forties told me that she would be voting DUP this time round, even if it was with a heavy heart. She had done so at the European election last year and saw no reason not to do so again. She told me she had always voted Ulster Unionist and her family had always voted Ulster Unionist, but she could not be easily persuaded to come back the UUP. She said that when she voted DUP in the last election she had returned home with many doubts in her mind. As she was preparing to go out that evening, her mother's death notice fell from her jewellery box. She told me in all sincerity she felt it was a sign her mother was ashamed of her for what she had just done.

I fear this is our big problem. The time has passed when traditional Ulster Unionist voters are, by and large, too ashamed to vote for the DUP to send a message that they do not accept the direction the political process is going in.

On 6 May, the UUP were officially reduced to one seat in the House of Commons, its lowest standing in British politics in its one hundred year history. The party received 127,314 votes or 17.7 per cent of the total poll. Returned in North Down, Sylvia Hermon would be joining nine DUP members on the opposition benches at Westminster. They had triumphed as Northern Ireland's largest party after 241,856 people had turned out to give them a mandate to oppose government including Sinn Féin with 33.7 per cent of the vote. The DUP's team of MPs was bolstered by newcomers David Simpson, Sammy Wilson and William McCrea. They looked set to radically transform Northern Ireland's representation and image at the House of Commons. It was almost an exact reversal of Unionist fortunes in the 1997 general election when the UUP won 32.7 per cent of the vote and were returned to Parliament with ten members.

The SDLP held the line against Sinn Féin while polling just less than the UUP with 17.5 per cent. However, they won South Belfast, held South Down with a majority of over 9,000, and against all the odds left themselves with almost a 6,000 majority to defend in Foyle. The Nationalist party's hard work on the ground, plus the fall-out Sinn Féin suffered from the Northern Bank robbery and the McCartney murder helped Mark Durkan. The SDLP did not just survive politically, their performance left the Republican movement with a lot of work to do over the next parliament if they were to overturn their majorities.

Losing South Belfast had been a crushing blow for many Ulster Unionists as Michael McGimpsey was seen by some as a potential successor to David Trimble. Others, however, were aghast that the party had been foolish enough to turn down the possibility of having at least one seat before the election. Lord Kilclooney remarked, 'I told the party leadership before the election that we'll lose both seats to Irish nationalism and we did. We lost South Belfast and we lost Fermanagh and South Tyrone. I suggested to senior party figures, including David Trimble, we should do a deal with the DUP, they had made a reasonable offer and we would have one seat.'[10]

Its outgoing MP argued that the seat had in fact gone to Nationalism because the UUP had dishonestly split the vote. Martin Smyth argued that 'if Michael had been telling the truth, Spratt would have won'. He claimed people in the constituency were telling him, 'I'm sorry I didn't vote with my instincts but because Michael said the UUP had done surveys, that he was ahead, and that Spratt was in third place, I voted for him to keep McDonnell out. Not necessarily to get Michael in and if I'd realized Spratt was ahead I would have voted for Spratt.'[11] I put it to Martin Smyth after the election that had he backed Michael McGimpsey the UUP most likely would have held the seat, to which he responded, 'he didn't even ask me to'.[12]

Campaign Chief Tim Lemon disputed this analysis of the South Belfast situation. He said,

> I'm not too sure how many votes we lost because of the Molyneaux/Smyth incident. I think those people were lost already and it was just another thing which validated their decision not to vote for us. It was the sort of thing which probably galvanized core UUP support. They would have been thinking, *look at those fools, they are betraying us yet again.* So it probably motivated the people who were always going to support us, but the people who had already switched off or switched over, it just validated their reasoning – *look at that, they're fighting among themselves again, I'm glad I'm voting DUP.*[13]

Communications Director Alex Benjamin took a different view, arguing the party could not 'come back' after 'the patron of its party and the outgoing MP' appeared with an opposition candidate. He said it just looked 'utterly ridiculous'.[14]

Party Vice-Chairman, David Campbell, highlighted the impossibility of the situation David Trimble faced over the proposed deal with the DUP:

> With hindsight, we should have opted for South Belfast. Although we were hearing that even if we had there were moves to put up an independent Unionist candidate in South Belfast which, I have no doubt, was inspired by the DUP but they've attempted to wash their hands of it. In Fermanagh, we would have had a huge party management problem if we had forgone that seat to keep South Belfast. Common sense says it should have been done and if there is a chance to do it again next time, it probably will have to be done. But how could you have gone to Fermanagh, which is one of first constituencies to pay its dues every year, which has just gone through what it has gone through over the past 30 years and said no, you can have Sinn Féin's Michelle Gildernew because we want Michael to get elected in South Belfast? The same problem in Belfast ... or even worse considering we still held the seat. We were cursed whatever we did. People were crying for unity, and in the case of South Belfast they ignored the party that had held the seat for 20 years and whose MP Robert Bradford was murdered by the IRA holding the seat ... so the people got what they deserve.[15]

At last, in his eightieth year, Ian Paisley was the undisputed and triumphant leader of Unionism. He had come a long way since he was chided by Loyalists after the Belfast Agreement was concluded, but where would he take Unionism once Northern Ireland had recovered from the shock of the 2005 election result? In his acceptance speech, the DUP leader warned the two governments that they 'had better listen to what the people of Northern Ireland were saying', and that 'we cannot tolerate Sinn Féin/IRA anymore'.[16] His deputy leader, Peter Robinson, repeated his call for the SDLP to join his party in a voluntary coalition and establish an 'executive that will be representative of the people of Northern Ireland', without Sinn Féin.[17]

Cunningham House was in turmoil and many found it hard to grasp the scale of the defeat their leader had suffered and the implications it had for the party and for Unionism as a whole. David Campbell summed up how most of the war room staff were feeling that evening.

> ...at the end of the day, the DUP have spent the last three or four elections hammering Trimble and demonizing the man completely unfairly. He could probably get elected anywhere else in the UK. It may be no consolation to David now, but in the context of when he resigned, what every commentator of note was saying was that history will regard this man very highly. At this moment in time the electorate of Upper Bann and Northern Ireland may not, but quite frankly if they want David Simpson then they can have him and they deserve him.[18]

In Foyle, Sinn Féin described Mark Durkan's success as a pyrrhic victory achieved by Unionist tactical voting. But the SDLP leader, who had been politically written off months ago, said he was 'delighted for the people of Derry'.[19] Sinn Féin did increase its share of the vote to 24.3 per cent, gaining Newry and South Armagh from the SDLP, but they failed to deliver the expected knock-out blow to their Nationalist rivals. Their candidates took the line that they were now, by far, the largest pro-Agreement party.[20] This was not an opinion shared by Sinn Féin's party strategist, Jim Gibney, who took a different view of the DUP's negotiating position on the basis of the December 2004 deal. He said the DUP had 'faltered' before Christmas, but that theirs was a 'tactical stall and not a fundamental retreat'.[21]

David Trimble responded to early questions over his leadership, to which he said he would 'consult broadly' within his party before coming to a 'collective decision'. His resignation, however, was expected to take place within days. At the count he said he believed the situation in Northern Ireland was 'now a much better one' as a result of the work his party had done and that he was very 'proud' of that achievement.[22] On 7 May, David Trimble had discussions at

Cunningham House with Party Officers over the way forward as the impact of the results bedded in.

The UUP leader issued a statement saying that, having met with the President and the Chairman of the party, he had 'indicated to them' that he did 'not wish to continue as leader'. David Trimble thanked party members for their support over the last decade, stating his belief that Unionism had 'greatly advantaged' as a result of their efforts. Tony Blair was the first to pay tribute to his 'leadership, vision and courage' and 'sheer dogged determination' in the face of the surmounting difficulties he faced in the search for peace. The British Prime Minister said the political process was not yet complete, but the efforts David Trimble had made 'and the price he has paid, places a responsibility on all of us to finish the job'. Tony Blair also remarked, with no sense of irony, that without David Trimble 'there would have been no Belfast Agreement'. A sentiment, oddly enough, that had echoed across Northern Ireland from Ian Paisley's pulpit every weekend since 10 April 1998.

7 The Trimble Project

Republicans should have carried out their commitments under the Belfast Agreement, but one has to look at the wider goals being achieved. At the end of the day, we haven't had to rely on policemen and soldiers giving up their lives to move this forward and protect us. My children just have no conception of The Troubles, there's even very little exposure to sectarianism now and you have to say, well is that worth losing six or seven seats in parliament? For them, it probably is. For me, having been part of the party that had ten seats in parliament, I don't know, the jury's still out on that.

David Campbell, 8 June 2005

In 2005 the UUC had been the predominant voice of Unionism for one hundred years. They had met the challenge of Home Rule by creating Northern Ireland and survived repeated attempts by Republicans to destroy its political union with Britain. In the aftermath of both the 2005 general election and the search to find a successor to David Trimble, their party lay in tatters having suffered the greatest electoral defeat in its history. What then was the task that lay ahead for the new UUP leader? Had the party finally exhausted itself? Had David Trimble driven the political process as far as he could at the expense of his party's future? Or could those following in his footsteps recover the UUP's fortunes and find a new role for the party in maintaining the union?

To be successful in reviving the UUP's fortunes, its new leader must take the opportunity to make a fresh start in rebuilding the party from top to bottom and re-establishing its electoral constituency. If Ulster Unionists disagree with the party taking on radical reform and maintaining an inherently conservative attitude towards change, as some undoubtedly will, then the party can survive their loss. For the UUP in 2005, it is a case of radical reform or managed decline. Primarily, the next leader needs to re-define what Ulster Unionism is if he or she is to successfully attract new people to the party and if it is to imaginatively re-invent itself. This is not the same thing as 'bringing in new blood', which is political speak for rewarding some of those the old leadership did not favour and who helped the new one establish itself.

To undertake this task successfully the new leader must learn from the mistakes of the past, drawing a line in the sand regarding those failures. What then were those mistakes and how can the UUP go about learning from them? In order to satisfactorily answer these questions an analysis of the Trimble Project itself is required. The party must examine why David Trimble repeatedly engaged in power-sharing with Republicans while lacking a broad and stable support base within the Unionist community. What did the UUP leader set out to achieve? Why did he accept and support an agreement that failed to tie prisoner releases to decommissioning or one that did not require weapons to be handed over prior to executive formation?

After leaving office Trimble candidly hinted at his intentions during that period. He told me that:

> It did not seem to me in 2003 to be good politics for us to be actually saying very loudly in Northern Ireland what was true. We did in fact achieve more – perhaps in retrospect I shouldn't say more – we achieved more in terms of renegotiating the Agreement afterwards than the DUP ever did because suspension, the International Monitoring Commission (IMC) and exclusion undoubtedly go an awful long way to repairing what we saw on 10 April 1998 as a weakness in the Agreement. But it has taken so many years to get it. Now along the way you can't just turn round and say well I'm going to have nothing further to do with the government, because if you do that you might as well resign from politics. The question is what do you do to put some steel into the process and the idea emerged of an IMC and it has had a degree of success. In terms of what we pushed the government to do – adding a suspension power to the Agreement, which was a huge amendment to it, gaining an oversight body regarding paramilitaries and the government's

139

response to them, and getting the government to take a power to exclude from the Northern Ireland Executive – these were huge changes to the Belfast Agreement.[1]

The whole issue of decommissioning and the Agreement was a political red herring, but the principle behind decommissioning was not. Decommissioning was all about trust and this is where David Trimble was unfortunate, especially after 2001. In order to reach a settlement in 1998 that secured Northern Ireland's future within the UK he had to trust both Tony Blair and Sinn Féin, or at least rely heavily on their actions. He had to trust Republicans to follow through on their side of the bargain and, in turn, to trust Tony Blair to ensure that they did just that. The problem for David Trimble was that the British government's security side of the Agreement with Sinn Féin was more important to Blair than maintaining devolved government, and Sinn Féin knew it. Consequently, they both let David Trimble down, and the Unionist electorate, having witnessed this, lost all faith in his ability to satisfactorily represent their interests.

For some Cunningham House insiders this destroyed the UUP on polling day 2005. UUP Policy Officer Brian Crowe argues that,

> Ultimately, the failure of the Trimble Project damned the party at the polls. The inability/unwillingness of the Republican movement to democratize made that failure inevitable. David Trimble's leadership, as far as the Unionist electorate was concerned, was intimately bound up with the project and its failure. With or without David Trimble, Ulster Unionism was going to pay an electoral price for the failure of the project – with Trimble the price was going to be very, very high.[2]

David Trimble, however, argues that he did not 'trust' Republicans and it is mistaken to imagine that he did so. Commenting on the failed sequence of 2003, which should have led to the restoration of Northern Ireland's institutions he contends that:

> I never trusted Republicans and we tried to take out our own insurance during that sequencing. We were not going to commit to anything until we were satisfied that decommissioning had

taken place in a transparent manner. When it did not take place in a transparent manner we had no reservations about putting the brakes on.

Defending his decision to enter into that sequence with Sinn Féin, David Trimble argues that,

> ... our objective ever since the Belfast Agreement has not been to simply just have nothing. The whole point of negotiating a settlement was in order to restore democratic political institutions in Northern Ireland. So while we were ready to blow the whistle on the Republicans when they did wrong – and I am glad there was at our insistence a power of suspension in reserve to deal with that – having no Assembly was not our objective and to sit with no Assembly was not our objective. So, inevitably, in a post-suspension or any suspension situation, the question we were asking ourselves was: Is it possible to get things to go right?[3]

The result of such thinking was, as Campaign Chief Tim Lemon argues, that

> ... the UUP were actually asking people to vote for us in 2005 on the things we had delivered in 1998 – a peaceful society, a society more at ease with itself and a more economically prosperous society. We were still operating on the basis that we had done something which was good, which was morally necessary and which was a great thing. We were still instinctively trying to persuade people about the Agreement when in fact people had either accepted or not accepted the Agreement and moved on. They had become dissatisfied with the implementation of the Agreement and we simply ignored that. People were actually dissatisfied at what they had at the minute and weren't looking at the fact that it was worse five or ten years ago.[4]

I compared David Trimble and Brian Faulkner at the beginning of this book, but that was by no means a personal or stylistic appraisal. The two Unionist leaders, while facing very similar political situations, were complete opposites in terms of approach and political

141

orientation. David Trimble had the benefit of hindsight when approaching the question of power-sharing and often used it to his advantage. While there are obvious comparisons with Brian Faulkner to be made, David Trimble also learnt political lessons from his mentor, William Craig, and his untimely exit from politics after the constitutional convention in 1975. Like Brian Faulkner, William Craig came to recognize the need for a political accommodation with Nationalism and like Brian Faulkner, he too became the victim of anti-Agreement Unionism when his deal with moderate Nationalists looked like it might well succeed.[5]

For all his efforts, Brian Faulkner was a man who lacked both conviction and the political qualities a great leader must possess if he is to succeed. Consequently, he was bullied into accepting power-sharing by Edward Heath and was as much a victim of circumstance as was the Executive he agreed to form. This is not to say that Brian Faulkner did not take risks or engage whole-heartedly in the power-sharing government experiment. He most certainly did. The risks Brian Faulkner took, however, were based on short-term thinking, as they were a direct response to pressure from Downing Street. Consequently, they were not based on the long-term interests of Unionism.

David Trimble, on the other hand, tricked the Unionist political establishment into electing him as the most straight-talking, sharp-minded, hard-line Unionist of the five MPs in the 1995 leadership contest. There were few UUC delegates present that night who would have considered the victor either in comparison to Brian Faulkner or his power-sharing Executive. After all, David Trimble himself had played a role in deconstructing it twenty-one years earlier. David Campbell argues that he got elected 'on the back of Drumcree and was therefore perceived as someone not to be messed with. As far as the British and Irish governments were concerned, he was very much an unknown quantity.'[6] David Trimble's former adviser, David Kerr, highlights two reasons for his shock victory that evening: 'Firstly, a lot of people voting for Trimble thought they were electing the most right-wing leader of Unionism imaginable at that time. A few years later they realised they hadn't. Secondly, on the night John Taylor made a very poor speech and Trimble spoke very well and when the two were compared, Trimble had the edge.'[7]

David Trimble quickly proved himself to be a leader who did indeed possess the qualities needed to survive tactically the internal and external challenges all reform-minded Unionist leaders face. To his credit he did so during one of the most difficult periods of Northern Ireland's troubled history. Within two years of becoming UUP leader he had to gather cross-party support for the sort of venture that saw Brian Faulkner out of office in 1974. For David Trimble this meant forging a relationship with the British government that put Unionism back on the UK's political map after two decades of isolation. His emerging support base in 1996/97 were delighted to have a Unionist leader who was finally making the running in a political process over Northern Ireland's future.[8] As David Kerr put it, when David Trimble came and took office there were no 'great structural changes in the party but what you did sense around the place was a buzz. Here was someone who was a fairly dynamic individual who was good at handling the media, very intellectual, very clued up on the mechanics of any future talks process and knew where we stood in relation to any negotiations. He had a very good idea of where the party needed to go in terms of the years ahead and the negotiations in particular.'[9] However, the direction David Trimble was determined to take his party in would not prove popular with many of his colleagues, who had no desire to sacrifice their electoral positions for his power-sharing project.

The problem David Trimble faced in 1995 was very different from Brian Faulkner's dilemma in 1972. The oppositionist politics of the 1980s had achieved absolutely nothing for Ulster Unionism. The party's policy of taking the same position on political reform as Ian Paisley had held Ulster Unionism back and James Molyneaux's leadership epitomized this. Campbell argued that,

> Unionists were losing out badly both internally in Northern Ireland and internationally. Molyneaux really hadn't focused at all on Europe or North America whereas John Hume and latterly Sinn Féin were able to monopolize both areas to our detriment. We had eleven MPs and the fact that they clearly made no impact whatsoever really made me very sceptical of Unionist MPs, particularly with the Conservative Party who were meant to be Unionist. I just wondered what on earth they were being paid to do. My personal position in 1985 was that every Unionist MP should have resigned out of shame.

For Trimbleites like Campbell the Downing Street Declaration was 'the final straw'. From his perspective,

> the rest of the UK were really telling Northern Ireland that it no longer had any interest in it and Unionism was doing nothing about it. It was a symptom of Unionism's declining influence in Westminster if we were getting something like the Downing Street Declaration in a parliament where Unionists were actually in many ways propping up Major's dwindling majority.[10]

David Trimble directly attempted to solve that problem. To do so he had to reverse Unionism out of the cul-de-sac of 1980s oppositionist politics; undertake a fundamental political U-turn on accepting an inclusive settlement; and grasp the initiative in a political process that had moved well beyond his party since the signing of the AIA. In contrast, Republicans had been involved in a process of engagement with constitutional Nationalism and the two governments for some time. This enabled Gerry Adams and Martin McGuinness to coax their organization towards a settlement with the British government at the pace of the slowest Republican. Consequently, Sinn Féin only moved politically when almost the entire Republican movement was behind its policy. For David Trimble there was no such luxury. He simply could not afford to continue at the pace of Seamus Mallon's slow learners. Had he attempted such an approach to reaching a settlement there would have been no Belfast Agreement in his time. This set David Trimble at a distinct disadvantage from his Nationalist counterparts. The responsibility therefore fell on Tony Blair's government to ensure lessons were learnt from Edward Heath's mistakes in 1973/74. The Unionist leader was reliant on Tony Blair to keep the balance for Unionism in the substantive negotiations.

The problem Brian Faulkner faced was similar in many respects. He was attempting to engage in power-sharing after the outbreak of violence and the imposition of direct rule. He was also confronted with serious intra-Unionist challenges from William Craig and Ian Paisley. The UUP had governed Northern Ireland for the previous 50 years. As such, many Unionists were not psychologically prepared to support power-sharing with an Irish dimension. To have had any chance of success Brian Faulkner needed strong leadership, strong ministers, the support of the

British government and a great deal of good fortune. He possessed none of these things. First, he was not greatly respected by his colleagues in the UUP and this was reflected when it split over the British government's White Paper proposals on devolved power-sharing government. He was left with a negotiating team made up almost entirely of the party's liberal wing. Crucially, Faulkner lacked the ability to carry with him the section of the UUP who might have enhanced his ability to sell the power-sharing Agreement to Unionism. Second, sections of the British government viewed Sunningdale and Faulkner's weakness as an opportunity to break the traditional Unionist mould and create a centre-ground through which the conflict could be regulated. Edward Heath saw Sunningdale as an opportunity to end Unionist rule in Northern Ireland and stop the escalating violence. Third, events conspired against Faulkner that were indicative of the British and Irish government's domestic inability to work Sunningdale. Take Edward Heath's decision to call an early election in February 1974 for example. This left Faulkner's Executive without a mandate for government having been in office only a number of weeks.[11]

David Trimble's position was not dissimilar in 1995. Having taken an isolationist view of Northern Ireland's conflict and acted as the voice of Unionist opposition during the 1980s, his party had neither learnt the lessons of Sunningdale nor prepared itself to negotiate a political settlement with Nationalism. Like Brian Faulkner, David Trimble also needed a strong negotiating team, the support of the British Government and a good deal of good fortune. When he re-entered the government talks process in 1997, he had built around him a strong and youthful group driven by the personal dynamism he brought to the process. They were also eager to reach a deal that secured Northern Ireland's constitutional union with Britain and one that enshrined the principle of consent into any future change to that status. David Trimble had broken new ground within British politics and a lot of people in Northern Ireland responded to this.

For its part the British government had learnt lessons from its Sunningdale experience, and as such had kept the balance between Unionism and Nationalism during the substantive negotiations. Tony Blair supported David Trimble, but the government did not fully compensate for the section of Unionism that had excluded itself from those talks. Arguably, this was the part of the circle that could not have been squared. Unlike Brian Faulkner, fortune shone for David Trimble on many occasions. He barely secured a majority of support from the Unionist community during the 1999 referendum campaign, narrowly won a majority of the UUC in favour of going into government with Sinn Féin and survived repeated attempts to displace him as UUP leader. He did not become known as the 'Harry Houdini of Northern Ireland politics' for no good reason.[12]

In terms of where David Trimble took Unionism, his legacy mirrors the achievements of John Hume within northern Nationalism. The Ulster Unionist leader convinced the bulk of the Unionist political élite of his analysis of the conflict – a political settlement with Nationalism was in the interests of Unionism. While John Hume had persuaded Gerry Adams that IRA violence was an impediment to a united Ireland,[13] David Trimble convinced Unionists that political intransigence regarding a settlement with Nationalism threatened the union. This argument is borne out by the fact that the DUP came to accept fully the Belfast Agreement under the 2004 comprehensive proposals.

The DUP, however, had a number of difficulties with following in David Trimble's footsteps. First, had they completed a deal with Sinn Féin in 2004 that lacked transparency and confidence-building measures, they would then find it very difficult to attempt the same thing in the future. Second, the DUP appeared to have no clear policy on how they would gather support for such an agreement or advocate power-sharing with Sinn Féin. In fact, their 'fair deal' policy proposals were based on the premise of rejecting the concept of inclusivity. If they were going to agree a deal with Republicans then it had to appear both to reject some aspects of the Trimble Project and to contain some major symbolic concession from Sinn Féin concerning the IRA's future. The comprehensive proposals did neither of those two things. How, then could the DUP sell such a massive U-turn to the Unionist electorate?

It is the IRA's continued existence that is important in the political process and not the cosmetic issue of decommissioning. Sinn Féin have illustrated their ability to completely side-step any agreement with the DUP and deal with this issue. This may have come as a surprise to many Unionists but Sinn Féin's concern is with the British government and not Ian Paisley. The fact that the government responded with demilitarization so quickly after the IRA's historic decommissioning announcement on 28 July 2005[14] illustrates this point.[15]

Before completion Sinn Féin will have to be convinced that they have squeezed every last concession out of the Belfast Agreement. Their statement telling IRA units to dump arms would indicate they are reaching that point. The problem with Sinn Féin's approach to the political process is that they have practically destroyed the Agreement through achieving their electoral goals without having fully abandoned the 'armalite and the ballot box' strategy. The question to consider here is whether this is something Republicans are concerned about or have an interest in avoiding. This is a dilemma the DUP should concern itself with immediately. Their response to the IRA's announcement indicates that they are incapable of doing so. If, as some people suspect, Sinn Féin are no longer interested in the Belfast Agreement and are now ready to press for an all-Ireland settlement, the two governments are going to struggle to maintain the equilibrium that has existed uneasily since 1998. Some, such as Reg Empey, already fear this problem has led government and the leading political parties in Northern Ireland to consider creating a society where 'Sinn Féin looks after the Catholics and Paisley looks after the Prods.' Empey argues that 'while that might have short-term attractions for some people, in the long term it will be very bad for the union with Britain'.[16]

There is an alternative approach to this. The two governments have exhausted the 'carrot' side of their strategy towards intransigent parties over the last seven years. Given the polarization that now exists there is a strong argument to be made for using the 'stick' in their diplomacy.[17] For Sinn Féin's part they may ignore the DUP and concentrate on advancing their political position in the Republic having successfully done so in Northern Ireland. This will not be the case if the DUP quickly show a willingness to engage with Republicans and the two governments. What then can be expected of Republicans in a situation where, paradoxically, they are actually the more likely of the two main parties to be capable of working devolution in Northern Ireland? This question is at the heart of the crisis facing modern Unionism in 2005. The difference between the UUP and the DUP over the last decade illustrates this problem. For David Trimble the political process was all about challenging Republicans and changing the dynamics of politics in Northern Ireland. In contrast, for the DUP, it has been about destroying Ulster Unionism. This is something that had its attractions to sections of the

Republican movement – those who see no interest in making Northern Ireland work.

If the DUP are to negotiate a settlement they will need a deal that Ian Paisley can comfortably advocate and, at the same time, avoid serious splits within his party over. The DUP have the potential to rupture in a similar fashion as the UUP did when David Trimble entered government with Sinn Féin in the absence of decommissioning. Following the IRA's July 2005 statement, division seemed increasingly obvious with Ian Paisley Junior positioning himself as the new right-wing leader of Unionism and Peter Robinson looking increasingly isolated. The DUP remains fundamentally fractured between those who have steadfastly opposed the concept of political pluralism in principle, Ian Paisley and his Free Presbyterian followers, and the party's reformers, Robinson and Dodds, who are tempted by the trappings of power the Belfast Agreement affords.

In terms of winning a general election, however, it made political sense in 2005 for the DUP to go to the electorate seeking a mandate to rule out power-sharing with Sinn Féin. Consequently, they face severe difficulties in advocating the idea of power-sharing with Republicans to their constituency. It will, however, be much easier for them to do so having won a landslide victory over Ulster Unionism in the 2005 election. Without having begun to promote a policy of power-sharing with Sinn Féin, and having defeated the UUP on the basis of their long-term opposition to political pluralism, it is far from obvious how the DUP will go about it. Ian Paisley's return to health, however, rapidly heralded the return to dominance of his policy line on power-sharing within the party – he was ruling it out. In doing so he risks once again isolating Unionism from its government in Westminster.

I now wish to return to the question of how David Trimble survived for almost a decade as UUP leader despite being neither loved nor feared by his party. There is no doubt that he was by far the most intellectually gifted politician of his generation, tactically clever, and personally impressive. He failed, however, to manage successfully his political party. David Trimble had the presence and skill of a great parliamentarian, yet he lacked the political ruthlessness to instil discipline within the UUP and manage the debate over policy within it. The problem he faced was that if he had attempted consensus politics he would have found it very difficult to have come to an agreed position on anything. Furthermore, consensus politics was neither his political instinct nor personal leadership style. Lord Kilclooney argues that 'David became very distant from the rest of us in his final two years as leader. He never spoke about his policies and he didn't consult in the way he did right up through the negotiations of the Belfast Agreement. I think he just went ahead and did his own thing and I suspect the party officers were compliant and just did as he expected.'[18]

If there was a happy medium to be found in the party David Trimble never satisfactorily attempted to find it. When I asked Trimble's press officer, Alex Benjamin, about this he recalled being in Hillsborough Castle during the negotiations and

> ... Trimble had gone off to meet the Prime Minister. When he came back Michael McGimpsey and a couple of others were sitting around the table and Michael asked him about what happened in the meeting. Trimble's response was: *If you weren't in the meeting you don't need to know what it was about.* That was a senior negotiator, supposedly a senior negotiator to the UUP, and he was effectively cut out of the loop because, I don't know why, but whatever the reason, that was Trimble's style. He wasn't particularly good at bringing people with him or explaining the logic of his reasoning and, if he had been, a lot more people would have followed him you know.[19]

As Lord Maginnis put it, Trimble's 'people power was lacking and where he was seen initially as being courageous in having taken the Ulster Unionists to the fore, the follow-up aspect in terms of getting out and explaining it in detail to people just wasn't there'.[20]

To make matters worse for the UUP leader, many of his opponents had their own local power bases. This was largely due to the nature of the UUP's constitution and structure. The party operates with a great deal of autonomy given to its constituency branches and far too often as if it were eighteen different parties. David Kerr argues that the

> ... lack of central control and power of the party leader within the UUP seriously weakened Trimble's hand in terms of policy direction and day-to-day tactics. What you find is that within the

149

> structure you have to operate on a basis of consensus all the time or virtually all the time, bringing as many people with you as possible. Now, in politics that's a fairly healthy way to operate but in situations where you are faced with very difficult negotiations and day-to-day management sometimes you need a bit of a free hand. I think Trimble was hamstrung by dissident voices and a lack of overall discipline in the party during and after the talks process.[21]

Consequently, David Trimble faced frequent challenges from quarters of his party which would have been of little relevance in a modern, centrally structured political party. So what could he have done about it?

Take, for example, the Conservative Party leader Michael Howard's decision to sack outgoing MP for Arundel and South Downs, Howard Flight, for contradicting Conservative Central Office over a policy message at the beginning of his last election campaign. Howard's actions, while brutally harsh, sent a clear signal to all potential dissenters within the party. Particularly since Flight had a sizeable majority and was being punished for a relatively innocuous offence. David Trimble never dealt with internal dissent in such a fashion. His enemies knew they could get away with opposing him to further their own positions within the party and therefore they continuously did so. When it came to implementing the Belfast Agreement and fighting elections he allowed a process of relentless bickering to become his and the party's Achilles heel.

His supporters would argue that Trimble was so busy negotiating the Agreement's implementation, fighting elections and setting up devolved government that he had neither the time nor the capacity to deal with internal discipline and party modernization.[22] There is certainly a lot of truth in this argument. For prolonged periods of his tenure as UUP leader David Trimble experienced enormous political pressure and, at critical junctures of the political process where he had to lead his party, he was very successful in doing so. I once heard him comment that he absolutely hated administration. By that I think he might have meant the day-to-day running of the UUP.

Sylvia Hermon describes David Trimble as an 'extremely courageous leader'.

He knew well the criticism that would be heaped upon his head and in the end he felt, I think, very isolated. He had been leading from the front for such a long time and that is what leadership is all about. It's about making the tough decisions, making the hard calls, knowing the UUC is going to be critical and that there is still going to be division. And in his heart of hearts Trimble had the moral courage and personal integrity to say, this is the way I want to go, this is the way I want you to go, now give me your support, come with me and I will take you there. That is leadership and despite all the criticism he was never afraid of it.[23]

My personal view is that Trimble's opponents would have used any significant learning process the UUP might have undertaken after the 2001 election to undermine his position further. As Alex Benjamin put it,

> ... in order to actually tackle the issues that 2001 brought up, a fundamental reassessment of Trimble's style, the policy he advocated and the direction in which he was trying to take the party would have been required. Effectively after 2001, the fissures which were always there started to get bigger and bigger and ultimately, that's really when you started to see the party fracturing, moving into different cabals and the cabal Trimble had around him and who were advising him politically weren't going to rock the boat because they had other interests. So those people around him were not going to come out and say 'hold on a minute'. Effectively, he surrounded himself with 'yes' men and those that weren't had problems. They were either marginalized or he did not listen to their advice.[24]

I would not argue, however, that had that not been the case, the UUP under David Trimble would have successfully employed such a learning process. The lack of required critical thinking within the party and, in fact, within its culture was a fundamental problem facing any UUP leader. Having never experienced losing an election in a normal democratic fashion, the UUP had never developed into a modern, election-winning machine. When Northern Ireland went to the polls the party certainly faced challenges, but the UUP had never actually

151

challenged any other party politically and in politics these are two very different things. I raised this question with David Campbell, who remarked: 'I think that actually the problem the party has always had in the aftermath of elections, whether they have been good or bad, is that to my knowledge they have never sat down and analyzed what went wrong or what went right. Certainly, in my time, that appears to have been the case. We have just gone through one election after the other and we haven't really learned anything from them.'[25]

After 2003 a learning process or a change would have surely meant the end of the Trimble Project. Party President Lord Rogan admitted that the UUP 'could have been less adventurous' following that election. He said, however, that 'none of the senior people, to my knowledge, made the suggestion that Trimble should leave in 2003. Trimble now says, in retrospect, that perhaps he should have left then. There was no move after 2003 to change direction or reunite the people.'[26]

This cultural problem stemmed from the fact that historically the UUP had effectively been the government of Northern Ireland as of right until 1972, and was the party of opposition to political reform until the Trimble era. The 2005 election was the first time the UUP actually had to defeat someone else in order to come out on top. I put this question to the man who had contested and won the most elections as a UUP candidate, Lord Kilclooney. His response was, 'yes, that's absolutely true. This was the first time we'd actually had to recover lost ground in an election. It wasn't in the party's culture, but not only is it not in the culture or in the history of the UUP, I suspect that even today, in 2005, the party still hasn't recognized that things have to change. Therefore I'm worried that we're going on as if nothing has happened.'[27]

It is debatable whether the UUP won or lost the 2001 election. Some argue that the party effectively lost in 2001, and 'because we didn't treat it as a loss, we suffered death by a thousand cuts in 2005'.[28] The result certainly could have been far worse for the party, therefore the leadership did not treat it as a failure.[29] Roy Beggs held his East Antrim seat by just 128 votes. David Trimble and David Burnside both won with relatively slim majorities, the former boosted by a not insignificant Catholic vote in Upper Bann. Had Beggs decided that at 65 he was too old to run again, the DUP's Sammy Wilson would certainly have taken the seat. While Beggs' personal standing within

Larne and the wider farming community made it difficult for the DUP challenger, he had no obvious successor within the party. This was a province-wide problem for the UUP, highlighting one practical lesson of the 2001 election the party had failed to act on. The UUP might have concentrated its limited resources on contesting seats that were there to be won instead of maximizing its overall vote share. To have done so would have meant publicly accepting before the election that the party believed the *Belfast Telegraph* poll was accurate. This was something the leadership was not pre-disposed to do.

Steven King made the point that, 'the main problem of 2005 was that we just didn't understand what the election was about. It was about five seats, holding on to our seats. We pretended that we were fighting some sort of province-wide election. It was nonsense.'[30] Whilst resource concentration would have made no difference to the number of seats the party won, the deficit at the next election would certainly have been smaller. This argument, however, ignores the fact that the party did not have a great deal of manpower to plough into selected areas, certainly in comparison with Sinn Féin or the DUP.

The 2001 election was extremely difficult in the sense that the party was campaigning amid negotiations to set up the political institutions. This was during a post-Agreement phase when acceptance of the idea of power-sharing among Unionists was declining.[31] As David Campbell put it,

> Unionists hadn't decisively made up their mind[s] and I think were still actually there to be persuaded. This is why at one time during the count we were looking at the prospect of only winning two seats; but in the event we ended up winning six – a couple by the skin of our teeth. We didn't take note of that message but at the same time we were embarked on a journey with the Agreement and the institutions in the hope that everything would turn out right and that people who had made commitments would stand by those commitments. That didn't happen either. Principally from Republicans but also from our own government and the Dublin government, who really from 2001 onwards had embarked very much on a policy of coaxing and appeasement rather than a policy of punishment and exclusion, which is obviously what we were demanding of them.[32]

The UUP also had the advantage in 2001 of being Northern Ireland's largest political party. The DUP was damaged by the stigma of running away from the challenge of negotiating a settlement with Irish Nationalism. David Trimble was still Northern Ireland's First Minister and publicly viewed as the man who had taken bold risks in bringing peace to the Province. He was followed by the media wherever he went and this, to some extent, enabled the Unionist leader to set the political agenda during the election on the basis of what he had achieved to date. In contrast, the UUP made almost no impact whatsoever in shaping the media agenda in 2005. As Stormont press officer Geoffrey McGimpsey put it 'a factor to our election performance was the media's total unwillingness to deal with positive messages or our policy issues which were very much in the public interest. They just gave up on it and went through the motions.'[33] Campaign Chief Tim Lemon commented that 'the media had absolutely no interest in the UUP's campaign. They weren't expecting us to do anything other than fail miserably and during the campaign we gave them nothing to persuade them otherwise. They were right.'[34]

In 2001, while the campaign slogan of *'Ulster Unionism – Delivering'* was not particularly inspiring, it did resonate with the electorate. There was still something David Trimble could deliver. Despite the DUP's cartoon campaign which taunted him for having delivered Sinn Féin in Government before decommissioning, prisoner releases and the destruction of the RUC, enough Unionists appreciated the socio-economic benefits and peace that came with devolved government. Many Unionists retained high hopes that David Trimble would make the Agreement work. While Unionism was still in shock from what the Belfast Agreement entailed in practice, enough Unionists remained prepared to reward David Trimble for securing Unionism's political future, for the positivism he had brought to Unionism, and for the economic and political face-lift the Belfast Agreement had given Northern Ireland. Equally, enough Unionists remained unprepared to punish him by voting for his sectarian rivals.

During the failed implementation process that followed the 2001 campaign Unionists and Nationalists began to move back into the ethno-national zero-sum mindset that has defined politics in Northern Ireland throughout the years of the recent conflict. Failure for that process lay with the duplicitous approach of Republicans to that

Agreement and, equally damningly, of the British and Irish governments' unwillingness to implement it in its cross-communal spirit. This, however, was not an argument that created any sympathy for David Trimble among the Unionist community. As far as it was concerned, the Agreement had failed them. In 2001, it was not Sinn Féin in government or the loss of the RUC that motivated the majority of anti-Agreement Unionists who opposed the accord. The single most important variable in their opposition was the perception that all the 'concessions were to Nationalists' in the Belfast Agreement.[35]

After 2001, the DUP successfully tapped into the deep well of mistrust and anxiety that existed within the Unionist community. They built on the prevalent feeling amongst Unionists that the Belfast Agreement had granted Nationalism a victory on the political issues that were sacred to them. Those who had taken risks in cutting that historic deal with Irish Nationalism, who had subsequently proved ineffective in pressuring the two governments to uphold its inter-communal balance and who had been repeatedly let down by the Republican movement and the British government paid the price.

The UUP had never undergone a modernization process nor had it undertaken the structural changes necessary to win elections in the media age. Consequently David Trimble left the party as badly in need of modernization in 2005 than when he inherited it ten years earlier. The UUP's composition was disparate, its administration cumbersome and its communication system ineffective. The party's central press office was in fact counter-productive during the Trimble years. Headquarters would frequently send out policy messages to the media, which were immediately followed up by statements from constituency offices directly contradicting the leadership's line. UUP spin doctor Alex Benjamin summed up this situation: 'Since 1999 I have not been in a position to articulate a position or sell any message because if you try to spin something from headquarters, 40 per cent of the party then counteracts it with something else, so you're not a spin doctor in any normal sense.'[36] The radical political reforms David Trimble envisaged in negotiating the Belfast Agreement might have been more easily digested had the party been fine-tuned to modern politics. Exactly how much difference this would have made is debatable, but it would have reduced the number of people estranged from David Trimble's leadership.

The criticism here is that Trimble did not use the qualities he possessed to minimize the damage internal dissent caused him in the long term. His style often alienated people and once friends became enemies he did little either to compensate them or to get rid of them. For example, JefferyDonaldson felt sidelined by Trimble towards the end of the negotiations leading up to the Belfast Agreement. David Kerr argued that Donaldson was, 'deeply hurt at the way Trimble behaved in the last week of the talks'. There were other talks team members, such as Peter Weir, who 'felt greatly let down that on the last day of the talks process, when they didn't agree with certain aspects of the Agreement, that their opinion counted for nothing. They felt very, very offended personally by that after having put in so much effort. And they felt that if all the hands were not in the air in the negotiating team room then the party shouldn't have signed up.'[37]

Personal bitterness within the party grew around Jeffery Donaldson from that day and David Trimble failed to address this. He relied far too much on being the fox and never enough on being the lion when it was most needed domestically. It struck me as highly ironic that while his voice was heard loud and clear in London, Dublin and Washington, it was often drowned out by Donaldson's whispers in his own backyard. Much of this discontent had less to do with anti-Agreement Unionism and more to do with the bitterness of the hangover of the 1995 leadership election. As Campbell put it, 'with some elements in the party there would certainly have been a personal element against Trimble leading back to that election. There would have been failed candidates, their dented egos and the Agreement. And whilst they may have agreed with the Agreement, the Agreement gave them their opportunity to re-launch an attack on the leadership.'[38] While concurring with this view Sylvia Hermon argues that David Trimble's tolerance of disloyalty 'was one of the things that in the end led to his downfall, as those who were loyal and who were fighting very hard for the Belfast Agreement felt undermined all the time'.[39] As Alex Benjamin put it, when it came to disciplining senior party figures, 'he always tried to let it lie and hope it would go away'.[40]

For others the problems of discipline should have been conducted on the basis of democratic decision-making. David Campbell, for example, who supported Taylor in the 1995 leadership contest and who was actually against accepting the Agreement in its final draft as he felt it was weak on the key issues of decommissioning and prisoners, felt honour-bound to accept the majority position after the negotiations were complete and support David Trimble. He recalls:

> Whenever the Agreement was first put to the party, David Trimble got about 75 per cent endorsement. My position was that I hadn't actually agree with the Agreement at that time, but when 75 per cent of the party endorsed it, I personally felt honour-bound to accept that and others didn't. I think it was at that point the party should have moved against those that didn't. It's one thing to maintain your position of principle against something, but it is a completely different matter when the party is fighting elections. You had a significant element of the party doing everything it could to actually undermine the party, their own party, of which they were candidates. I think the party should have taken a much harder line against figures like Peter Weir, Pauline Armitage, Jeffery Donaldson and nipped it in the bud at a very early stage. Instead, it was allowed to fester until that 75 per cent was reduced down to about 55 per cent. Trimble would argue that he was working with a team of party officers whose main priority was holding the party together. Now you can't fault people for wanting to do that, but in the context of trying to deliver really significant reforms, both inside the party and in Northern Ireland generally ... it was a miracle we actually got as far as we did. With hindsight, and I think that if we were ever to do it again, we would need to reform the party first and then the Belfast Agreement, rather than the other way around.[41]

On the question of a leader being popular within his party and the Unionist community, Northern Ireland and Unionism is an unusual case in terms of public opinion. Ulster Unionists have never had a political hero. As one of David Trimble's most ardent critics put it, he 'kept the sympathy but not the support of a large section of Unionism for a long time, even after mistake, after mistake ... due to their desire not to be pushed into an inward-looking narrow DUP position'.[42] Their mentality is one of a people caught between a rock and a hard place. When times are tough they often revel in the sort of political obstinacy that Ian Paisley came to epitomize, regardless of the political and social consequences.

As for Ian Paisley, he is neither hero nor anti-hero to the Unionist electorate. He represents the deep-seated cultural and political fears that have become embedded in the Unionist psyche since partition – fear of the Republic, fear of the traitor in their midst, fear of the insurgent waiting in the wings for that moment of weakness, and fear of perfidious Albion. It was this style of leadership that led Unionism to the isolated position it found itself in by the early 1990s. Unionism had been static in terms of its day-to-day tactics and ideology. It had been stagnating for almost two decades. Unionism had not psychologically modernized and by the time the paramilitary ceasefires came the political process had advanced rapidly without it. Unionism desperately needed someone who was capable of catching up with those political developments and that was David Trimble.

Trimble himself did not quite fit the bill of Unionist hero. He was very popular at one time and not just as a Unionist leader, but universally in his role as Northern Ireland's First Minister. This is something no Unionist leader before him achieved. Something similar can be said of Seamus Mallon as Northern Ireland's Deputy First Minister. As with Brian Faulkner's Sunningdale Executive, when the Belfast Agreement worked it worked for everyone in Northern Ireland. Both power-sharing governments were popular when they were fully operational. Faulkner's opponents in 1974 were forced to resort to the unconstitutional method of a mass Protestant strike to finally destroy his Executive. Paradoxically, David Trimble's opponents were actually forced to work the Agreement they opposed by taking up ministerial positions while not sitting on the Executive. This resulted in the bizarre arrangement whereby DUP ministers carried out their ministerial duties but refused to attend Executive meetings. This enabled them to keep up their pretence that they did not work with Sinn Féin. This fudging marked a critical departure from Unionist opposition during the Sunningdale period. It had as much to do with the British government's approach to implementing the Belfast Agreement as it did David Trimble's engagement in it. The d'Hondt formula which both main Unionist parties sought the abolition of in 2005, ensured the DUP could not easily exclude themselves from the Executive. Any such refusal would have ensured their ministerial portfolios were automatically re-allocated to other parties. Not only would they have been blamed for running away from negotiating a settlement with Nationalism and for running away from the opportunity to govern Northern Ireland, but they would also have been blamed for allowing Nationalists to gain extra ministerial posts through their own intransigence. Furthermore, it was actually the public's perception that the DUP had backed away from negotiating with Nationalism over Northern Ireland's future in 1997/98 that damaged their prospects in the 1998 and 2001 elections.

David Trimble also achieved political respectability for Unionism on the international stage and within British politics. This political quality may be unimportant to the idiosyncratic Ulster Protestant, but it is of fundamental importance to maintaining Northern Ireland's political union with Britain. This point I shall address fully in the concluding chapter. David Trimble's difficulties within the Unionist political élite, however, are best illustrated by his oft-quoted reference to the question he asked his wife, Daphne, concerning whether she thought he would have enough support to carry the UUC in the political process and survive on the deal he had brokered in 1998. His wife famously told him that she thought he would gain just enough support at every stage to survive and implement the deal. As UUP Communications Director put it, Trimble thought, 'To hell with it, 51 per cent is good enough for me.'[43]

To carry the UUP and Unionism through Northern Ireland's recent political process with only just enough support was arguably no mandate at all. It was politics based on short- to medium-term risk taking. In that sense, there can be little surprise that the UUP was politically decimated in 2005. Some Ulster Unionists were surprised that it was such a long time coming. David Trimble had been stretching his party against the will of almost half its governing council and against what became the majority of Unionist opinion after the 2003 Assembly election. This makes his achievements even more astonishing. He candidly admits that 'I lasted longer than I thought I was going to last in 1998.'[44]

This poses the question as to what his long-term intentions were in entering the political process. He had gone far out in front of his party and constituency in order to secure the union with Britain and compensate Unionism for its lost years of opposition to reform.

However, he also seemed to be taking the sort of risks in the political process that indicated he put the primacy of that process both ahead of his position as leader and of his own party's electoral fortunes. As one of his arch critics put it, 'never have we been decimated in the British House of Commons, never. He's almost destroyed the Unionist party.'[45] What is certain is that any leader that depends almost entirely on forces and events outside his control cannot survive for long. David Trimble defied that logic for some time. During an interview following his political defeat I put this question to him:

Kerr: A lot of your critics accuse you of keeping the political process alive at the expense of your position or that of your party.

Trimble: Well it's a matter of judgement on this and it's very easy after the event to say, oh well, it would have been safer to have done this, but before the event it is not clear whether that is the case. You have to go back to 2003 and factor in the government's decision to postpone the Assembly election in the spring. This plays very badly politically for the government and no political element says it is the sensible thing to do. We then came out of the summer and all the commentators were saying to us that there is going to be an Assembly election. They said Blair is going to call an election. But what we did not know that and what came out of that sequencing was that in the negotiations in the autumn, Blair had apparently given a commitment to the Irish government that there would be an election some time that year.

Kerr: How significant was that?

Trimble: That was a hugely significant factor. I feel that the government who we were trying to work closely with should have been clear about this position. They weren't. Had that been clear to us we would have steered more towards caution, perhaps. But you know, as I say, it's a matter of judgement as to what is the best way to go.[46]

* * * *

What, then, can any new leader learn from Trimble's predicament and how can these lessons help to revive the fortunes of the party? In answering that question we have to consider whether Sinn Féin actually wanted Northern Ireland to work between 1998 and 2005, whether David Trimble could rely on them to go about a process of constructively engaging in devolution and whether they were structurally capable of doing so. These were the questions the UUP leader had to ask himself throughout the political process. Once he attempted something outside Northern Ireland's zero-sum politics, his position was always going to be vulnerable to the risks involved in taking political decisions based on an assessment of these problems. What David Trimble certainly did do by taking risks was to make life difficult for the Republicans who were attempting to undermine the Belfast Agreement. While this was zero-sum politics in terms of the political blame game that implementing the Agreement became, it certainly added a new dimension to it. This phase of the process came to an end in October 2003 when David Trimble was seen to be on the verge of doing a deal with Sinn Féin. As it turned out this sequence offered none of the confidence-building measures he required to re-market the Agreement to Unionism. By then Trimbleism had been demonized by his opponents and he was let down by all his partners in the political process. Consequently, it was only a matter of time before the electorate called time on the Trimble Project.

From David Trimble's perspective 'Republicans have also wrecked their own political project in Northern Ireland because they have lost their potential partner.' He contends that one of the reasons for the failure of their attempted sequence with the DUP at the end of 2004 was a 'Republican reluctance to a deal with the DUP, as Paisley and his party are hate figures within a large part of the Nationalist community'. David Trimble was convinced that 'there was always the suspicion that no matter what was being said publicly, at the heart of it, Republicans were not prepared to engage with the DUP. They were not prepared to do a deal or could not do a deal that would satisfy the DUP. That means they are left without the prospect of an inclusive process within Northern Ireland.'[47] Sinn Féin's analysis of the Belfast Agreement substantiates Trimble's argument. Republican strategist Jim Gibney explains that one of the reasons Sinn Féin accepted the Belfast Agreement was, that 'properly implemented, it creates a level playing field within which Nationalists have access to all levers of power, influence, respect, integrity and parity of esteem for their cultural identity'.[48] As Sylvia Hermon puts it, 'perversely and ironically, Sinn Féin needs the Northern Ireland Assembly ... in order to deliver and to take forward its agenda for social inclusion because they can do nothing at Westminster'.[49]

Trimble's successor as UUP leader will have the luxury of not having a great deal of political influence over what form any renegotiation the Belfast Agreement might take. The new leadership will have time to concentrate on doing the things in politics his predecessor neglected. By that I mean reforming the UUP and turning it into an election-winning machine. The UUP must centralize the selection of its Westminster and Assembly candidates and convince fresh people with political ability to stand for election. The leadership must exert a degree of control over the selection of candidates, because when this has been left to constituencies in the past they have not always chosen the appropriate person for a particular seat. People of quality or substance are not and will not be prepared to submit themselves to a selection processes in which they may get humiliated and fail to be selected because of personal power struggles or grievances in their constituency. It is not simply selection that is the problem as Rodney McCune highlights. 'Poor candidates can actually succeed within a clear, effective and energetic party, while the reverse is true of able candidates in a rudderless and apathetic one.'[50]

As Roy Beggs comments,

> ... the current arrangement of having eighteen individual constituencies doing their own thing hasn't worked in the past and won't work in the future. We desperately need a party machine that puts a team in place and insists on the team working, because there's no place for individuals any longer. It is absolutely vital that at the earliest possible date that we can clearly demonstrate that we have a united party supporting the chosen leader of the party. The first person that steps out of line should be kicked out and we must never again allow ourselves to be undermined from within by those who have been given respect for past services which perhaps was a loyalty extended too long.[51]

A similar argument can be made regarding the UUP Officer Team. Lord Kilclooney suggests that 'there is a great responsibility on members of the UUC who elect the officer team to not simply vote for names that are well known in the press but for people who they really think can give a fresh impetus to the UUP. Some officers have been there for a generation and really, decent souls as they are, their days are over.' He argues that a 'fresh break, fresh policies and a fresh regime in the UUC and Officers Board is what is needed'. His former assistant, Steven King, concurs with the Strangford MLA suggesting that 'the officer team is desperately weak. Any member of the party should be able to run for the officer team and it should be the twelve best people in the party. Merit should be the only qualification.'[53] Ken Maginnis argues that 'party officers shouldn't be officers unless they have a special talent, be it finance, policy, or people'.[54] This is an issue at least where there appears to be cross-party consensus over what sort of reforms are necessary.

In terms of winning elections the party has another serious problem, which is cultural rather than structural. This is the way in which it approaches constituency politics. When the DUP win Westminster seats they consolidate their position through visible high street offices and solid constituency work. UUP MPs have historically viewed their role as representing their constituency, the Unionist people and Northern Ireland in Parliament. By contrast, the DUP largely undertake tasks that benefit the Protestant population in their areas or as a whole. As Steven King put it, 'they see themselves as being sectarian social workers' in their communities.[52] Consequently, most UUP MPs have tended to neglect their constituencies and have not undertaken the sort of high-profile grass roots constituency work required to win elections in Northern Ireland today.

Returning to the question of what David Trimble's legacy means for the future of the UUP, he advanced Unionism politically to a far greater extent than could have been imagined in 1995. Edward Heath's government after he came to power in 1970 is a fine example. The Conservative Prime Minister's manifesto was almost identical to the one Margaret Thatcher implemented following her election victory over Labour Prime Minister James Callaghan in 1979. Sections of Heath's government knew what was wrong with Britain in what seemed to be its terminal decline from empire by the early 1970s. Some also knew what needed to be done in order to recover from this decline. By 1979 the ideas of economic monetarism and anti-corporatism were not new schools of thought in British politics. The crucial difference between Heath and Thatcher was that she followed through on her electoral promises. David Trimble, like Margaret Thatcher, firmly implemented the policies he came to power intending to advance. Neither leader had a clear mandate on taking office to deliver their reforms. In fact, they both succeeded in driving through reformist agendas despite lacking broad-based political support within their parties.

David Trimble drove Unionism through a period of transition that was taking place with or without his party and, like Margaret Thatcher, his conviction for the political project he epitomized led him to make ill-conceived judgements towards the end of his tenure. He is a conviction politician. He believed that negotiating the Belfast Agreement was intellectually and morally the correct thing for Ulster Unionism to do. By 2003, however, it had become as popular within Unionism as Thatcher's Poll Tax was with the British electorate in the late 1980s. However, just as there was no turning back from Thatcherism, it seems safe to conclude that Unionism will never look back from the Trimble era.

In terms of party policy any new UUP leader should make no apology for the UUP's mistakes during the Belfast Agreement's implementation phase. Nor should the leadership apologize for negotiating it. The party must continue in the same vein as it has since that agreement was signed. By that I mean working constructively with the other Northern Ireland parties to fully implement devolved government. The UUP were right to negotiate the Belfast Agreement and those who made its implementation impossible are now faced with the responsibility of resuscitating it or finding an alternative form of political administration for Northern Ireland's government, acceptable to both governments and both communities. Having done all the hard work, or the 'heavy lifting' as Seamus Mallon puts it, it would be a mistake for the UUP to oppose suddenly power-sharing with Republicans in principle, or make its implementation difficult should the DUP go forward with a deal.

The UUP must quickly come to terms with the fact that it has lost its position for the foreseeable future and be realistic about what it can achieve over the coming years. It should be generous to the DUP and end the cycle of pointless in-fighting. The sooner the UUP does this the sooner the DUP will be free to engage openly in pro-Agreement politics. There is a key role for the UUP to play in the coming years as facilitators between the British government, Irish nationalism and the DUP. This will not sound like a very attractive option to those within the party who have still to grasp the significance of the UUP's defeat. The party can, however, begin its psychological and electoral recovery in such a role.

This is not a view that is likely to be shared by everyone in the party. As Steven King argues,

> ... the key issue is that it's very difficult for the UUP to make up ground until the DUP do a deal, if they ever do a deal. Our way back is if they eventually get cajoled by the British government into doing a deal with Sinn Féin and it's whether we take the right attitude to that or not that will decide the future of the UUP. If, in the event of the deal we go into government and provide a fireguard for the DUP then we might as well pack up and leave, because, for the sake of two ministerial posts, we'd lose any opportunity to criticize the DUP. We're just too nice about politics – we were saying that if it brings back devolution then that has to be welcomed. Well no, I'm sorry, we're just a political party. We're not a government in exile. I think sometimes we tend to put Northern Ireland first a bit too much.[55]

This is the question the party has to ask itself. Are its interest in securing a quick recovery on the basis of traditional sectarian zero-sum politics or are they in putting the union with Britain first? I ask that question from the premise that the union is very much at risk with the DUP as Unionism's dominant voice. The dilemma facing Unionism goes well beyond party politics. It is about the future of Unionism in the post-Trimble era. In order to address these challenges Unionists urgently need to enter into a new debate on what it means to be Irish and Unionist in the twenty-first century.

The internal and external pressures that hampered David Trimble in his attempts to implement the Agreement will continue to affect parties endeavouring to undertake the same thing. New symbolic issues will arise that will stall the implementation process and potentially cause further splits. This is the nature of the power-sharing model of government. The UUP must carve out a position of constructive opposition within the structures of devolved government that offers a positive secular alternative to the zero sum approach of the DUP and Sinn Féin. By doing so, it can advance its long-term goal of nurturing stable devolved government in Northern Ireland. This must remain the party's overriding aim, as only through consolidating stable devolved government can the UUP stabilize and maintain the union. This means taking seats in a government. Any refusal to do so will make it impossible for the DUP to work the Agreement and much harder for lasting devolved government in Northern Ireland to be achieved.

Those who advocate the alternative approach should think long and hard about what it is the UUP wishes to achieve in Northern Ireland and what form modern Ulster Unionism should take. Ulster Unionism has not begun a lengthy and painful transition process suddenly to sit on its hands and revert to the sort of negativity that left Trimble playing catch up in the political process when Tony Blair came to power. What David Trimble achieved is not enough and must be built on quickly before the momentum is lost. Once the party recovers from the shock of the 2005 defeat it must learn from the mistakes of the Conservative Party in the wake of their 1997 electoral disaster. The advantage the UUP has in this respect is that unlike the challenge New Labour posed to the Conservatives after 1997, the DUP are not a better vehicle for pursuing the interests of the Unionist community or those of the people of Northern Ireland as a whole, which ultimately should be the aim of any Unionist party. They cannot naturally build on David Trimble's achievements both in strengthening Unionism within the UK and bringing back the distinction of being both Irish and Unionist to British national politics. Inevitably it will take some time for the Unionist electorate to begin to see this. Just as the Conservative Party does not attack Tony Blair relentlessly for being a Thatcherite, the UUP must resist the temptation to attack their political rivals for having converted to pro-Agreement politics, even if it is at their expense in the short term. This will be the short- to medium-term cost the UUP has to pay for winning the argument over power-sharing in Northern Ireland. The SDLP have already begun this process with Sinn Féin and are showing healthy signs of recovery. The UUP can do the same thing.

A major problem facing Unionism today is that those in the Republican movement that have used the red herring of decommissioning as a stalling mechanism on working Northern Ireland will find the

DUP far easier to out-manœuvre than the UUP. I suspect those Republicans who saw the political benefits of making Northern Ireland work in the short- to medium-term are beginning to see the error of their zero-sum approach towards the UUP. Those who saw no benefit will be pressing their all-Ireland agenda if the DUP opts out. If Sinn Féin and the DUP fail to work the Agreement then the blame for political inertia in Northern Ireland will lie with Unionists. Given how Ian Paisley came to power, it will be harder for him to make it work and easier for Republicans to ensure it fails. Given that analysis, Ian Paisley appears to have two options.

The first is to behave like the PLO's former leader, Yasser Arafat, and end his political life having fought off all enemies, and refusing to compromise on his principles regarding power-sharing. The second option will be to take up the position of First Minister of Northern Ireland, having defeated all his Unionist rivals and the British political establishment who have, in the past, done much to ensure that such a situation never occurred. The UUP and the SDLP must offer a credible alternative to either of these scenarios. By that I mean opposing those who are incapable of or unwilling to make Northern Ireland work in the interests of everyone, rather than opposing the framework within which that failure takes place. As such, opposition as a policy within the constitutional framework that we have in Northern Ireland is no policy at all. The Belfast Agreement was designed to make the politics of intransigence difficult. That, however, does not mean that smaller parties should lose their identity by joining an Executive that includes their opponents. This is something the UUP needs to think carefully about. In spite of all their failings Republicans have shown a degree of willingness to work devolution. Unionism made it simple for them to disentangle themselves from that scenario. They will have no incentive to do so again in the future unless Unionism gets its act together and provides it.

There is also no longer any reason to have three schools of political thought within the UUP. The far right has failed, the pro-Agreement centre-right is where most Unionists sit and the left is simply the centre in its unelectable form. This gives the new leader the opportunity to work out an inclusive centre-right policy, allowing all strands of opinion to feel accommodated and begin rebuilding the party on a solid platform across Northern Ireland. The much-vaunted speculation that the party may cease to exist should not be taken too seriously. Unionism in Northern Ireland has always had two faces. In its modern form, the UUP represents the civic nationalism that inter-communal power-sharing and pluralism have come to symbolize. The DUP, regardless of what political veneer its reformers attempt to disguise it with, represents ethnic nationalism as its political language remains based on fear, religious prejudice and political isolationism. The UUP should use its recent break with the Orange Order as an historical turning point to look beyond its traditional support base towards the 100,000 plus pro-British people in Northern Ireland who do not vote any more. If the ethnic nationalist Unionist party cannot tap into that constituency then surely the UUP should try.

There is an argument to be made for the UUP re-aligning itself or merging with the Conservative and Unionist Party. Senior party figures such as Lord Kilclooney and David Burnside favour such a move. Others such as the party's only sitting MP, Sylvia Hermon, do not.[56] The merits of this viewpoint rest on how the Conservative Party would view such overtures from the depleted UUP. Based on their approach to Unionism under Ted Heath, Margaret Thatcher and John Major, I feel somewhat sceptical about that. It would, however, give the party a strong basis on which to rebuild, it might attract tens of thousands of small 'c' Unionists who never come out on polling day and begin to redress the serious imbalance between Unionism and the British political establishment. Lord Kilclooney argues that

> ... if the UUP were to link up with the UK Conservative Party – the Conservative and Unionist Party of Great Britain and Northern Ireland – people in Northern Ireland, particularly those voters who are now abstaining, not voting, the middle-class conservative people, would begin to say, 'Ah, at last we've got a party that's really different from the DUP. We can go out and vote again and we could be electing people who might be in the government next time round.' This would give them a real reason to get involved in politics again.[57]

He also argues that 'the UUP have got to attract some of these 100,000 non-voting Unionists back to us in order to start winning back seats for the UUP'.[58]

The Conservatives, however, will naturally be more concerned with forging a working relationship with the DUP now that they are the main representatives of Unionism, yet they will hardly want to get too Paisley-friendly, having just rid themselves of their extreme, right-wing elements. Sylvia Hermon's argument that she is not a Conservative for me holds little water, as she has survived well as a Unionist in the UUP. This illustrates, however, the problems the party would have with such a policy. There are Ulster Unionists who view themselves as conservatives and others who see themselves as socialists or liberals. They are all members of the UUP because they are Unionists first, and conservatives, liberals or socialists second. Theoretically, whether Ulster Unionists are aligned to a mainstream British party or not should be of secondary importance if it furthered the interests of Unionism. The debate within the party over British ideological positions is rather skewed as there is little distinction between the British Labour Party and the Conservative Party any longer.

Moreover, regardless of how most Unionists or Nationalists view themselves in relation to British political parties, both cultures in Northern Ireland are inherently socially and politically conservative in comparison to British society. For example, a liberal Unionist in the UUP may well have very little in common with a British liberal, or for that matter reflect British liberal ideals. David Trimble addressed this question in his first major public interview following his resignation. When asked by the BBC's John Humphrys about the contradiction between his Vanguard past and his liberal image, Trimble replied 'there is this misapprehension that liberalism is soft, liberalism isn't soft. Historically, liberals can also be tough minded – when you have got a situation which involves conflict, tough minded in being able to actually cope with it.'[59] Some Conservatives within the party admit that the idea of a closer relationship with the Conservative Party is something that might 'undermine the coalition that is Ulster Unionism'.[60] This has been an historic feature of Ulster Unionism from the first Home Rule crisis when Ulster Liberals and Tories began to define themselves first as Unionists with other allegiances coming second. The counter-argument to this is that if it advanced the Unionist cause or position then those secondary allegiances would remain just that.

Many think there has been a permanent re-alignment within Unionism and this is reinforced by the fact that many Unionists would prefer there to be only one Unionist party. This is because they are frightened of Sinn Féin's advances and dissatisfied up with a political process that, from their perspective, has been completely one-sided. They were not voting DUP in 2005 because they had fundamentally hardened to the concept of power-sharing with Nationalism. The fact that it took the electorate so long finally to remove David Trimble bears out this argument, indicating how patient the majority of Unionists were in giving the Agreement a chance to work. It is not because Ian Paisley suddenly represents the views of Ulster Unionists, or has captured the centre ground of politics in Northern Ireland. Unionists have been hearing the same language and the same message from Ian Paisley for 40 years. Yet this is the first time they have voted for him across the board. They did so because Tony Blair allowed Sinn Féin to renege on its commitments under the Agreement and allowed Republicans to manipulate the political process in order to manage their own internal problems. Voters switched to Ian Paisley because the Unionist champion of the Belfast Agreement had been publicly let down in its implementation phase. They did so because the views and concerns of the Unionist population were seen to be secondary to those of the Republican movement because it had a paramilitary wing. The big problem now facing the DUP as a result of this is that David Trimble has finally gone. They relied on him getting his hands dirty in negotiating the Agreement and they relied on him to break the taboo of going into government with Sinn Féin. The DUP lost their unelectable image on a platform of personally demonizing David Trimble and the Agreement he came to symbolize. The problem for Ian Paisley now is that with Trimble gone, his DUP is on its own. They can either enter into negotiations with Sinn Féin or re-enter political obscurity within British politics and isolationism within the UK.

People also voted DUP because of the widespread perception among Unionists that Nationalism had gained much more from the Belfast Agreement than Unionism. This is something the UUP were well aware of in 2001 yet did nothing about. The UUP's failure to have learnt from the 2001 election result and the fact that David Trimble carried on with the Agreement regardless of Unionist popular opinion makes the reform process ahead of the UUP both difficult and lengthy. However, the painful symbolic issues that dominated the first implementation phase of the Belfast Agreement will pass, and the voice of civic Unionism will be heard again. The UUP have lost many of those moderate Unionists. Jeffery Donaldson's effective representation of Unionist fears and concerns before he left the UUP eased the conscience of traditional Unionists in their conversion to voting DUP. As David Burnside put it, 'mainline Ulster Unionists, down-the-middle Ulster Unionists, were always turned off by the traditional Protestant Orange DUP. The majority of Protestants felt very uneasy with "the old people dancing on a Saturday in a town hall is a sin" style of Protestantism. Jeffery, however, gave them that middle-of-the-road respectability.'[61]

In order to be heard, the party must seriously re-brand and target an electorate from all age groups. This is something the DUP and Sinn Féin have already done with considerable skill. If you take, for example, the generation of people who are under 25 that vote DUP or Sinn Féin, these are not people who are voting for them for the same reasons as the generation before them. The older generations of Sinn Féin and DUP voters lived through the civil strife of the 1980s and 1990s and knew they were voting for conflict and sectarianism. As such their appeal, even at the height of Northern Ireland's ethnic conflict, had a relatively low glass ceiling. The new generation are voting for two radical parties offering leadership that is dynamic, highly effective on the ground and challenging towards the opposite community within Northern Ireland. The DUP and Sinn Féin are two sides of the same coin and, as such, need each other to a certain extent. Gone, however, is the Republican talk of 'smash Stormont' and the DUP mantra of 'smash Sinn Féin'. Many Nationalists would now prefer to live in a Northern Ireland that works rather than existing under the cloud of Republican and Loyalist violence in one that does not. They see Sinn Féin as the most likely party to ensure that it does so to their advantage, while advancing their national aspirations. For their part, Unionists have largely accepted that some form of political settlement with Nationalism in Northern Ireland is inevitable, but they no longer trust the UUP to ensure that it works to their benefit and not at their expense.

The challenge facing Unionism is that the DUP cannot deliver any of the things Sinn Féin has achieved for its community under the Belfast Agreement. To a certain extent Unionism had to lose on some of the symbolic issues of the conflict to facilitate the entry of Republicans into a workable inclusive political process. The fact that anti-Agreement Unionists hampered David Trimble's attempts to work it at every stage enabled Republicans to benefit from many of those symbolic victories without having to work the Belfast Agreement in return. This is what David Trimble was seeking to achieve by engaging with Sinn Féin. The slow learners have come full circle, but it seems unclear how they can deliver on the mandate the Unionist electorate granted them in May 2005. Ruling out power-sharing with Republicans in principle is not a realistic goal and if it is pursued as a long-term policy by the DUP it will seriously damage the union as we know it. They should remember that an agreement only lasts as long as it lasts. The one they opposed in 1998 was as good as it is likely to get for Unionism in the foreseeable future, so they should work it while they still can. The best Ian Paisley can hope to achieve is to re-package the Belfast Agreement as a better deal than the one David Trimble negotiated. The DUP can then offer this to the Unionist community, blaming David Trimble for all the bitter reforms they had to endure in order for him to bring that agreement about. The UUP should swallow its pride and help them do it.

8 His Master's Voice

I do not believe that creating a society in Northern Ireland where Sinn Féin looks after the Catholics and Paisley looks after the Prods is viable. It might have short-term attractions to some people, but in the long-term it is bad for the union because we have got to market it to a new generation and to those potential Nationalists who might be persuaded that it is to their benefit. There is no sense in trying to motivate within your own circle all the time. Unionism has to be dynamic and outward looking if it is to have a long-term future. We've got to think long-term here. I'm opposed to going into this kind of tribal, separate development, South African-style, which I fear the British government may find temporarily attractive.

Reg Empey, 25 July 2005

David Trimble, the most influential and controversial Ulster Unionist to have entered British politics in the history of Northern Ireland, had finally been defeated by the DUP. Who then would be the thirteenth leader of the UUP as it lay decimated at the beginning of its second century? Was there anyone within the UUP who could successfully take on the task of rebuilding the party and conducting root and branch reform in the wake of such an election defeat? Or, as Peter Robinson put it, does it really matter who Trimble's successor is?[1] Ironically, while many of his colleagues had made successive attempts to displace him as leader, the party was totally unprepared for the post-Trimble era. The UUP leader himself had not prepared a successor and there was an enormous age gap between the party's old guard and its bright young things. In fact, the youngest potential candidate was the party's only remaining MP, Sylvia Hermon, who was the first to declare an interest in the vacancy on the first floor of Cunningham House. Its current resident, however, had not had his final say.[2]

On Monday 9 May everyone who was anyone in Ireland's media made the trip to the Holywood Road to hear David Trimble make his resignation speech in the foyer of Cunningham House. Gathered around him were his remaining colleagues and the staff who had assisted him during his final campaign. When David Trimble emerged from the backstairs to face a chattering throng of journalists and cameramen, there was no sign of the ruddy-faced defeated parliamentary candidate who had stood alone three days before at the count in Upper Bann. The UUP leader had recovered his spirits and fielded questions, speaking candidly of the highs and lows of his political career over the previous decade.

David Trimble said he had 'no regrets' about the 'strategic decision' he had taken in brokering the Belfast Agreement, no regrets as to what it entailed and no regrets regarding the approach he had taken in negotiating it. He laid the blame for its failure squarely with the Republican movement. He also blamed the British government in which he had placed the trust of the Unionist community that it would be fully implemented. David Trimble then warned the new Secretary of State for Northern Ireland, Peter Hain, that he too would fail in his oft-stated hope of seeing the political process succeed unless the government changed its approach to the Agreement. He asked him to consider whether any other Unionist leader would 'make an effort to implement the Agreement when they see what has happened to the one leader who did unambiguously endeavour to do so'.[3]

9 May

'Trimble prepares to resign with his party in tatters after Paisley's success'[4]

An Historic Day at UUP HQ if ever there was one. People are walking on glass as we wait for DT to arrive to make his resignation speech.

By 10am the lobby is awash with journalists, security guards and staff. It is the moment they have all been waiting for. The last word from the great David Trimble.

When they do arrive the UUP leadership certainly do not look like men who are about to resign. Party President Lord Rogan and Chairman James Cooper are huddled around Trimble in the conference room putting the final touches to his statement – it's business as usual.

At 10.20 silence fills the lobby as Alex puts the word out that they are about to come down the backstairs. Trimble finally emerges to the sound of frantic snappers clicking and lights flashing. No sooner is he in front of the microphone than he is on his toes, sparkling, cracking jokes, and exuding positive energy from the stand. It is like an enormous weight has been lifted from the man's shoulders and he cannot resist letting the world know how relieved he is. In recent years the chains of office have often seemed like an albatross around the UUP leader's neck.

He tells the spectators that he had considered standing down after the 2003 Assembly election defeat, but that it was now his firm intention to resign once a new leader has been found.

It is a bizarre performance, but one that has us all smiling. I guess it is just what we have come to expect from the unpredictable man that is Trimble. The journalists enjoy it equally and the question-and-answer session is thoroughly entertaining.

Before the show ends Ken Maginnis calls me upstairs to tell me that he intends to run in the leadership contest to replace DT. He says the contenders are Empey, Hermon, himself, Burnside, Rogan and Cooper in that order. It must have slipped his mind to mention his old colleague and adversary, John Taylor. Even in defeat, politics is fun.

Upstairs the Local Council Election results are coming in thick and fast and attention has soon reverted to business as usual – losing another election. We were polling around 17 per cent of the first preference vote – a figure which neatly reflects our Westminster performance.

After lunch I clear my desk, say goodbye to my war room colleagues, and head back to London with Claire. I am looking forward to escaping the paranoid environment of Cunningham House, the siege mentality that affects you after working twelve-hour shifts in there, and the shell shock that its war-torn inhabitants are now experiencing.

As we step off the plane in London I have a message on my phone telling me that Ken has failed to win a council seat in Dungannon. The caller is most amused that the UUP has suffered the loss of its leader and the first casualty in its campaign to find his successor on the very same day.

The news is also not good for many aspiring councillors. UUP stalwart Chris McGimpsey looks set to lose his seat in West Belfast. To me this says it all. We have lost the working-class vote in our capital and for a candidate like Chris, who has always done the groundwork over the years in his local community, indicates exactly where the UUP stand. If McGimpsey, or Fred Cobain for that matter, can't make a significant impact in the city with the best will in the world, then it is back to basics for the UUP. We've basically lost the working-class vote almost in its entirety. Even well-known candidates, with impressive records of representing working-class communities, perform abysmally.

Yet it was not basics the first leadership hopeful had in mind. Hermon spelt out her electoral platform on 11 May, signalling she wanted to see the UUP move in a 'more liberal direction'. Hermon, however, indicated that she would have to consider her family situation before deciding whether to formally enter the leadership race. She said that she would not let her husband, Sir John Hermon, who suffers from Alzheimer's disease, 'down in his hour of need'.[5] While her liberal stance was unlikely to win her much support amongst her senior colleagues, or in the UUC, as the party's only remaining MP she was a serious contender. Regardless of who took over the leadership or on what platform they did so, the party had three issues it needed to address urgently: it had to stop the haemorrhaging of votes and prepare for the next Assembly election; it had to unite around the new leader whoever he/she might be; and it had to undertake a learning process and use this opportunity to implement serious structural, financial and personnel reforms. Who was fit for such a task?

11 May

'UUP in search for new leader'[6]

To my mind there are only two serious contenders and I have no doubt they will both be in the race. The first is Reg Empey who has to be seen, even at this stage, as the favourite, given his predominance amongst the Assembly group, his strong track record as a Stormont minister, his broad centre-ground appeal, and the stark lack of heavyweight competition amongst his peers.

He does of course come with a good deal of baggage. He was Trimble's Chief-Lieutenant during the negotiation of the Belfast Agreement and as Finance Minister under the Northern Ireland Executive. He apparently had stage fright when the possibility of challenging Trimble for the leadership arose after the 2003 election defeat and, as such, is widely viewed as indecisive and lacking the killer instinct needed to lead the party.

He is without a doubt, however, a unifying figure. And while he is tainted with the failures of the implementation phase of the Belfast Agreement he has distanced himself from Trimble over the last eighteen months. As the party's diplomatic gent he is also someone who has presented and can present Ulster Unionism in its best light.

The second serious contender is Kilclooney, who has by far the most impressive CV among his rivals. He has ministerial experience from the last pre-1972 Stormont government, is both former MEP and Strangford MP, represents the UK on the Council of Europe and has the respect of the British political establishment. No one could argue he did not have the ability to do the job in spades but, having lost to Trimble in 1995, I doubt whether he will accept it unless it is offered on a plate.

Kilclooney's critics argue that he is never in Northern Ireland and that he would not take the job on full-time even if he was given it. Not only that, but he has certainly not become one of the 'big beasts' of Unionism without standing on a few toes over the years.

In my mind, however, Kilclooney has the best political judgement and instinct among his colleagues. He is infuriatingly always right! Equally, Kilclooney has the ruthless streak required to implement the painful reforms the party must undergo if it is to survive.

Hedging my bets I phone Trimble's former Communications Chief, David Kerr, to gauge his view of the contest. He tells me he will be supporting an Empey/Burnside ticket if one emerges, as Empey represents the centre ground and Burnside can carry out the tough decisions the party needs to reform.

'What about the others?' I ask.

He says, 'Do you remember the beginning of Steven Speilberg's *Saving Private Ryan*?'

I do.

'As the boats approach the shore on the morning of the D-Day Landing, packed solid with troops, they stop a hundred yards out to sea before the hatches open. Bullets then fly everywhere from the DUP gunners upon the shore. Men are hit and fall before they get off the boat – that's Ken Maginnis and David McNarry.

Troops rush through the water to get to dry land and attack. Again, men are hit and some of them fall and drown. Some are helped forward by their comrades – that's Empey – while others are left to their fate – that's Hermon.

The only two that make it onto the beach alone are Burnside and Taylor. What happens next is open to question.

Taylor most likely ducks for cover and then holds the line until reinforcements arrive from the mainland.

Burnside either joins the Germans or puts up a serious fight, again holding the fort until reinforcements arrive.'

I tell him that Taylor is the best bet then. He laughs and says 'Fair enough, Mike, but what will we do if he gets a job as a French interpreter and sits it out until the end of the war?'

I take his point, but there is no doubt in my mind that Taylor is the candidate the DUP would fear the most.

On 11 May, Northern Ireland's new MPs took their seats for the first time at Parliament, with the exception of Sinn Féin's Connor Murphy. In the Commons' chamber, Ian Paisley sat in David Trimble's prized position on the opposition benches, with his namesake, Sylvia Hermon, (whose maiden name is Paisley), at the opposite end looking decidedly uncomfortable in her new role as the lone UUP representative. The same day Lord Kilclooney wrote a letter to the Party Officers, Peers and MLAs from Strasbourg, where he sits on the Council of Europe, indicating that he would be prepared to 'offer firm and decisive leadership' in replacing David Trimble. This would be in 'co-operation with colleagues in Stormont and Westminster – until the next AGM in April 2006', when he indicated he would resign. He highlighted the urgency with which the party needed to address its financial situation, to develop a policy which would 'make a clear distinction between the UUP and the DUP' and to end the 'sniping' between the two main Unionist parties.[7] Lord Kilclooney was not so much throwing his hat into the ring, as dangling it across the English Channel should the party care for his wisdom and experience in its hour of need.

On 14 May, the UUP's 200-strong Party Executive met to discuss the election result and receive the formal resignation of its leader, who won a standing ovation as he left the stage.[8] In contrast, Sylvia Hermon, who received scant praise at the Executive meeting for having topped the poll in North Down, was dealt a blow by David Burnside, who left early to deliver an impromptu media briefing. The South Antrim MLA indicated that he did not believe she had 'the presence in the House of Commons to be a leader of the UUP'. He also ruled himself out of the contest and threw his weight behind Lord Kilclooney, who had since publicly commented that he would be prepared to lead if he had 'two deputies'.[9] Following that meeting, Cunningham House announced that a new leader would be elected at a special meeting of the party's Ruling Council on 23 June (later changed to 24 June). In the meantime the party would be run by a troika of Reg Empey, Sylvia Hermon, and Lord Rogan.[10]

12 May

'Gang of three to run Ulster Unionists'[11]

Today we have to finish packing up and vacating our Westminster offices. The DUP are set to move in next week. Robinson has long had his eye on the fourth Party Leader's Office that Trimble has occupied since 1995.

DT is next door clearing out his shelves and chucking lots of things out – to my horror! It's a historian's treasure-trove in there.

Fearghal McKinney and his crew have been in filming this historic eviction for a UTV special on Trimble, which is to be screened next week. A moment to remember? I think not.

Rumours abound that he is set for the Lords. He looks somewhat unenthusiastic about this prospect. Like a football player who has been taken off the pitch in extra time and will miss out on the penalty shoot-out. I can't say I blame him. He's far too young and has too much to offer to take his place in Heaven's Waiting Room just yet.

I first met David Trimble in November 2000. I remember distinctly how shocked I was when I did, as he looked to me like a man that had not had a night's sleep literally in years. Beneath Trimble's eyes, his face was like a cement garden and he shook with what I thought was a mixture of nervousness and restlessness.

I quickly came to learn that he worked incredibly hard. I remember

180

one morning I got to work and he was standing impatiently outside his office waiting for someone to let him in. It was five past nine and he had arrived at Parliament before me, travelling from his home in Northern Ireland. I only lived half way up the Tottenham Court Road.

When I went back to Glengall Street for the 2001 election, during our first war room meeting the then Chief of Staff, David Kerr, divided up the roles each of us were to [have]. I left the meeting feeling very lucky to have been appointed the role of accompanying DT around Northern Ireland and keeping in touch with HQ. It wasn't too long before I realized I had got it because no one else wanted the job.

I did not mind, however, and was very glad of the experience. For me, canvassing in places such as Bangor and Larne with the Ulster Unionist leader was absolutely thrilling. I remember nipping out of his car one afternoon and grabbing the *Belfast Telegraph* so he would have it when he came back from a meeting. His face brightened when he saw the front page. It was their pre-election political poll – it was all glad tidings for Mr Trimble.

One afternoon we had been strolling down Bangor High Street and he sent me into Woolworth's to get a copy of the *Spectator*. Like a complete idiot I came back with a copy of the *North Down Spectator* in my hand. It was of course the English political digest the UUP leader had been looking for. Oh well, the best way to learn is always the hard way as my grandmother used to say to me.

Later that same day DT was ambushed by Mid Ulster MLA Billy Armstrong who made the UUP leader ride with him in his Mercedes ahead of me in the armoured-plated police car. This was to the total horror of DT's bodyguards, who were cursing and shouting the whole way up the road. Looking back on 2001 the contrast was dramatic. DT shot all over Northern Ireland, creating news stories every time he walked out of Glengall Street. He even hired a helicopter for a province-wide tour. This was a far cry from 2005, when our clapped-out London bus didn't look like it could get us to Belfast, nevermind Parliament Square.

There has been much written about Trimble's personality and his quirky nature but it only paints part of the picture. If I were to describe him in a sentence, I'd say he was without doubt the most contradictory man I had ever met. That is neither a compliment nor a criticism, it's just David Trimble.

As an individual in Northern Ireland, I imagine he never really fitted in. He certainly doesn't think the way most people from Northern Ireland think and he doesn't always have the patience to work out how people from Northern Ireland think either.

It has been said often enough that he prefers being in London or America than Bangor or Banbridge. I think the anonymity of London was a great relief to Trimble during his years as leader, as was the fact that his courageous leadership was readily appreciated by the British political establishment.

One of his favourite things was simply to disappear off to Oxford Street on his own on a quiet sunny afternoon without any security. If he was in the mood, he was often good humoured and engaging, in contrast to the shy or aloof behaviour he was renowned for.

I remember once Claire and I had spent weeks arranging an evening event at the House of Commons for young professionals from Northern Ireland to meet the UUP's senior party members. The media came and DT made a speech welcoming everyone. Ten minutes later he was gone to do an interview with the BBC at Millbank. My heart sank, as the whole point of the evening was for people to get the opportunity to engage with him and find out what was going on in the party. However, half an hour later he was back and by 9.30 he had spoken to almost everyone in the room. When I bumped into him he handed me an empty glass and asked me why on earth we had run out of wine. This was a side to Trimble that not a lot of people saw and one, sadly, that Northern Ireland very rarely encountered.

As I finish packing I see Sylvia and she seems deeply sad that Trimble is going. She has been one of his most loyal colleagues. She starts talking about DT at the Hillsborough Castle negotiations of

September 2003. When the UUP negotiating team arrived and was shocked by the lack of resources there for the different parties. They certainly weren't being wined and dined by the British government. They were served a flask of bitter coffee and a plate of chocolate biscuits at 10 in the morning and scarcely anything else. Sinn Féin were huddled up in one room and the UUP were working in an adjoining room.

At one stage on a Saturday evening when hunger was getting the better of everyone, Gerry Adams and Martin McGuinness came bursting into the UUP's room, announcing that they were sending out for pizza. They asked the UUP delegation if any of them would like to order pizza! David Trimble, who goes extremely red when embarrassed or angry, went beetroot and did not know what to do. Sylvia teased him that he did not know what a pizza was and the UUP leader's complexion worsened before declining their kind offer. No doubt the Republicans were in fits of laughter when they retreated back to their partitioned room. The UUP man was not for pizza and it was not because they had no anchovies. But it was telling that after all the years of negotiation the party could not even eat a pizza bought for them by Sinn Féin.

Sylvia seems highly amused by this recollection and there was no doubt she got away with saying things to Trimble that others would not have dared.

After lunch he comes in and sits down for a chat. He is in a very pensive mood. He tells me where he thinks we went wrong in the election. For him the big political lesson is the deep disenchantment within the Unionist community towards the idea of Republicans in a fully inclusive government. He says that disenchantment was greater than he had expected.

On the more practical issues the party can work on, he highlights canvassing. He says mail drops should be paralleled with vigorous doorstep work. There is a lesson to be learnt with regards to Durkan's success in Foyle as the SDLP had been out on the doorsteps for ages before the election doing solid, focused and directed campaigning. Trimble argues that we have been operating a less aggressive, less forthright campaign.

He is right about Durkan. When I congratulated him on winning his seat he smiled and said the battle is only beginning and that he would be taking nothing for granted over the next four years. His result proved one thing and that is that the SDLP have finally got their act together.

When the packing is done, we look around the office and other than a 'Save Gibraltar' sticker and a calendar of past UUP leaders which has been left as a house-warming present for the DUP, you would never have known there had been a Unionist Party here at all.

After a long and memorable presence at the Commons the UUP has all but gone and no one is in any doubt that it will be a long time before it is returned as a significant political force. When I began working here in 1999 there were 10 UUP MPs, but now there is just 1. Quite sad really, but that's politics.

Once DT is finished he sticks his head around the door, smiles, shrugs his shoulders, and says 'see you sometime'.

Then he is gone. I rush out moments later to pinch the name-plate from his door for a keepsake, but he has beaten me to it! His office is completely bare, gone is the UUC's 'Ulster is Ours' election poster with James Craig on the front. Gone too is the Carlsberg cartoon on his wall that read 'Ulster, probably the best laager in the world'.

Last night Rodney McCune and I had bumped into DUP new boys, David Simpson and Willie McCrea, walking up Victoria Street with their bags looking lost. 'Westminster's that way,' Rodney shouted, pointing at Big Ben behind them, but there was no craic to be had from them at all.

On 18 May, Lord Maginnis officially confirmed he intended to join the leadership race, telling UTV's Alastair Stewart that he is 'up for the leadership'.[12] Maginnis said the UUP had to discover what 'caused people not just to vote against us, but not to come out to vote'. He did little, however, to distance himself from the man who beat him in the 1995 leadership contest, indicating that had he won that night he 'would not have done the job as well as David Trimble'.[13] The previous day, Sylvia Hermon threw her own hat back out of the ring, declaring she could not burden her family further with work commitments when her husband's condition was deteriorating. She regretted the 'disappointment' her decision would cause to colleagues and people across Northern Ireland, but at this stage of her career she felt it was the correct thing to do.[14] Sylvia Hermon's departure left the liberal wing of the party with no champion, but there was speculation that she might re-enter the contest at a later stage or that another candidate would emerge who could represent her values. No one could imagine who it might be. The other main contenders were very quiet indeed. Except for Lord Kilclooney that is, who immediately issued a statement requesting Sylvia Hermon take the position of 'Leader of the Ulster Unionist Parliamentary Party', while a new party leader was found.

On 23 May, the Westminster Unionist Association issued a statement indicating that they favoured Lord Kilclooney as a caretaker leader. A WUA spokesman said that the organization had met and agreed that Kilclooney's 'previous ministerial experience' and record 'in Westminster, Stormont and Europe' made him the most likely candidate 'to avoid further electoral losses'.[15] Not unsurprisingly, the DUP were fast to respond, with Ian Paisley quizzing Lord Kilclooney over his career aspirations when they met on a plane, and Strangford MP Iris Robinson attacking him in the media. While stressing that who led the UUP after David Trimble was 'of little interest' to her or the DUP, Robinson described Kilclooney as 'an architect of the failed Belfast Agreement' who represented the 'weak and inept pushover Unionism of an era that has passed'.[16] This was the first raw nerve of the UUP that had been touched since the election campaign.

30 May

'Unimportant who will follow on from Trimble – Robinson'[17]

So does it matter who Trimble's successor is and will it be a poisoned chalice? Empey, Hermon, Kilclooney and Maginnis certainly seem to think it does matter, as does Iris Robinson, if it is her rival for hearts and minds in Strangford who comes out victorious.

The obvious problem the party has in dealing with the legacy of Trimble is that there are no leadership contenders who are not tainted in varying degrees by the Trimble project.

Not that the party needs someone who has no involvement in the Belfast Agreement, just someone who does not have his or her finger-prints all over its failed implementation. Only Kilclooney fits that bill.

While he was crucial in negotiating and agreeing the accord, the party was not long into the implementation phase when he distanced himself from the process. Of course this was something he was often criticized for doing, as a lasting Trimble/Taylor leadership team, in my mind, would have been too robust for the likes of Donaldson to have challenged.

I have always wondered how the political process would have developed had Kilclooney won the 1995 leadership election, or, equally, had Trimble kept the UUP Peer on board.

On 1 June the *Belfast Telegraph* stirred things up in what was becoming a rather slow bicycle race, by printing Lord Kilclooney's 'caretaker' letter which had been leaked the previous day. The paper focused on his stark warning that if the UUP wasted more time and drifted politically, he feared it could lose 'at least half' its MLAs in the event of an Assembly election in the autumn or next spring.[18]

Meanwhile, Reg Empey was coming under 'extreme pressure' to reveal his intentions, having kept his cards close to his chest in the contest.[19] There was certainly a body of support gathering around him among the Assembly group but he was by no means the only person making the running at Stormont. Strangford MLA and former Trimble aide David McNarry had announced his intention to run as a reform candidate and there were also whispers that North Down MLA Alan McFarland was set to enter the race.[20] These two candidates would flank Reg Empey (58) on the right and left, respectively. McNarry (57) was the straight-talking, hot-headed Orangeman, whereas McFarland (55) was clearly Sylvia Hermon's softly-spoken standard-bearer from North Down.

David McNarry had written to as many of the UUC delegates as possible to seek support, having failed to gain a full list from Cunningham House. Headquarters were allowing one 'official' letter to be sent out by each of the candidates after nominations closed.[21] On 7 June the Strangford MLA formally made his ambitions known, stating his intention to 'take the party out of denial' should he become its new leader.[22] Two days later his main rival finally entered the race with a glossy campaign launch at Belfast's Holiday Inn. Surrounded by a strong team of MLAs, including Danny Kennedy, Tom Elliott and Fred Cobain, the former Enterprise and Trade Minister declared the UUP's days of 'high-handedness' over and that he intended to carry out the reform process necessary for electoral success.[23]

With equal doses of substance and style Reg Empey's campaign launch suggested that the 'pundit's favourite' deserved that tag. Lord Kilclooney reiterated that he was 'not interested in the longer term leadership' and it was not because he was suddenly backing Reg Empey.[24] In the same breath he labelled those vying for the UUP top job as 'has-beens', who were all associated with the demise of a party which, in his opinion, might struggle to survive if fresh leadership was not forthcoming.[25] Kilclooney argued that the party must be prepared to look outside its ranks to find its next leader and suggested Gulf War hero Colonel Tim Collins. The spoof internet newspaper, *The Portadown News*, subsequently ran a story on Tim Collins' potential leadership bid, erroneously quoting the Gulf War hero as saying he had no experience in politics and had in fact spent his 'entire adult life telling working-class men to stop thinking for themselves and obey his orders'. It then quoted Kilclooney as having said, 'see, he's perfect!'[26]

After the weekend Alan McFarland became the third candidate to launch a bid to become David Trimble's successor. Citing his military background as qualification to end the party's internal division, McFarland told a news conference at Holywood's Culloden Hotel that he was leading 'a grass-roots rebellion'.[27] UUP dissenters in his own constituency seemed unconvinced as, in a bizarre twist to what had

187

otherwise been a dull leadership campaign, his fellow North Down MLA, Robert McCartney, reported that he had been approached by people within the UUP to put himself forward as a candidate.[28] Having previously left the organization to forge and divide his own Unionist party, many joked that with a record of political intransigence in Northern Ireland second only to Ian Paisley's, he was in fact perfectly qualified to lead the UUP.

On Wednesday 15 June, with three days to go before nominations for the leadership closed, the contest's only remaining peer decided not to seek the top job and withdrew from the race. Ken Maginnis said he would now 'most likely support Empey' on the night.[29] There had also been speculation that another candidate was set to enter the race at the last minute and it was rumoured that Antrim Councillor Adrian Watson, who was close to David Burnside, had requested a leadership nomination form from Cunningham House.

The deadline passed at 5pm Friday 17 June and UUP election chief Tim Lemon had only received the papers of the three already-announced candidates.[30] On the evening of 24 June, at Belfast's Ramada Hotel, either Reg Empey, Alan McFarland or David McNarry would emerge as the next elected leader of the UUP.[31] By that stage Empey, who had since received the formal backing of the party's MEP, Jim Nicholson,[32] was seen as so far in front that local bookmakers were not offering odds on the contest. Eastwoods commented that they believed Empey was 'an absolute certainty' so there was 'no point' in doing so.[33] They were not alone and David Burnside, who had previously backed Lord Kilclooney, lent his last-minute support to the former Stormont minister.[34]

The electoral process was to be the same as ten years ago when Ken Maginnis, William Ross, Rev. Martin Smyth, John Taylor and David Trimble took the podium in search of the UUP crown.[35] Each candidate was required to gather twenty signatures from UUC delegates from at least three constituencies excluding their own.[36] The successful candidate would be the man who gathered over fifty per cent of the vote, with the lowest-ranking candidate being eliminated in the first round before a new party leader emerged.

23 June

'Bookies think it's a one-horse race'[37]

So, will Empey be the thirteenth leader of the UUP and the man who fills Trimble's boots? Common wisdom would indicate that this will be the case. It would also suggest that the thirteenth leader will need even more luck than his famous predecessor if he is to succeed.

Seven weeks have passed since Trimble fell in Upper Bann and the enormity of the task facing Empey, McFarland or McNarry if they are to revive the party's fortunes is sinking in.

There has been a fair bit of speculation this week that McFarland's campaign has, despite the lack of high-profile backers, had a considerable impact. Those who do not want more of the same are said to be quietly gathering around him. But who are they? No one in the party wants more of the same. Well, very few people anyway. So what exactly does this mean? Many view Empey as a dead cert. simply because he has the support of most of the Assembly team.

But I am not at all convinced this means 'it's in the bag' for him, as there is no way, despite what everyone is saying, that this Assembly group reflects the UUC. I have no doubt Empey knows this. That is the problem he faces.

So it is not clear-cut as to how the council will vote at all. On the surface the three candidates are offering very similar electoral packages, but on the basis of their campaigns it is far from clear what any of them would actually do if they were elected. Their brief electoral platforms have actually mirrored the election campaign. No policy, no message, no direction – just trust me and we'll hope things improve.

It's not that I don't think Empey won't win it, it's just that I don't sense he will win by the margin many are expecting him to. If he receives well over sixty per cent of the vote on the first count then he will have a good strong mandate for change. It's as simple as that. The problem he faces is that there are two other candidates and this makes it highly likely that it will either go to a second count or he will win in the first round by a very slender margin.

The question is, out of the three candidates who represent the Trimble project, which one will be seen as the best to build on the failures of that project? This, bearing in mind that two of them are candidates who were very close to Trimble and who completely failed to alter his course over the last three years.

McNarry won't win because the UUP has very definitely moved away from the right during Trimble's years and I have no sense that it will want to go there again. Perhaps the candidate that has the best quality of the three is McFarland, as other than his first name and the fact he was in the army and is from North Down, no one knows anything about him. On the other hand, the UUC is naturally conservative with a small- to medium-sized 'c', and that, of course, is where Empey hovers.

The real conservative here I think has been Barney Eastwood.

There is more to this contest than meets the eye.

The three candidates had sent out their election literature to the UUC delegates through Cunningham House days after the nominations had closed. David McNarry, who had officially been the first of them to publicly declare his hand, had written a personal note, with policy proposals sketched out on the side. In a sense it was just that, a personal and emotive statement, and as such not only did it lack substance but it also lacked style. For McNarry change was all about 'reconnecting' with the UUP's lost voters, restoring 'the trust of the people' and embracing the traditional UUP core voter.[38] The UUP had neglected the Orange Order and the working-class Protestants who had supported the party over the previous century. McNarry was going to bring them back. His main problem was that he was widely perceived within the party as hot-tempered and not someone who could easily unite the diverse strands of Unionist opinion that made up the party's Ruling Council. He had also been very close to David Trimble in recent years, which would ultimately count against him too.

Alan McFarland's literature was a standard UUP election canvass card, only with a personal note identifying what he saw as the party's failings. He spoke of ridding the UUP of its 'cabals and cliques', returning to 'bread and butter politics' and forging a 'coalition of all the talents' in the party.[39] While it was more professional than McNarry's and much less earthy, McFarland's literature and last-minute campaign came across as just that, something that had been thrown together at the last moment to champion Sylvia Hermon's cause. McFarland's other asset was the fact that while he did come from the left of the party, he had not been central to any of the failures the UUP had incurred since 2001. He was also relatively young and had a solid family history in the party and was liked by those who knew him. This, after the bitter years of pro- and anti-Agreement infighting, was another factor in his favour. There were few unknown quantities in the UUP, thus any truly fresh approach on offer would certainly be as attractive to some as his repeated rhetoric of an 'internal revolution' might be to others.[40]

Reg Empey's campaign and literature was well-conceived and well-delivered.[41] He had clearly been preparing his campaign for some time. The front runner had long since carved out his own style within the party and his glossy literature reflected the hard work his campaign team had been putting in behind the scenes. It was very much a leader's leaflet, hitting all the right notes, offering clear and structured policy objectives, and reminding his audience that he was the man with the experience to do the job. It was in fact a very well constructed mini-manifesto, stating where he would gently steer the party and, as such, was packed with promises and good ideas. Like the other candidates, however, he gave no clear indication as to how he would deliver the radical reform the UUP so desperately needed. On paper at least, the way he did not say it put him in a different political class to his rivals. He had singled out just about everything that was wrong with the party and voiced his determination to address those very issues. The crucial question was whether enough people would be convinced he would do just that. Reg Empey was widely regarded as the 'no change' candidate who lacked the stomach for confrontation and had a reputation for indecision. This stemmed from the perception that he lost his nerve when there was a movement within the party to replace David Trimble with a 'leadership team of Smyth, Donaldson, Empey and Burnside'.[42] Of the three candidates, if elected, the weight of expectation would be greatest upon Reg Empey's shoulders, as he had played a key part in the Trimble Project.

24 June

'Empey tipped to grab UUP crown'[43]

I arrive at Cunningham House after lunch to meet with the old team before heading up to Belfast for the election. In the weeks I have been away things have changed a great deal. The war room has been dismantled, Steven King has disappeared, as has Policy Director Cyril Donnan, and the building seems calm in the wake of the hustle and bustle of Trimble's last election campaign. The door to his old office is ajar as I walk upstairs, so I peer in. I see that it has been cleared for the man who will take up the chair the following morning. As I stand there I imagine the UUP leader taking his Nobel Peace Prize down from the wall beside the window, shrugging his shoulders and marching out with it under his arm.

I go up to visit Alex and I am pleasantly surprised to see he has taken up smoking in his office again, a sure sign that the king is really dead! At 6pm I arrive at the Ramada Hotel with Geoff McGimpsey and UUP special advisors Stephen Barr and Mark Neale. Mark, who was present the last time the UUC elected its leader, is predicting a low turn out and is hoping that, whatever the result, a unanimous result will emerge by the end of the night with the party falling in behind the newly-anointed leader.

We are early, but so too are hundreds of others. It seems there will be a very strong crowd for the three candidates to address after all. As we walk into the foyer, members of Empey's campaign team are chatting to delegates while the media films the only part of the evening's proceedings they can witness.

No sooner am I in the building than a friend greets me and asks if I have seen Trimble. I have not. He is not coming I tell him. It's unlike DT to read the thoughts of his colleagues and gracefully disappear. People find it notoriously difficult to express themselves when he is around. But it would be rather ironic if he were sitting in the front row listening to his successor's sales pitch.

It does make me think that this is the first UUC meeting or conference I have ever attended where DT is not the star of the show. Tonight's agenda looks rather light without him. If it had been yet another leadership challenge to oust him the world's media would have been banging at the doors. As it is, we are lucky to have the local press observing the election of his successor. I bump into Rodney McCune, who had been delayed in Heathrow. He tells me he met UTV's chief political correspondent Ken Reid on the way. Reid was heading in the opposite direction. It seemed the UUP's leadership contest was not important enough for him to attend. This was a cruel sign of where the UUP now stands.

I guess there was simply no controversy or occasion without Trimble, and as UUC delegates huddled in corners around the building, for the first time in years, it was not of him they spoke.

I chat to Ray Haden and Mark Graham, two of the brains behind Empey's campaign. They seem pretty tense and the beers in their hands have done little to dull their senses or steady their nerves.

There is a certain buzz about the place but it is in an atmosphere of strained interest and most people I speak to say they just want to get it over and done with. But who are people voting for? I have been in London some weeks and find myself out of touch.

Lots of people are speaking about it being very close and Empey's team are not expecting to get a result over 60 per cent on the first count, 52 per cent or 53 per cent are their average projections.

193

I see both McNarry and McFarland in the lobby before the proceedings get underway. Both look very nervous indeed, especially McFarland, as if the weight of expectation has suddenly landed on his shoulders. He seems to be getting quite a lot of warm remarks and support from passers-by.

Party President Lord Rogan conducts a ballot and McNarry is to speak first, followed by McFarland and then Empey. A distinct advantage for the favourite as he can see where the other candidates are coming from and what sort of questions to expect from the delegates.

To me, there is also an advantage in speaking last in the sense that what you say will be in the minds of the electors just before they vote. But that could of course work the other way around.

Each candidate is allowed ten minutes to speak before taking questions from the floor for a further twenty minutes. Rogan opens the election to a packed conference room of elderly delegates from the eighteen electoral constituencies across Northern Ireland. I turn to one of the party's Westminster candidates and ask him if he is excited.

'Excited!' he laughs, 'about tonight's line up? McNarry, McFarland and Empey? It's a sad reflection of just how low we have sunk in our centenary year.'

Silence falls as Rogan announces that McNarry will be the first candidate to speak.

McNarry begins with well-prepared and emotionally engaging sound-bites, talking of 'renewing [the] trust' of the party's 'natural supporters', of a UUP that had 'undersold its achievements' and of 'restoring parity of esteem for Loyalist Unionist communities'.

I am surprised by his speech. It's as good as it is off key. He has prepared well and said many things that should have struck a chord with the delegates. They were simply in no mood to be rallied. They

194

want to know when and how he is going to fix the party. McNarry responds confidently with well-rehearsed answers to the well-rehearsed, planted questions he fields. He gets into his stride so well that he begins to sound arrogant. When asked if he would remove all the party officers if elected, McNarry replies that 'if at the end of the evening I am the leader it will be me that will be talking to the officers and they will not be talking to me'.

When David Burnside asks him if, as party leader, he will take his ministerial seats with Sinn Féin should the DUP complete their elusive deal and form an executive with Republicans, McNarry asks the delegates 'when did this party ever go into opposition just for the sake of it?' He says it was now up to the DUP as to whether Unionism formed an executive with Republicans and dismissed the idea that the UUP should sit on the Opposition benches to 'moan and groan'. He concluded by saying that he would 'play no part in sitting in opposition'.

As he leaves the stage he receives a good and measured response despite the pensive atmosphere. I don't think his performance improves his chances considerably, but it is certainly an act for Alan McFarland, who is next up, to follow.

As he begins to make his leadership speech, McFarland appears to be very nervous. He begins in an informal style, almost introducing himself and apologizing for not being that well-known to all the delegates.

He tells them that he is less well-known because he has been getting on 'with bread-and-butter politics' while others have 'hogged and abused the limelight for personal rather than party interests'. He tells the UUC that he has a very 'clear position' and a 'very clear idea of what the UUP needs to do to regain the high ground'. He promises to bring accountability to the UUP, to ensure it 'becomes the property of its members' and to end the era of 'them and us' between an 'unaccountable inner circle' and the party's grass roots.

195

It is at this point that the audience pricks up its ears and begins interrupting McFarland with bursts of applause. He then distances himself from McNarry and Empey, reminding the ruling council that he has never been a party officer, a senior advisor or played a central role in the Belfast Agreement's failed implementation phase. This is why he is standing. He says others had 'already had their chance to promote and deliver the reforms that they now supposedly champion. They did not succeed then and this party has now paid the price.'

It was at this point that I prick up my ears. McFarland is getting into his stride and pressing all the right buttons.

He receives a long round of applause when he points out that the UUP must be 'the only political party that had the majority of its opponents within its own ranks'.

Stamping his mark on the contest, McFarland said 'that every member of this council knows what has to be done' and if elected he pledged to recall the council in September to seek a mandate for a 'package of constitutional reforms' to transform the party into a modern election-winning machine.

I was surprised by how positively he was received. Had he run a stronger campaign more delegates might have come here tonight prepared to think of him as a credible alternative to Empey.

Burnside rose and asked the same question as to where McFarland stood on Sinn Féin in government and McFarland gave the same answer as McNarry, arguing that he did 'not believe the UUP' were a 'party of opposition'.

It was obvious what was coming and I was extremely surprised by the huge error I feared Empey was about to make. When he finally took to the stage the delegates had been seated for well over an hour and an atmosphere of excitement and expectation was beginning to fill the air.

But when he rose to speak it was the old Empey on the stage, the former First Minister's Chief-Lieutenant, the man who had never really stepped out of Trimble's shadow.

Empey told the UUC they shared 'a common goal to put things right', promising to 'harness all the talents' of the party's membership and 'draw a line in the sand'.

He said his priority would be to 'heal the wounds of the last seven years', 'listen to the grass roots' and re-engage with the party's 'traditional support base' in representing the 'wider orange family'. Empey made a general speech to the broad centre-ground that would register with every Unionist anywhere. It was inoffensive and appealing, yet it lacked the substance and dynamism of his literature.

In conclusion, Empey said that he had spelt out 'a vision of what it is to be an Ulster Unionist and a strategy for recovery'.

The problem with his election platform was that he had not done so, whereas McFarland had at least attempted to. Empey had said little to rouse the spirits of the delegates.

I don't think they were expecting much from McNarry or McFarland, but they certainly were from Empey, as this is his defining moment. Where McFarland had seemed nervous and McNarry arrogant, Empey came across as frightened of saying anything which might result in him actually losing the contest. He was simply not prepared to stamp his authority on this election and take whatever risk winning it convincingly might entail. He had decided on the cautious conservative approach, decided on playing it safe, and decided not to rock the boat in any way. Consequently, he ran the risk of winning over no one.

When asked questions on whether he would press the officers to go and why he had shied away from challenging Trimble in the past, he fudged a diplomatic course. If Empey had to shrug off his 'indecisive' image this evening in order to decisively win over the hearts and minds of the UUC then he was failing to do so.

When Burnside took the floor for the third and final time, asking the candidate he had publicly supported how he would address the hypothetical Sinn Féin/DUP conundrum, Empey delivered what his team thought would be the knock-out punch. The former architect of the Belfast Agreement, who had supported Trimble's past U-turns on this very issue, said that he would not take up ministerial positions in a Sinn Féin/DUP Government during this Assembly, giving the indication that he would take his party into a period of opposition.

Empey said he did 'not believe that this party should be in any executive including Sinn Féin during the lifetime of this Assembly'.

Burnside sat down and Empey waited for the rapturous applause from the delegates.

It did not come.

Instead, there were isolated pockets of clapping, mostly from the back of the hall where some of his Assembly team were gathered.

I was astounded that the favourite had taken this position and equally shocked that he had been advised to do so. It was, paradoxically, an enormous risk. The criticism he had to shake off this evening was that he was indecisive. Ruling out power-sharing with Sinn Féin in the lifetime of this Assembly was, however, a complete fudge as the DUP had already done so and there would most likely be an Assembly election if Paisley agreed a deal with Republicans in the near future.

Aside from that, avoiding an Assembly election might have been a viable policy as this would enable the UUP to avoid more electoral losses.

I was here as an observer from the Westminster Unionist Association, which does not have delegate status. As such I did not have a vote. Had I held the responsibility of voting on their behalf this evening, I would have arrived intending to vote for the man leaving the stage at this moment. We had discussed the leadership contest as a group and whilst we had come to a unanimous decision to back Kilclooney,

Empey had clearly been the second choice should the UUP peer fall out of contention. Yet this position might well have swayed my mind had I been voting. I wondered how many others in the room were thinking the same thing. Hypothetically, if the IRA decommissioned next week and Assembly elections were called with the DUP seeking a mandate to go into government with Sinn Féin, Empey was giving the impression that the UUP were going to oppose the Agreement that he had fought to keep alive over the last seven years.

The question was obviously a plant and a very bad one at that. I'd heard people close to Empey arguing that Burnside would bring 10 or 15 per cent of the delegates with him, but they clearly weren't factoring in the 15 or 20 per cent he might alienate.

With that the conference voted and broke for twenty minutes as the staff did the count.

As I walked from the hall people were joking that if Trimble walked in now and made a speech like he had at last year's conference he'd win by a landslide.

I headed straight for the bar where Empey's team were nervously sipping beers. They turned grey, appearing momentarily sober, when I told them what had happened. When the delegates reconvened for the result Rogan took the stage and informed the UUC that over 81 per cent of its eligible membership had attended and voted this evening, a total of 619.

'Ladies and gentlemen, there were 615 votes cast with four spoilt.

The result was Sir Reg Empey 295, 47.96%;

Mr Alan McFarland 266, 43.25%;

And Mr David McNarry 54 votes, 8.78%.

No candidate has received 50% plus one so Mr McNarry is eliminated and delegates must vote again.'

Chatter filled the hall as the delegates reached for their ballot papers.

I met members of Empey's team outside and they were aghast at the result. What had gone wrong.

I told them.

The hall erupted with noise as the result sunk in. Most people had expected it to be decided on the first count, with McNarry trailing McFarland and Empey the clear winner. Yet he had polled only 29 votes more than his unknown challenger. McFarland hinted at the beginning of his speech that he was a dark horse candidate. He couldn't have been more right.

As the delegates then voted for a second time the shock amongst Empey's supporters became evident, as was the realization that their candidate, should he win, would do so with a far weaker mandate than hoped for. Had Empey gained close to 50 per cent with the other two candidates evenly split perhaps more people would have swung in behind him and provided a firm result to rebuild the party with. But as things stood, both candidates could still win so all the talk of Empey only needing 19 transfers from McNarry that was filling the hall was nonsense.

Delegates where soon called to return and Rogan rose for the last time and announced the result.

'This time there were 608 valid votes and 5 spoilt votes.

The result was Sir Reg Empey 321 votes, 52.79% and Mr Alan McFarland 287 47.2%

Sir Reg is our new leader.'

Empey had won by 34 votes, polling 321 to McFarland's 287, increasing his lead by only four votes from the first round.

When Empey emerged to make his acceptance speech we saw a totally different man. The new UUP leader warmed to the huge round of applause and standing ovation he got when he took the stage for the second time that evening. He joked with the crowd and lightened the atmosphere with the charm that had eluded him earlier on.

Sir Reg said he was 'immensely grateful to the UUC for their support', and graciously praised his predecessor, David Trimble, for the 'efforts that he had made'.

He said that Trimble had been 'badly let down by our government and our prime minister' and to have 'stayed the course through such a betrayal was a considerable mark [of] his character'.

The lights suddenly went out at the back of the hall and Sir Reg commented, to roars of applause, that 'they needn't turn out the lights on this party. We are going to relight it.' He said this party is 'going to fight its way back to where we belong'.

Reg had finally won the much coveted prize of leader of the UUP, and, boy, did he look relieved.

So, on 24 June 2005, Sir Reg Empey became the Ulster Unionist who would lead the party's revival in the wake of David Trimble's collapse. While enjoying the backing of the vast majority of the party's household names and Assembly members he had received just 52.7 per cent of the UUC vote. Sources close to Empey indicated that he would soon forge a young leadership team which had Newry and Armagh MLA Danny Kennedy as his deputy.[44] After the election contest Empey outlined his policy on devolution, indicating that Unionists should wait until the spring of 2006 before making any definitive judgement on the IRA's position on standing down and ending illegal activity.[45] The new leader said he had made it clear in his literature that the UUP would 'not participate in an Executive which includes Sinn Féin in the lifetime of this Assembly'.[46] He stressed the difficult tasks in front of the UUP and spoke of restructuring the party and bringing in new blood. He also said he did not expect to lead the UUP for more than five years.[47]

Empey had ruled out power-sharing with Sinn Féin. Of course this pledge was only for the lifetime of the current Northern Ireland Assembly, which had been elected in 2003. Therefore, should a deal emerge in the near future between the two largest parties, the subsequent Assembly elections would allow Empey to shift from that position. This stance most likely came from the fact that he had gathered an unlikely coalition of supporters around him during the campaign. He clearly had to deliver on this point during the contest, but given the result he could be fairly confident that their support had failed to deliver him the UUC votes he needed to gain the mandate his supporters had sought.

While the result was indecisive, it certainly confirmed that the party did not want the sort of lurch to the right some favoured. The UUC delegates at the Ramada Hotel treated the leadership candidates and the party officers in the same fashion as the electorate had treated the UUP on 5 May. They accepted the literature, smiled politely at the politicians, and then voted in the opposite direction to which they said they would. The UUC did, however, unite around the new leader and, as with the 2005 general election campaign, the bitterness of the Trimble years and the civil war within Unionism over the Belfast Agreement had been tempered. The result, of course, and the nature in which it was delivered, suggested nothing of the sort.

9 The State of the Union

What the British Government needs to do in terms of making any agreement work is protect the basic principles which that agreement was founded on, such as democracy and its core values. What the government must do is vigorously police and uphold those principles. That does not mean that it has to be partial towards a political party. What it means is that it has to be very firmly in defence of the democratic process and in defence of people being law abiding. To do this it must ensure that everyone is playing the game by the same set of rules.

David Trimble, 8 June 2005

Having assessed why the UUP negotiated the Belfast Agreement and subsequently attempted to implement it, an analysis of the role of the British government, Tony Blair's relationship with David Trimble and the state of the political union between Britain and Northern Ireland is necessary to understand fully the predicament Ulster Unionism faces today. The first point to make here is that David Trimble proactively changed the relationship between Unionism and the British political establishment, worked it to its most productive end and influenced it as far as he could. In many respects in doing so he was very successful. Many of his critics, however, argue that he placed too much emphasis on his relationship with Tony Blair at the expense of his party's electoral standing in Northern Ireland. The question many Trimble supporters have asked me over the last years is – why did Tony Blair let the UUP leader down so badly? The answer to this question is a very simple one. To my mind, he let Trimble down because he could. David Trimble faced the same problem as Brian Faulkner in his dealings with the British Prime Minister. It is the same problem facing any Unionist leader when negotiating with the British government and a problem that is at the core of the dilemma facing Ulster Unionism today. David Trimble had absolutely no alternative but to trust Tony Blair at critical junctures in the political process. Having been let down by Blair on one occasion meant that Trimble could not rely on his word the next time he gave it, but he simply had to reconsider the option of trusting him again if he was to further the political process. In 2001 I asked Lord Kilclooney about this in light of his support for the Agreement, knowing he had held reservations about decommissioning and the formation of an Executive that included Republicans. His response illustrates this problem:

> We got this letter from the Prime Minister delivered to our rooms stating that it required decommissioning to take place first, which he expected to start in July 1998. After that I couldn't oppose the Agreement any further. One had to accept the Prime Minister's word even though one suspected its accuracy. So I finally accepted, in the interests of unity in the party and standing with David, and secondly, because we had this new assurance from the Prime Minister in writing.[1]

If David Trimble had not trusted that Tony Blair would hold Republicans to their commitments under the Belfast Agreement, it would never have been agreed. For Trimble, Good Friday 1998 was the high-water mark of what he was prepared to accept as the leader of Ulster Unionism and what he believed Unionists could support. He thought he could subsequently renegotiate the issues where the Belfast Agreement had been weak from a Unionist perspective during its implementation. He successfully achieved this, securing the IMC and convincing the government to take the powers to suspend and exclude. For UUP insiders like Alex Benjamin, the problem with David Trimble's strategy was that he 'had embarked on a project, he wanted to see it through and it probably could have worked had he not been let down at every stage by the government'.[2] David Trimble's critics argue that it was obvious that Tony Blair was going to let him down. Speaking after the 2005 election Trimble commented that, 'Blair still says that his preferred option is to have Republicans included. No matter how bad they are, no matter what wrong they do, there is always another chance to give to them and there is nothing but a few token words of condemnation.'[3]

I then asked David Trimble how he felt about Sinn Féin's failure to deliver the confidence-building measures in 2003:

Kerr: Were you in a no-win situation in 2003 because Blair seemed certain to let Republicans off the hook should they fail to deliver?'

Trimble: Which is what he did. This is what he did on that occasion and this is the mode he is still engaged in. He is so obsessed with keeping Republicans in that he is sacrificing everything else on the board. The UUP has suffered badly and the SDLP have suffered too. As a result, the political process in Northern Ireland is in danger of going into deep freeze, but still, in terms of the government's strategy, the obsession is with Sinn Féin.[4]

* * * *

The problem David Trimble faced after 1998 was that where the British Government sought to break the Unionist mould of politics in Northern Ireland under Sunningdale, under the Belfast Agreement their aim was to end permanently Republican violence. Consequently, Tony Blair needed Gerry Adams slightly more than he needed David Trimble throughout the process. The very fact that David Trimble was negotiating the Agreement after Ian Paisley and Robert McCartney excluded their parties from the political talks process illustrates that point. Tony Blair did not feel it necessary to have all the Unionist parties present and negotiating an agreement over Northern Ireland's constitutional future. In fact, he most likely hoped the DUP would feel unable to negotiate it, as agreement was far more likely to be forthcoming in their absence.

This left David Trimble in the same position as Brian Faulkner in 1973. He needed the British Prime Minister to keep the balance for Unionism in the negotiations and to allow him to score heavily on the issues that were imperative to the Unionist cause. Ted Heath had no concept of this at all. Tony Blair on the other hand, fully understood David Trimble's predicament and while using it to his advantage on occasions, ensured the UUP leader secured a settlement he could at least sell to the majority of the Unionist community at that point. It was not the Prime Minister's fault that large sections of the Unionist élite were too intransigent to negotiate the accord and subsequently worked to undermine it. Tony Blair and David Trimble had a meeting of minds on the constitutional aspects of the Agreement. As David Kerr put it,

> ... for all the criticism we have of Blair over the RUC, prisoners and decommissioning, he was guided by an acute sense of fairness on the constitutional question. Blair was determined to ensure that Trimble was not shafted or that Unionism was not shafted by any settlement in terms of its constitutional future. But you will find that if you look at it that Blair was the key factor in terms of stabilizing the negotiations over North–South linkages and the consent principle and you have to respect him for that.[5]

Others within the party take a more negative view of the Prime Minister's role, such as David Burnside, who labelled Blair's promises under the Belfast Agreement 'as a con job'.[6]

Tony Blair's fairness in handling the strand two aspects of the Agreement is a point the Ulster Unionist leader was been consistently grateful for in the political process. It is also a point that reflects the deeply uncomfortable position Unionism holds with regard to its relationship with the British government. Historically, British interests and Ulster Unionist interests have rarely matched. Consequently, Unionist leaders are on the one hand reluctant to negotiate over the union with Britain, while on the other, duty-bound to trust the government to act in good faith when they do. Tony Blair therefore put David Trimble under an enormous amount of pressure to negotiate a settlement and, having delivered for him on strand two of the Agreement, expected the UUP leader to return the favour in transforming Unionism.

David Campbell describes David Trimble's predicament in 1998:

> Blair was a new Prime Minister so therefore we believed what he was telling us: Sinn Féin would not be allowed to be in government unless they disarmed. Where are we from that promise? Certainly it was the Blair letter that turned the party to support the Agreement and then it was the Blair pledges that turned the Unionist public opinion to support the Agreement. Whereas I suspect Bertie Ahern just bullied Nationalists and told

the SDLP: 'Look, you are going to get nothing unless you become much more realistic here.' Particularly since Blair was such a powerful Prime Minister. The fact Labour had a majority of 178 would certainly have informed Trimble's decision-making at the time. If Trimble hadn't made that Agreement then what were they going to do? Probably take a much greener view of things. Since the Agreement, partly because of David's personal relationship with Blair, the Labour Party is very different on Northern Ireland. You just couldn't compare its attitude in government to Kevin McNamara's time, which was Irish unity or nothing.[7]

Unfortunately for David Trimble the Prime Minister did not act in good faith in keeping his promises during the Belfast Agreement's implementation phase. Reg Empey said, 'He had a good relationship with Blair and that's a positive thing but the reality is he didn't get the delivery on those promises and that was the big problem.'[8] On the Blair–Trimble relationship Ken Maginnis said, 'I didn't know Blair until he became Prime Minister. David Trimble came into the House of Commons and knew him straight away. He picked him out and [developed] a relationship immediately. That is, I suppose, the saddest things about Trimble's political life – he invested everything in Blair – that's my opinion.'[9]

In October 2003, when it appeared David Trimble had nowhere left to turn politically, Tony Blair deserted him. UUP communications chief Alex Benjamin argues that the turning-point in the Blair–Trimble relationship was Hillsborough 1999: 'Trimble probably had Blair totally on side up until that point.' In his view, 'one of the fundamental flaws Trimble made was in going into government with Sinn Féin. Trimble had said *no guns, no government*. That was a huge thing to concede and he took the risk. Once he conceded that I think Blair and his Chief of Staff Jonathan Powell thought, *well these guys are totally on board and we can mould them and shape them into doing what we want to do*. So if Trimble hadn't conceded on that one, if he'd dug his heels in on that one, I think we'd be in a better position. But he didn't do it.'[10]

The former UUP leader, however, has not been candid in his criticism of Tony Blair in this process. But when I asked him after the election, his remarks regarding the government's overall handling of the political process were telling.

Kerr: You disassociated yourself with the terms 'trust' and 'Republicans', but surely the key to making the Belfast Agreement work was Tony Blair and your relationship of trust with him. He let you down, didn't he?

Trimble: Well of course he did. But the way I would look at it is like this. What Blair should actually have done was to have been more vigorous in defending the Agreement and defending the principles of the Agreement.

Kerr: Well you can only trust Republicans to keep their end of the bargain if you can trust the government, or governments, to ensure they do so. So what do you do?

Trimble: Well that's the question. What we did was to try and put pressure on the governments to behave and that is what the fight over the Independent Monitoring Commission was [about]. That is why the then Secretary of State John Reid resisted the IMC. He was going to take decisions. He wasn't going to have some people exercising oversight over him. That is why the IMC was potentially, and still is potentially, a huge success provided it maintains the credibility it has. So what do you do when governments are not actually being robust enough? You try to change them.[11]

Kerr: How can you do this without trust?

Trimble: When you have got so many variables in this and so many parties it becomes enormously difficult to deliver unless all the parties are actually playing the game and playing the game fairly with others. I have mentioned my irritation with Downing Street not confiding in us about the very key factor of when the 2003 Assembly election was going to be. I think that is not playing the game properly. It's also hugely important in this context that each of the major players have a very clear understanding of what the others' position is. It is not, and should not, be seen as a game in which your object is to wipe the eye of the other parties. It should be a question of how do we collectively as parties deliver the result. And that means having a clear view of what the position of various other parties is. Now, some parties have been selfish. The most selfish of all, the Cuckoo in the nest, has been the Republicans. They have been entirely selfish in their approach and certainly predatory towards the SDLP. They have also been quite dismissive of the difficult position of the Unionists. As a result of this they pump themselves up but fail to deliver when they see the seriousness of the situation they have got themselves into. Then they are surprised to find that some of the other players have indeed become toughly disenchanted with them.

Kerr: How did the rules get bent?

Trimble: I think it is quite right for the government to ensure that everybody has to play by the same rule book and that we are not going to tolerate people who are engaged in violence. The government was running with that until it fudged. It is simple when you are dealing with outright terrorism, but when you move away from terrorism to what is now a political party with its own private armed wing which is used for raising finances and intimidation, it is not simple. The government isn't being clear-cut in maintaining the basic democratic principles in the situation. In the post-ceasefire period things got foggy. Initially it was terrorism that you were dealing with, a bombing campaign, and then we moved with the ceasefires into a less clear situation. The government has not managed to uphold that and steer a clear course through that. Now, while I am being critical of government, I've got to be clear about it, the main reason why the project went onto the rocks was because of the wrongdoing of Republicans. The failure of the government to be firm with those committing that wrongdoing was a contributory factor.[12] That poses the question as to how Republicans would have acted had they thought failure to honour their side of the bargain would have resulted in significant political sanctions from the two governments. That is a question to which, unfortunately, I have no answer and Republicans never really had to worry about.

When I questioned David Trimble's successor on the issue of Blair's role in policing the Agreement I found him in broad agreement with the former leader:

Kerr: In terms of gaining things like the IMC and exclusion, gaining amendments that make up for weaknesses through renegotiating the Agreement, they couldn't really be sold to the electorate as making up for those weaknesses, could they?'

Empey: The Agreement wasn't renegotiated. They weren't amendments, they were additional aspects. Ironically, the IMC, which we encouraged, is now being used by alleged opponents of the Agreement as the measuring stick. Nothing is going to compensate for failure, no matter what you do. Nothing is going to compensate for that, so the only solution is that people will have to honour their obligations. The government has to honour its obligations to deal with those people. If you have an agreement and people don't honour that agreement you have to pursue a course to get them to do so. In political terms, the weakness has been that the government hasn't honoured its part of the bargain, nor has the SDLP. That's the weakness, no matter what agreement you have. If there is no enforcement of the mechanisms that were designed to implement it, then the question must be asked: why have those mechanisms regarding exclusion if we weren't going to use them when necessary? But of course we are a regional party dependent on a national government – we don't make the law.[13]

* * * *

The Belfast Agreement certainly marked a departure for Britain in terms of its policy towards Northern Ireland, but just how significant this policy shift will be in terms of regulating the conflict remains to be seen. The core principles of British policy on Northern Ireland have not changed fundamentally since 1972. What has changed significantly is the way in which Britain has gone about achieving its policy objectives there, and the style and approach with which it has done so. David Trimble argues that 'the British government's policy now is not the same as it was in the 1970s or 1980s. It may be achieving or pursuing the same fundamental objectives but in terms of its approach to things it is different. This ought to be a reassurance to Unionists, or Unionism collectively, as we are now in a position to be real players. In the 1970s and 1980s British governments prevented us from being real players by marginalising us and trying to impose things on us.'[14]

British policy on Northern Ireland before and after the Belfast Agreement was to contain and then end Republican terrorism – particularly in its mainland cities. In a sense, the Belfast Agreement was about bringing Republicans into a political process where they were part of a level political playing-field and one that gave them time to unwind their military structures. The problem for Unionism here is reflective of David Trimble's position when he entered the political process. Unionism was not a driving force in that process and it had very little in terms of power to negotiate with other than offering its consent to political reform. Trimble's problem was working out what he could do politically while the Republicans slowly unwound those military structures. One option was to force their hand and go into government with them. When Trimble did this it bought him time, illustrated the Belfast Agreement could work, gained international recognition for Unionism, and ensured that someone else received the blame when it collapsed.

The problem for David Trimble was that there was a limit to the number of times that he could get away with going into government with Sinn Féin and collapsing the Assembly when they failed to deliver what he needed to sell the Agreement. As for the Republican movement, their engagement with the British government was at a snail's pace compared to the speed Trimble needed to travel at. In that sense, the UUP needed the Belfast Agreement to work immediately and certainly more so than any of Northern Ireland's other political parties. Trimble was a hostage to time and constantly reliant on the actions of others regarding how successful he would be in his attempts to draw Republicans into power-sharing. He denies he entirely trusted any of the other players in the political process. He dismisses any such suggestion remarking that 'it is foolish to proceed in politics, particularly in the situation that I was in, on a basis of trust because you do not know what pressures the other chap is going to be under'.[15]

In analyzing this situation, I think it is safe to argue that none of the parties involved in the political process expected David Trimble to last much longer than 2001. His prolonged political survival illustrates two things. First, he was highly adroit at strategically positioning himself within the political game and out-manœuvring his rivals. Second, the longer he remained leader of the UUP the more obvious it became that he would ultimately be let down by his partners in the political process – Tony Blair and Gerry Adams. Tony Blair had four years from 2001 to press Sinn Féin finally to deliver for David Trimble and, despite the fact that the UUP's arguments were consistently backed up by IMC reports, the Prime Minister would not do so.[16] Not only that, he did nothing to compensate the UUP for the fact that when Unionists voted against David Trimble in 2003, they were actually voting against the British government's mishandling of the political process in Northern Ireland. The same argument can be made regarding the Irish government and the SDLP. As for Sinn Féin, while they clearly had huge internal problems with their inability or unwillingness to deconstruct the IRA, why should they have helped David Trimble in the absence of serious pressure from the two governments? They might have done more to meet the Unionist leader's needs in 2003, as those who favoured devolution within Sinn Féin had some interest in delivering on that deal with David Trimble. It was always going to be easier for Republicans to sell the merits of accepting devolution to their constituency with the UUP rather than the DUP. By 2003, however, it was becoming obvious that David Trimble could no longer carry Unionism in any agreement with Sinn Féin. So why then would Gerry Adams and Martin McGuinness have expended the confidence-building measures on a deal with Trimble in 2003 that he might not be able to deliver on? The fact that Trimble was prepared to take a similar risk with Blair and Adams in 2003 highlights the Unionist leader's reliance on the actions of others to deliver in the process.

During the sequencing that was to establish institutions it appeared as though Republicans were going through the motions, the two governments were crossing their fingers and Trimble was on his last throw of the dice. As it turned out, fortune faded for the UUP leader. In the final analysis, Trimble was the only player in the political process whose future depended on the success or failure of that deal. Reg Empey's description of that afternoon's events illustrates this point: 'While David might have been prepared to give it his best shot, I think when he went into a room where a lot of staff were seated watching this, he knew from their reaction that it just wasn't going to work. So he was left pretty much with no choice.'[17]

In essence, Sinn Féin did not need to complete a deal with David Trimble in October 2003. From the British government's perspective, while the UUP leader was no longer the political force he once was, there was no harm in trying. The fact that they decommissioned weapons and then made their historic statement on 28 July 2005, without a deal, illustrates the dangerous position Unionism is in now.

The government has no great expectation that Paisley will deliver, therefore it is content to proceed with the political process with Sinn Féin. In the absence of a Sinn Féin–DUP agreement, the IRA have committed themselves to acts of verifiable decommissioning and decriminalization with the British government in return for demilitarization and speaking rights in the Irish Parliament. If the DUP does not engage, the British government has signalled its willingness to proceed with the political process without them. The dilemma here for Unionism is that, while David Trimble was always at least 'two or three steps ahead of his troops', Ian Paisley is 'at least one step behind his', as Denis Rogan puts it.[18]

The fact that the DUP is facing the prospect of being in a political process with the IRA in the absence of David Trimble is a very worrying development for them. Republicans were able to wrong-foot Unionism so easily again in 2005 as the DUP lags behind Sinn Féin in that process. The very fact that they came to a position of power in 2005 on the basis of ruling out power-sharing with Sinn Féin has suddenly become their main problem. Consequently, Republicans acted quickly following the election in order to remove the logic behind the DUP's argument for exclusion. The only way for the DUP to catch up is to call the IRA's bluff. The crucial issue here again is not decommissioning but policing and justice. If Republicans accept policing and justice in Northern Ireland then the political process will have come full circle from 1972. Direct Rule was imposed on Northern Ireland in 1972 partly due to Brian Faulkner's refusal to accept a Stormont government without the devolution of security powers. The irony is that the phase of the conflict that saw Stormont prorogued will truly have ended if policing and justice powers are devolved and Republicans accept and support them.

In 2003, the IRA's handling of de Chastelain and, in turn, de Chastelain's handling of the press conference which was supposed to provide the confidence-building measures, seemed purposely to rule out any possibility of a deal. The fact that the British government then went ahead with the Assembly elections they had promised as part of the sequencing bears out the argument that they had given up on the UUP as the vehicle with which to take the political process forward. The Northern Bank robbery and the McCartney murder did, however, illustrate just how difficult Gerry

Adams' position was with the hard-liners in his movement, something which is almost completely lost on the Unionist community. Adams and McGuinness were asking people who are prepared to shoot soldiers and policemen, to accept politics without violence, or the threat of violence, as the sole means of delivering their national aspirations. The UUP knew from British security briefings the problems Sinn Féin were having with their people. David Campbell said: 'It was almost a paradox that at times, Adams and McGuiness were actually personally in danger, whereas we weren't, at least, personally in danger, our politics were in danger.'[19]

What I am arguing here is that Unionists should not be too surprised at all by the position that David Trimble found himself in. In terms of winning votes and consolidating support amongst the electorate for his position as UUP leader, he should not have gone back into government with Sinn Féin after they failed to complete their side of the bargain on decommissioning. He did so because it advanced the Belfast Agreement. This is something he saw as being in the long-term interests of the Unionist community. Where he failed in taking this and other momentous decisions was that he did so without the backing of his party as a whole or the Unionist community. I am arguing, however, that David Trimble punched well above his weight during and after the Belfast Agreement was negotiated. To grasp the significance of this argument one only has to consider the disarray Unionism was in when it entered those negotiations, how the British government went about excluding Unionism from the AIA's negotiation, the limited issues David Trimble had to negotiate with in 1998 and the internal and external opposition he faced when doing so.

Unionism had come from nowhere in the political process and consequently its leader had very few cards to play in the political game that ensued after Good Friday 1998. During the implementation phase David Trimble convinced the government to set up the IMC, which tracked the activities of paramilitary organizations in Northern Ireland. This was a serious symbolic victory for Trimble, but one which had little impact on the Unionist community.[20] The DUP and Trimble's internal opponents actually opposed the IMC. Ironically, Trimble 'actually ended up rectifying the Belfast Agreement's shortcomings through the creation of IMC and the government actually legislating to allow for exclusion without a cross-community vote, and that should have

214

satisfied', in David Campbell's opinion, 'the anti-Agreement element in the party. But it was at that point it became clear that nothing would satisfy them other than David Trimble's head. Donaldson, Foster and Weir left the party and Smyth and Burnside withdrew the whip, supposedly over the creation of the IMC, yet the DUP have used it as the main plank of their argument for accepting the main principles of the Agreement. We've just turned full circle.'[21]

There is also the question as to how David Trimble and the Belfast Agreement changed Northern Ireland's political union with Britain. For all the hype on 'sell-outs' and 'one-way tickets to a united Ireland', emanating from the anti-Agreement camp over the last decade, the argument seems to have been finally settled. No serious Unionist politician will now make an argument that the Belfast Agreement was not in the interests of Unionism. During that period there were three kinds of anti-Agreement Unionist politicians. The first kind were genuinely psychologically unprepared to accept terrorists being let out of prison as their colleagues waited to enter government having refused to disarm; the second kind simply had not grasped where the long-term interests of the Unionist community lay; the third kind had, but chose to cynically exploit the deep apprehension within the Unionist community about negotiating with Republicans over the future of Northern Ireland in order to supplant David Trimble as the voice of Unionism. This, of course, is not a new phenomenon in Unionist politics. It is, however, indicative of a political situation (zero-sum game) where a leader goes out ahead of his electoral constituency to further the interests of that community.

So, in the first instance, David Trimble secured the constitutional position of Northern Ireland within the UK, attained the acceptance of the principle of consent over its future, secured the agreement of the Irish government to amend Articles 2 and 3 of the Irish Constitution, and enabled Sinn Féin to accept a settlement that fell short of a united Ireland. While this agreement clearly ticked all the right boxes in terms of Unionism's constitutional aspirations, it did not give David Trimble something tangible with which he could walk out onto Belfast High Street and sell. Conversely, the Agreement provided Sinn Féin and the DUP with exactly that. Sinn Féin's popularity soared among the Nationalist community after the Agreement as it gained credit on the issues of prisoners and police reform. As for the DUP, it won over large sections of Unionism through its opposition campaigns on those two issues. The irony of this was that Sinn Féin did not actually negotiate the Belfast Agreement, the SDLP did, and Irish officials indicate that so worried were Republicans about being seen to have done so that they actually considered running an anti-Agreement campaign in the Republic and a pro-Agreement campaign in Northern Ireland. This is an accusation Sinn Féin vehemently denies.[22] This nervousness about the Agreement is illustrated by the fact that they abstained when a vote was taken among the parties to ascertain if there was sufficient consensus for the agreement at the end of the negotiations. As David Trimble commented recently, 'Republicans did not that day vote for the Agreement … and if it had been a signing matter, I'd dearly love to know at what point they actually would have signed.'[23]

As for the DUP, police reform and prisoners were issues the UUP were weak on for three reasons. David Trimble's team were focused on negotiating the constitutional issues of strand two; they were reliant on the two small loyalist parties to enable them to represent a majority of Unionism in the negotiations; and they were weakened on those issues by the fact the DUP and the UKUP excluded themselves. Consequently, there was no emotive or symbolic card for Trimble to wave to his supporters. Decommissioning should have been that card but he failed to hold the Prime Minister to live up to his commitments under that agreement. If Tony Blair did not feel it was necessary to do so then why would the Republican movement. David Trimble blames Republicans for this but the British government is the sovereign power in Northern Ireland and as it made the rules by which the parties had to play under the Belfast Agreement only it can ultimately be responsible for enforcing them. David Trimble did, however, achieve decommissioning on three separate occasions, but it was 'always against major division within the party'. David Campbell argues that, 'IRA decommissioning was always set against a background of 49 per cent of our own party either denying it or minimizing it. That was our biggest problem – the division within the party, the lack of discipline within the party and the sheer selfishness of some individuals.'[24]

It is not simply, however, the constitutional position of Northern Ireland that is important in its political union with Britain. This union is like an arranged marriage two people enter into out of compulsion rather than love. In order to make it work, the two partners need either to have the same interests or for one partner to make it impossible for the other to leave the union. There is also, of course, the possibility that they will fall in love at a later date as their interests merge, but until that happens we should make our judgements based on the facts. Until 1998 Britain never fully committed itself to that political union after Stormont was prorogued. The Conservative Party's minimalist approach to Northern Ireland from Edward Heath to Margaret Thatcher and the Labour Party's complete misunderstanding of the dynamics of Northern Ireland's ethno-national conflict during that period illustrate this point.

The problem with Sunningdale for some Unionists was not with what the Agreement actually entailed, but what the British government's intentions might have been had they supported or accepted it. Having left Northern Ireland to be governed by the UUP from partition until 1972, no one outside the Republican movement was under any illusion that Downing Street had a great interest in the Province. However, under the Belfast Agreement the British government had signed an international agreement stating its intent to ensure Northern Ireland remained within the UK provided that that was the wish of a majority of its citizens.

Unionists had spent the previous 25 years attempting to make it impossible for the British government to alter the status of Northern Ireland. The signing of the AIA was a clear indication from the government that it would no longer tolerate political intransigence over internal reforms from Unionism. Reg Empey argues that the UUP had learnt the lessons of the AIA period but 'with Unionism represented as it now is by the DUP my fear is that we could go back to a position where they could repeat those mistakes – we should be very cautious about that'.[25] The choice facing Unionism in 2005 then is whether to return to the old politics of intransigence and its approach to dealing with the government or build on the approach David Trimble took regarding this relationship. While he was repeatedly let down by his government, he made it very difficult for them to do so and when they did the world noticed.

Unionists can continue to strengthen Northern Ireland's political union with Britain in this respect. The British government let David Trimble down because it was in its interests to do so with regard to keeping Sinn Féin comfortably within the process. That need not always be the case. If the Belfast Agreement works in the future and Republicans give up the IRA, the threat of violence and criminality will no longer hang over the political process and Sinn Féin will have to behave as a constitutional western democratic party. David Trimble's approach to the British government and the Agreement was tactically and politically clever. Consequently, Unionism reaped the rewards of his efforts both internationally and within the UK. A new modern UUP must emerge and build on these achievements as they can all too easily be undone. The government must also consider this view, as it is not in its long-term interest to see Northern Ireland divided between the DUP and Sinn Féin.

There may be those who consider joint authority a viable long-term policy option for Britain and therefore view autonomous ethnic segregation in Northern Ireland as attractive. This is hardly a new idea but one only has to look at a demographic map of Northern Ireland to understand the geopolitical and socio-economic costs Britain and Northern Ireland would incur from such a policy. It would also be unethical, but that is a personal moral judgement. It is, however, up to the government to engineer the conditions to avoid such a scenario. It is in the DUP's political instinct to play the 'fear card' and pursue such thinking, which is what they may do should the government call an assembly election in the near future.[26] There is, of course, no requirement for the government to do this until 2007, which would be one way of avoiding an election where the DUP sought a mandate to go into power with Sinn Féin with the argument that the only way to be safe from Republicanism was to ensure that the DUP remained Northern Ireland's largest party. The government would need to alter its approach to the management of the process to achieve this. Ruling out an election would also give the moderate parties time to regroup.

Unionism has experienced deep unpopularity in the international community and been a serious embarrassment to the British government for decades. David Trimble was the first Unionist leader to address this problem successfully. The anxiety for Unionists must be that those who have replaced him possess the qualities to undo those achievements. Without meaning to take too negative a view towards the DUP, they are exactly why Unionism was so unpopular both at home and abroad during the years of conflict. As Roy Beggs put it,

> ... the people of Great Britain, Europe, America and inter-
> nationally looked at Northern Ireland and all they could see was
> Paisley with his fist in the air and his mouth open shouting
> 'Ulster Says No, Never', and 'No Surrender'. And that really is
> about the height of it, apart from the fact that his troops on the
> ground are absolute experts in putting up flags and painting
> curbstones. David Trimble, I have to say, had greater faith,
> greater hope and greater vision than that. The legacy of Trimble's
> decision to sign the Belfast Agreement and the international role
> he has played was acknowledged when he was awarded the
> Nobel Peace Prize. He became the widely accepted spokesperson
> of the Ulster Unionist people. He presented the acceptable face of
> Unionism internationally. This is something we never previously
> had before him.[27]

By 2005 the DUP had stolen the UUP's political clothes. Now that
they have done so the UUP must be generous enough not to hinder
their development socially within the UK and Ireland. The DUP's
deep aversion to Westminster and the British political establishment
is actually reflected in their hatred and contempt for the UUP. This
argument is illustrated by the fact that during the election their goal
was not to smash Sinn Féin, but to smash the UUP in every constituency, regardless of whether a Nationalist took the seat or not. For Ian
Paisley, winning 2005 was as much about finally conquering
traditional Unionism as it was about defying Downing Street.
Whether Ian Paisley's new position of power will be tempered with
political realism or whether he will use his platform to re-establish
the politics of intransigence for which he is world-renowned remains
to be seen. Either way, this question highlights the dangers that lie
ahead for the Unionist people now that the DUP are their main
representatives.

There is nothing unusual about being a British Unionist in the
twenty-first century. It is the unusual position of being Irish and
being a Unionist that needs understanding within British politics
today. There is no reason why it cannot become as fashionable and
politically correct a position as being a Scottish nationalist and a

unionist, or a Pakistani cricket fanatic and a die-hard English football fan at the same time for that matter. Irish Unionists must now proactively engage in British political life and feel confident in doing so. David Trimble's UUP began this re-engagement process and it is now in the interests of the DUP at least to attempt to follow it through to its logical conclusion. In practical terms this means attending Westminster on a regular basis, socializing with British people that are not from Northern Ireland, taking part in British political life and lobbying for the Unionist cause in the UK, Ireland and America. One of the most painful ironies of life in the British Isles is that it is Unionists who very often struggle to fit in anywhere. The Unionist community must engage in positive political activity and put the years of opposition politics behind it. To do so it needs a modern, centralized, secular Unionist party in touch with both its immediate electorate and its natural connection to British political life. Unionism must begin to play a vibrant role in British society and to do so with the same enthusiasm and confidence as northern Nationalists engage in both the Republic of Ireland and Great Britain.

Turning to the question of Britain's relationship with Unionism and its approach to conflict regulation, I argued that its policy towards Northern Ireland had not changed. I mean this in the most generic sense and do not argue that the changes in style and substance were insignificant. Britain has a strategic and economic interest in making Northern Ireland work. It must therefore continue to improve its relationship with Unionism. The British government needs Ulster Unionism if it is to achieve long-term political stability in Northern Ireland. Britain and Ireland's interest in Northern Ireland has been primarily based on containing and stemming Republican violence over the last 30 years. A process that had its origins in the Sunningdale Agreement developed whereby the two governments actually established an interest in regulating the conflict as a policy goal in itself. What this meant for Britain was that while its objectives in Northern Ireland remained the same, it was prepared to go to much greater lengths to achieve them.

Tony Blair brought many things to the political process but most importantly he brought a sense of fairness to the negotiations when they took place. He also committed an abundance of time and patience to that process, something that no other Prime Minister had ever given

Northern Ireland. He brought with him the full resources of the British State in attempting to make the Belfast Agreement work. As David Campbell puts it, 'in terms of commitment to Northern Ireland, we got fifty times more out the Blair Administration than we ever got out of the Thatcher or Major Administrations. I think Labour activists on the mainland would have complained that the Prime Minister was spending much more time on and in Northern Ireland than with them. At one point, a Cabinet Minister said to David Trimble: you see much more of the Prime Minister than I do – what's he like?'[28]

The reason it failed in the short-term was, ironically, because British security interests took primacy over that Agreement, but it does not mean that this will always be the case. What it meant in 2005 was that the UUP became a sacrificial lamb in that phase of the process, something which commentators had been saying about John Hume and the SDLP a number of years ago. Just as the SDLP needed to concede political ground to give Sinn Féin credibility after 1998, the UUP needed to legitimize power-sharing with both forms of Nationalism to pave the way for a future where Northern Ireland can be stabilized through voluntary, multi-party sharing of power. In this sense the British government's long-term political interests and those of the UUP are not that different. The UUP, however, is no longer a political force of any significance, so the government's task, therefore, must now be to create the confidence within the Unionist community to re-engage in power-sharing without David Trimble. Ulster Unionists must assist the government in that process and through doing so, work towards reviving their political fortunes. This will take some time but it marks an important shift in British political thinking. The British approach to Northern Ireland has moved away from the short-termism of the political minimalism that epitomized Margaret Thatcher's handling of Northern Ireland in the 1980s. In 2005 government seems to be taking a short- to medium-term view that the Belfast Agreement is as good as Northern Ireland gets. How they manage that process, or with whom, appears to be a secondary concern.

There is one major drawback to such political thinking although it is far from insurmountable. Just as previous British Prime Ministers have underestimated or dismissed the uncertainty and fear amongst Unionists regarding political reform in Northern Ireland, in pursuit of its goals, Tony Blair's government has done the same thing. Not only that, but unlike other British Prime Ministers, Blair made it obvious that he understood the eggshell sensibilities of Irish Unionism and chose to ignore them all the same. My concern about this approach to conflict regulation in Northern Ireland is that while Northern Ireland might become a place where Nationalists are happy to live it may become unworkable as a result of Unionist instability. It is a delicate balance and policy-makers must be very careful when they attempt to create an equilibrium between the two communities. While Unionism had to concede things in the Agreement, Britain's interest is to end the conflict in Northern Ireland and to stabilize devolution. It must not lose sight of the fact that it needs Unionists to make that happen. Replacing terrorism with criminality will not work in the long term. This idea appears to be seen in some government circles as the price of bringing peace to Northern Ireland, just as previous governments took the view that Northern Ireland could be managed if the conflict was reduced to an acceptable level of violence. The government have good reason to step back from such thinking as we have a situation in Northern Ireland where all parties to the political process accept that they have to negotiate a settlement with the British and Irish governments. Therefore, stable and devolved democratic government based on power-sharing in Northern Ireland is indeed possible.

If Britain has come to the view that Northern Ireland is acceptable the way it is in 2005 it will miss the best opportunity it has ever had successfully to regulate its conflict in the long term. To my mind, the working Belfast Agreement *is* as good as it gets and the government was right to think that. The fact that the Agreement is not working and that there is still no violence is nothing to feel content about. It was this sort of complacent attitude both from Unionism and the British government that led Northern Ireland to the 30 years of conflict it recently experienced. Many of the problems that resulted in violence erupting between the two main communities lies beneath the surface and in some respects are worse than before. Ethno-national conflicts require long-term management and regulation if they are ever to be settled. The inter-ethnic tension in Northern Ireland is reflected in the behaviour of its élites. For example, Brian Faulkner's power-sharing coalition of 1974 worked well and most of its participants contend that good working relations quickly built up between its members.[29] This is certainly in contrast to Northern Ireland's recent power-sharing venture where relations between Unionists and Nationalists were quite often strained.[30] Social polarization in Northern Ireland has never been worse.

What then can the British government do about this? First, it can inject confidence-building measures into the political process by indicating to the Unionist community that it actually wants Northern Ireland to work. The Irish government should do the same thing. They spend a lot of time attacking Sinn Féin on the grounds of criminality and continued paramilitary violence so there should no longer be any difficulty in saying that it wants Northern Ireland to work politically. I know that would be useful from a Unionist perspective but there is no contradiction between the Irish government or Ireland's political parties repeatedly making such statements and actually holding an aspiration to have a united Ireland. Some people might respond to those points by arguing that both governments have made it very clear through the Belfast Agreement that they want Northern Ireland to work. I would respond that a lot of Unionists did not realize that and a brief glance at the 2005 election results should substantiate that point. Many Unionists felt that they had been deceived after experiencing the Agreement's implementation process. As Brendan O'Leary argues, 'By coercing the Northern Ireland parties to engage in power-sharing, the British government were asking people there to accept something it would never dream of imposing on mainland Britain.'[31]

Now, while a majority of Unionists came to view power-sharing with Republicans as something they should accept under Tony Blair's assurances, the government must not lose sight of those assurances and must in the future compensate politically for its failure to live up to them. This can be done in many ways and there is already a precedent for it. Secretary of State Peter Mandelson repeatedly acted in such a fashion as to maintain the balance between the communities and bolster the UUP in the absence of widespread support from their community. Mandelson approached his role in much the same way as Edward Heath's influential Secretary of State William Whitelaw in 1972 and 1973. William Whitelaw quickly realized that politics in Northern Ireland had many grey areas and that it was in those areas where the balance between the two communities could be struck. Sadly, both Whitelaw and Mandelson were forcibly removed from

Northern Ireland's political scene at critical junctures in the political process. I would not in any way underestimate the impact of their departures on either Sunningdale's negotiations or the Belfast Agreement's implementation phase. Their departures left both Brian Faulkner and David Trimble without the guidance from their government that might have enabled them to carry the process further.

When Mandelson took office in Northern Ireland he purposefully went out of his way to be impartial, while acting as a balance to the Irish government's position of supporting constitutional Nationalism when it was necessary. David Campbell argues that had he been Secretary of State from the Belfast Agreement onwards, 'things would have been radically different'.[32] This was crucial to David Trimble's capacity to work the Agreement. Not only did it give the Unionist leader confidence in negotiating with Irish Nationalism, he felt he had the backing of his government in doing so. This was fundamental to the Unionist side of the Agreement and fundamental to understanding the Unionist dilemma in the political process. In order to compensate for the failures of that process and the actions the government took during that period, it must be prepared to engage proactively with the Unionist community or the relationship will continue to be strained.

Of course, there is an argument to be made that the Unionist electorate want things entirely on their own terms; that they realize the political process has brought peace; that Northern Ireland is going to remain within the UK; that there is going to be economic prosperity; but that they do not actually want to engage in a process where there are symbolic difficulties for them. That is why they think that they can vote DUP without paying a price as a community or as individuals. They misunderstand the Unionist dilemma in the same way as many British policy-makers have. Imposing prisoner releases, police reform and Sinn Féin in government upon the Unionist community in Northern Ireland is not the same as forcing through university top-up fees or congestion charges in England. While voters in stable western democracies generally think with their economic pocketbooks, voters in Northern Ireland think in zero-sum nationalist terms. As UUP leader Reg Empey put it, 'the fundamental problem is that people felt, having supported the Belfast Agreement and taken the risk regarding prisoners and other unpalatable aspects, they never got the payback that they were entitled to and that was true'.[33]

It is not that this argument is fundamentally wrong in its orientation. In fact, it directly addresses certain aspects of the Unionist dilemma with the Agreement. Unionists voted the way they did because those symbolic reforms actually hurt them as a community. Subsequently, the DUP used that pain and the fear of further attacks on Unionist culture and society as a means of consolidating its vote. As David Burnside puts it,

> ... the UUP has been finally paid off by the electorate, and understandably so, because this was not the deal that 55 per cent of the Protestant people signed up to at the time of the Agreement. But it's more than that. It's not just the policy failure where the DUP are offering a better policy, people don't want terrorists and criminals in the government of Northern Ireland. And they were voting for the party which is less likely to put them there. Our leadership and our party's track record was that it couldn't wait to jump into government with Sinn Féin/IRA having achieved very little. So it was a mistake in the first place that they kept repeating, the Unionist people didn't trust them and the leadership was too clever by half. Every time they changed their tactics, it wasn't just clever, it was dishonest.[34]

This argument lies at the heart of why the UUP lost the 2005 election. As David Trimble put it, 'one of the most depressing things about politics in Northern Ireland in the last few years is that so many Nationalists have been able to turn a blind eye to criminality. So many Nationalists have been prepared to tolerate criminality, and consequently support has grown for Republicanism, despite their wrong-doing.' This is something the Nationalist community must think long and hard about.

This view also underestimates the fears and concerns that most Unionists have regarding their citizenship within the UK. UUP Policy Officer Brian Crowe's analysis is an illustration in part of these sentiments:

> Like most Unionists, I'm unconvinced that any British government will act on behalf of Unionism – and I remain

enough of a traditional Unionist to believe that when Dublin 'acts on behalf' of Nationalists in this part of the UK, it should be firmly told to mind its own business. Ultimately, my status as a British citizen does not depend on the charity of Westminster governments – it is my inherent right, which I cannot be deprived of without my consent. Perhaps all this is unrealistic and naive. But I therefore feel very uneasy about stressing the need to 'win' mainland opinion. Ulster Unionism should first and foremost be about winning the votes of Unionists in Northern Ireland, not seeking the favour of government.

Crowe surmises the distrust and distance that many Unionists feel when it comes to their relationship with Westminster. This is an inherent aspect of the siege mentality of Unionists in Northern Ireland. No better is it illustrated than by the paradox of believing on the one hand that citizenship is an inherent right, which it arguably should be in any democratic society one is born into; and on the other hand, the fact that Unionists like Crowe fought for the Belfast Agreement which secured that right through negotiation both with the British government and that of another state, the Republic of Ireland.

The Unionist community is not a single entity and, as such, the academic labels of civic and ethnic nationalism do not fit well when it comes to actual voting patterns. People from all spectrums of political Unionism voted DUP in 2005, and it had little to do with how they perceive themselves in terms of civic or ethnic identity. This does not mean that the Unionist community has not made a fundamental error in the 2005 election. As I said, it will now become easier for Republicans to ensure that Northern Ireland does not work and harder for those in Sinn Féin that believe they have an interest in working it to convince people of that view. Unionism should take note of this argument. Should the DUP fail where they hindered the UUP, the union will undoubtedly be in peril.

In coming to terms with accepting that it wants Northern Ireland to work, the British government must forge a new relationship with the new political representatives of Unionism in Northern Ireland, the DUP. Ulster Unionists should help them. The government has already done this very successfully with sections of the UUP, Nationalism, Republicanism and with the Irish government. It must do the same

226

with the DUP and re-engage with the Unionist community as a whole. It was right for the British government to be neutral in the negotiations that led up to the Belfast Agreement. It was necessary to enable the Republican movement to engage in that process. Consequently, there is no reason why the British government should not represent or favour the Unionist community or, for that matter, the citizens of Northern Ireland collectively who wish to maintain their political union with Britain. It has been an inherent weakness in the political process that they have not consistently sought to do so.

Being part of a nation, of course, is all about being recognized by other members of that nation. Survey data has consistently shown that large sections of British society are either ambivalent towards the future of Northern Ireland or would be happy to see a united Ireland. Survey data on Northern Ireland also indicates that for the first time more Protestants than Catholics think it is 'likely' that there will be a united Ireland in 'the next twenty years' by 32 per cent to 26 per cent.[35] In contrast, support for a united Ireland amongst the Catholic community has steadily decreased in recent years from 59 per cent in 2001 to 47 per cent in 2004.[36] This is a real problem for Unionism and one which until recently its leaders have done very little to address. They have, however, never had a better opportunity to do so than now as there are no Republican bombs going off in Belfast, Manchester or London. The argument that Unionists should not worry about seeking support for Northern Ireland's political union with Britain on the mainland has always been, and remains, the sort of narrow-minded thinking that has ensured Northern Ireland continues to be a place apart within the Kingdom since partition. The sooner Ulster Unionists begin to articulate this view as fundamental to the long-term interests of Unionism and act on it, the better. This problem is exemplified by the irony of the fact that Irish Nationalist communities are often more integrated in Britain than Irish Unionists. This is because Irish Unionists do not know how to think of themselves as a community when they move to Britain. They lose the rich cultural diversity they have to offer their society as a whole.

A long time ago, many Irish Unionists stopped believing that being Irish and being Unionist was a distinction worth bringing to British society. What I am arguing here is that there is more than enough room for the richness and diversity of Irish Unionism within British

227

political, cultural and national life. As leader of the Ulster Unionists and as the internationally respected voice of Unionism David Trimble began this transformation process. What I am proposing now is that Ulster Unionists collectively engage in the process of making that distinction something Britain can be proud of.

Notes

Chapter 1

1. *The Wizard of Oz* by Noel Langley, Florence Ryerson and Edgar Allen Woolf, Cutting Continuity Script, taken from Printer's Dupe,last revised 15 March 1939.
2. *Agreement between the Government of the United Kingdom of Great Britain and Northern Ireland and the Government of Ireland* (London: HMSO, 1998).
3. Harbinson, J., *The Ulster Unionist Party, 1882-1973: Its Development and Organisation* (Belfast: Black Staff Press, 1973).
4. See Stewart, A.T.Q., *The Narrow Ground: Aspects of Ulster, 1609–1969* (Belfast: Black Staff Press, 1977); Aughey, A., *Under Siege: Ulster Unionism and the Anglo-Irish Agreement* (Belfast: Black Staff Press, 1989); Cochrane, F., *Unionist Politics and the Politics of Unionism since the Anglo-Irish Agreement* (Cork: Cork University Press, 2001); Walker, G., *A History of the Ulster Unionist Party: Protest, Pragmatism and Pessimism* (Manchester: Manchester University Press, 2004).
5. Godson, D., *Himself Alone: David Trimble and the Ordeal of Unionism* (London: Harper Collins, 2004); Millar, F., *David Trimble: The Price of Peace* (Dublin: Liffey Press, 2004); McDonald, H., *Trimble* (London: Bloomsbury, 2000).
6. Buckland, P., *A History of Northern Ireland* (Dublin: Gill & Macmillan, 1981), p. 8.
7. Stewart, A.T.Q., *The Ulster Crisis* (London: Faber, 1967), p. 62.
8. Buckland, *A History of Northern Ireland*, p. 16.
9. O'Leary, B. and McGarry, J., *The Politics of Antagonism: Understanding Northern Ireland* (London: Athlone Press, 1996), pp. 94–5.

10. See McGarry, J. and O'Leary, B., *Explaining Northern Ireland* (Oxford: Blackwell, 1995), pp. 320–53; Coughlan, A., 'A Unitary Irish State', in McGarry, J. and O'Leary, B. (eds), *The Future of Northern Ireland* (Oxford: Oxford University Press, 1990), pp. 48–68.

11. See Miller, D., *Queen's Rebels: Ulster Loyalism in Historical Perspective* (Dublin: Gill and Macmillan, 1973); Gallagher, M., 'Do Unionists Have a Right to Self-Determination?' *Irish Political Studies*, 5, 1990, pp. 11–30; Stewart, *The Narrow Ground*. See also Aughey, *Under Siege*; O'Neill, T., *Autobiography* (London: Rupert Hart Davies. 1972).

12. O'Leary and McGarry, *The Politics of Antagonism*, p. 100.

13. Buckland, *A History of Northern Ireland*, p. 2.

14. The term, 'a place apart', was coined by Dervla Murphy in her famous book on Northern Ireland, *A Place Apart* (Middlesex: Penguin, 1978).

15. Buckland, *A History of Northern Ireland*, pp. 104–5.

16. O'Leary and McGarry, *The Politics of Antagonism*, pp. 153–77.

17. On O'Neillism, see Buckland, *A History of Northern Ireland*, pp. 110–31.

18. See Rose, R., *Governing Without Consensus* (London: Faber & Faber, 1971).

19. See Purdie, B., *Politics in the Streets: The Origins of the Civil Rights Movement in Northern Ireland* (Belfast: Black Staff Press 1990).

20. O'Leary and McGarry, *The Politics of Antagonism*, pp. 176–7.

21. See Kerr, M.R., *Imposing Power-Sharing: Conflict and Coexistence in Northern Ireland and Lebanon*, (Dublin: Irish Academic Press, 2005) Chapter 2; Fisk, R., *The Point of No Return: The Strike that Broke the British in Ulster* (London: Andre Deutsch, 1975).

22. *Agreement between the Government of the United Kingdom of Great Britain and Northern Ireland and the Government of Ireland* (London: HMSO, 1998).

23. *The Sunningdale Communiqué*, Paragraph 7 (London: HMSO, 1973).

24. Interview with Dermot Nally (Irish Diplomat at Sunningdale), Dublin, 10 May 2001.

25. Interview with James Molyneaux (Lord Molyneaux) (MP for South Antrim 1970–83 and Lagan Valley 1983–97, UUP Leader 1979–95), Westminster, 30 January 2001.

26. See Faulkner, B., *Memoirs of a Statesman* (London: Weidenfeld & Nicolson, 1978), p. 195.
27. See O'Neill, *Autobiography*; O'Leary and McGarry, *The Politics of Antagonism*, pp. 162–71; Interview with Leslie Morrell (Unionist Minister for Agriculture 1974), Belfast, 4 January 2001.
28. Interview with Sir Ken Bloomfield (Northern Ireland Executive Secretary 1974; Head of the Northern Ireland Civil service 1984–91), Craigavad, 23 August 2001.
29. This included members of Craig's Vanguard Unionist Progressive Party (VUPP), which originated from his Vanguard movement.
30. *Northern Ireland Assembly Debates*, Col. 1470, 5 December 1973.
31. Elliott, S. and Flackes, W.D., *Northern Ireland: A Political Directory*, (Belfast: Black Staff Press 1999), pp. 537–8.
32. See: http://www.linenhall.com/Troubled_Images/Online_Exhibition/List_of_Items/Item_6/item_6.html
33. Faulkner, B., *Memoirs of a Statesman*, pp 251–60.
34. See Fisk, *The Point of No Return*, pp. 24–8.
35. Interview with Glen Barr (Assembly Member for Londonderry 1973-4, Chairman of the UWC), Londonderry, 22 August 2001.
36. *Ibid.*
37. Interview with Lord Kilclooney, Westminster, 15 February 2001.
38. Rees, M., *Northern Ireland: A Personal Perspective* (London: Methuen, 1985), pp. 66–7.
39. FitzGerald, G., *All in a Life* (London: Macmillan, 1991) p. 237.
40. Fisk, *The Point of No Return*, p. 159.
41. Interview with Leslie Morrell (Agriculture Minister 1974), Belfast, 4 January 2001.
42. O'Leary and McGarry, *The Politics of Antagonism*, pp. 201–2.
43. *Anglo-Irish Agreement* (London: HMSO, 1985).
44. Interview with Lord Robin Butler, (Private Secretary to Margaret Thatcher 1982-85), Oxford, 9 October 2001.
45. See Cochrane, *Unionist Politics*, pp. 126–31.
46. O'Leary and McGarry, *The Politics of Antagonism*, p. 250.
47. Interview with Robin Butler, Oxford, 9 October 2001.
48. Unionists wanted the Republic of Ireland to relinquish the territorial claim Articles 2 and 3 of its constitution held over Northern Ireland. Chris McGimpsey unsuccessfully challenged

the Irish Government in the Irish Supreme Court in 1990 over this claim. (*McGimpsey* v. *An Taoiseach*); O'Leary and McGarry, *The Politics of Antagonism*, p. 225.

49. *Sinn Féin Ard-Fhéis* (Sinn Féin, 1986).

50. See *Scenario for Peace* (Sinn Féin, 1987); and *Towards a Lasting Peace in Ireland* (Sinn Féin, 1992); Sinn Féin's Danny Morrison said at the party's October 1981 Ard-Fheis, 'Who here really believes that we can win the war through the ballot box? But will anyone here object if, with a ballot paper in one hand and the Armalite in the other, we take power in Ireland?'

51. Interview with John Hume (SDLP Leader 1979–2001; Foyle MP 1983–2005), Londonderry/Derry, 13 September 2001.

52. Kerr, *Imposing Power-Sharing*, Chapter 3.

53. Interview with Peter Brooke (Lord Brooke) (Secretary of State for Northern Ireland 1989–92), London, 6 July 2001.

54. *The Times*, 4 November 1989.

55. *Financial Times*, 10 November 1990.

56. *The Downing Street Declaration* (London: HMSO, 1993); see also http://cain.ulst.ac.uk/events/peace/docs/dsd151293.htm

57. Interview with Robin Eames (Church of Ireland Primate), Armagh, 3 August 2001.

58. Interview with Albert Reynolds, Dublin, 20 September 2001.

59. *Ibid.*; O'Clery, C., *The Greening of the White House* (Dublin: Gill & Macmillan, 1996), pp. 89–100.

60. *The Irish Times*, 1 September 1994.

61. *The Times*, 12 September 1994.

62. *The Times*, 14 October 1994; Interview with Roy Magee (Fitzroy Presbyterian Church), Dundonald, 5 September 2001; Interview with David Adams (UDP negotiator 1996–98), Lisburn, 9 May 2001; See Rowan, B., *Behind the Lines: The Story of the IRA and Loyalist Ceasefires* (Belfast: Black Staff Press, 1995), pp. 75–123.

63. Interview with David Adams, Lisburn, 9 May 2001; Rowan, B., *Behind the Lines*, pp. 110–23.

64. *A Framework for Accountable Government in Northern Ireland* (London: HMSO, 1995); *A New Framework for Agreement: A Shared Understanding between the British and Irish Governments to Assist Discussion and Negotiation Involving the Northern Ireland Parties* (London: HMSO, 1995).

65. *The Times*, 26 June 1997.
66. *The Mitchell Commission's Report*:
    http://www.psr.keele.ac.uk/docs/mitch.htm 22 January 1996.
67. Interview with David Kerr (Personal Assistant to David Trimble during the Talks Process), Stormont, 5 September 2001.
68. *Propositions on Heads of Agreement* (London: HMSO, 1998).
69. Interview with Lord Kilclooney (Strangford MP 1983–2001), Westminster, 19 July 2000.
70. *Belfast Telegraph*, 7 April 1998.
71. *The Belfast Agreement*, pp. 11–12.
72. See O'Leary, B., 'The Nature of the British-Irish Agreement', *New Left Review*, 233, 1999, pp. 95–6; O'Leary, B., in 'Comparative Political Science and the British–Irish Agreement', McGarry (ed.) *Northern Ireland and the Divided World* (Oxford: Oxford University Press, 2001), pp. 53–88.
73. *The Belfast Agreement*, 1998, p. 22–5.
74. Interview with Rev. Martin Smyth (South Belfast MP 1982–2005), Westminster, 22 June 2005.
75. Interview with David Campbell (UUP Vice-Chairman), Stormont, 11 September 2001.
76. Interview with David Kerr (Personal Assistant to David Trimble), Stormont, 5 September 2001.
77. Interview with David Campbell, Stormont, 11 September 2001.
78. Interview with David Kerr, Stormont, 5 September 2001.
79. Interview with Lord Kilclooney, Westminster, 15 February 2001.
80. Ibid. For the full text of Blair's letter to Trimble see
    www.cain.ulst.ac.uk/events/peace/docs/tb100498.htm
81. BBC, 21 May 1998;
    www.news.bbc.co.uk/1/hi/events/northern_ireland/latest_news/97147.stm
82. *Belfast Newsletter*, 18 November 1999.
83. *The Independent*, 30 November 1999.
84. BBC, 27 November 1999;
    http://news.bbc.co.uk/1/hi/northern_ireland/539245.stm
85. *Financial Times*, 12 February 2000; Interview with Peter Mandelson (Secretary of State for Northern Ireland 1999–2000), Westminster, 2 July 2001.
86. *The Independent*, 7 May 2000.

87. *Belfast Newsletter*, 29 May 2000.
88. For a detailed account of this period see Godson, *Himself Alone*.
89. Interview with Jim Gibney (Sinn Féin Negotiator 1996–98), Belfast, 17 September 2004.
90. See *Key IRA Statements 1998–2003*, BBC, 30 October 2003; http://news.bbc.co.uk/1/hi/northern_ireland/2798801.stm
91. Interview with Jim Gibney, Belfast, 11/04/01 and 17/09/04.
92. *Daily Telegraph*, 15 October 2002,
93. *The Guardian*, 2 May 2003; see *Joint Declaration by the British and Irish Governments*, April 2003 (London: HMSO, 2003).
94. *Financial Times*, 18 June 2003.
95. *The Belfast Telegraph*, 23 June 2003.
96. Interview with Sylvia Hermon (North Down MP 2001–), Westminster, 7 July 2005.
97. Private conversation with David Trimble (First Minister of Northern Ireland 1999–2000; UUP Leader 1995–2005; Upper Bann MP 1990–2005), 29 October 2003.
98. BBC, 21 October 2003; http://news.bbc.co.uk/1/hi/northern_ireland/3212192.stm
99. BBC, 27 October 2003; http://news.bbc.co.uk/1/hi/northern_ireland/3218461.stm
100. Interview with Sylvia Hermon, Westminster, 7 July 2005.
101. *Ibid*.
102. *Ibid*.
103. *Daily Telegraph*, 6 January 2004.
104. Interview with David Campbell, Westminster, 8 June 2005.
105. Interview with David Trimble, Westminster, 8 June 2005.

Chapter 2
1. Interview with David Trimble, Westminster, 8 June 2005.
2. *The Irish Times*, 19 December 2003.
3. *The Belfast Telegraph*, 22 September 2000.
4. Private conversation with David Burnside (South Antrim MP 2001–5), Westminster, 16 March 2005.
5. *The Belfast Telegraph*, 10/11 March 2005, 'What Ulster Thinks Now', survey conducted by Millward Brown Ulster on 7 and 8 March 2005 with 1,010 adults at 56 randomly selected points across Northern Ireland.

6. *The Belfast Telegraph*, 21 December 2004.
7. *Irish News*, 1 February 2005.
8. BBC, 9 March 2005;
    http://news.bbc.co.uk/1/hi/northern_ireland/4331819.stm
9. BBC, 13 March 2005;
    http://news.bbc.co.uk/1/hi/northern_ireland/4344921.stm
10. *Belfast Newsletter*, 15 June 2004.
11. Interview with Alan McFarland (North Down MLA 2001–5), Westminster, 25 July 2005.
12. *Belfast Newsletter*, 15 June 2004.
13. Private conversation with Lord Kilclooney, Westminster, 24 March 2005.
14. *Belfast Newsletter*, 31 March 2005; see also www.jimallister.com
15. *Belfast Newsletter*, 31 March 2005.
16. See Proposals by the British and Irish Governments for a Comprehensive Agreement; (London: HMSO, 2004);
    http://www.nio.gov.uk/proposals_by_the_british_and_irish_governments_for_a_comprehensive_agreement.pdf
17. Ian Paisley's speech to the North Antrim DUP Association Annual Dinner, 27 November 2004.
18. Press statement by Roy Beggs, UUP Press Office, 18 February 2005.
19. See UUP's 'Campaign Against Criminality', leaflet, 21 February 2005.
20. Speech by David Trimble, UUP AGM, 5 March 2005:
    http://www.uup.org/media/media_05_03_05trimble.htm; On d'Hondt see O'Leary, B., 'The Nature of the British–Irish Agreement', *New Left Review*, 233, 1999, pp. 66–96.
21. *The Mirror*, Ulster Edition, 4 May 2005, Letter by Ian Paisley: 'In our manifesto we have pledged that inclusive, mandatory coalition government, which includes Sinn Féin under d'Hondt, or any other system, is out of the question.'
22. *The Belfast Telegraph*, 22 April 2005.
23. DUP 'Fair Deal Manifesto 2003': 'It's time for a Fair Deal'; www.dup2win.com
24. Interview with David Trimble, Westminster, 8 June 2005.
25. DUP 'Fair Deal Manifesto 2003': 'It's time for a Fair Deal'.
26. 'Inside Politics', BBC Radio Ulster, 1 March 2003.

27. Letter from Paul Murphy to Roy Beggs, 11 January 2005.
28. Interview with David Trimble, Westminster, 8 June 2005.
29. Proposals by the British and Irish Government for a Comprehensive Agreement, Annex D, Paragraph 5 (London: HMSO, 2004); http://www.nio.gov.uk/proposals_by_the_british_and_irish_governments_for_a_comprehensive_agreement.pdf
30. *Ibid.*
31. House of Commons Library Statistics Unit.
32. *Belfast Newsletter*, Letter by Jeffery Donaldson MP, 1 April 2005.
33. *The Belfast Telegraph*, 1 September 2005.
34. See Elliott and Flackes, *Northern Ireland: A Political Directory 1968–99*, p. 387.
35. *The Irish Times*, 9 January 1981.
36. *The Irish Times*, 7 April 2005.
37. *The Irish News*, 4 February 2005.
38. www.cain.ulst.ac.uk/othelem/chron/ch88.htm
38. *Hansard*, 6 April 2005 (London: HMSO).
40. *The Independent*, 7 April 2005, Adams' call on the IRA to end armed struggle.
41. www.uup.org press archive – Adams is talking to himself.
42. For the Patten Report see:
    http://cain.ulst.ac.uk/issues/police/patten/patten2001.pdf
    and on the DUP's response to it see *Hansard*, 6 June 2000, The Police (Northern Ireland) Bill.
43. PSNI Statement on Patten, 9 September 1999.
44. See Alex Kane, 'If you ask me', cartoon strip on the BBC's Hearts and Minds:
    www.bbc.co.uk/northernireland/heartsandminds/ifyouaskme/2005_iyam/20050324.shtml
45. *Sunday Mirror* (Northern Ireland edition), 1 May 2005.
46. www.ark.ac.uk/elections
47. 18 April 2005 http://www.allianceparty.org/news.asp?id=830
48. 21 April 2005 http://www.allianceparty.org/news.asp?id=847
49. 20 April 2005 http://www.allianceparty.org
50. www.ark.ac.uk/elections/fa03.htm
51. *The Mirror* (Northern Ireland Edition) April 15 2005
52. BBC, 'Hearts and Minds', 6 April 2005.

53. *Irish News*, 27 April 2005.
54. *Belfast Newsletter*, April 11 2005.
55. *Belfast Newsletter*, 11 April 2005.
56. Private correspondence with UUP Press Officer Geoffrey McGimpsey.
57. Interview with Rev. Martin Smyth, Westminster, 22 June 2005.
58. *Ibid.*
59. *Ibid.*
60. http://cain.ulst.ac.uk/othelem/chron/ch94.htm
61. Interview with David Campbell, Westminster, 8 June 2005.
62. Interview with David Burnside, London Embankment, 25 May 2005.
63. Interview with David Campbell, Westminster, 8 June 2005.
64. Interview with Alex Benjamin (UUP Director of Communications), Belfast, 24 June 2005.
65. Private conversation with Lord Kilclooney, Jerusalem, 7 January 2005.
66. Interview with David Burnside, London Embankment, 25 May 2005.
67. Interview with Sylvia Hermon, Westminster, 7 July 2005.
68. *Ibid.*
69. Interview with Alan McFarland (North Down MLA 1988–), Westminster, 25 July 2005.
70. Interview with Sylvia Hermon, Westminster, 7 July 2005.
71. *Belfast Newsletter*, 11 April 2005.

Chapter 3
1. DUP Political Election Broadcast, BBC, 12 April 2005.
2. Interview with Steven King (Personal Assistant to David Trimble), Westminster, 20 June 2005.
3. *Belfast Newsletter*, 12 April 2005.
4. *Belfast Newsletter*, 14 April 2005.
5. Interview with David Burnside, London Embankment, 25 May 2005.
6. Newsletter 14 April 2005; Mitchel McLaughlin's 'Report on Negotiations', speech to Sinn Féin Ard Fheis, 6 March 2005 http://www.sinnfein.ie/gaelic/news/details/8774
7. Interview with David Trimble, Westminster, 8 June 2005.

8. Private conversation with David Trimble, Belfast, 13 April 2005.
9. Interview with David Burnside, London, 25 May 2005.
10. Private conversation with Lord Kilclooney, 7 May 2005.
11. Interview with Alex Benjamin, Holywood, 24 June 2005.
12. *The Irish News*, 13 April 2005.
13. *The Irish News*, 14 April 2005.
14. *The Mirror* (Northern Ireland Edition) 15 April 2005
15. *The Mirror* (Northern Ireland Edition), 18 April 2005.
16. *The Belfast Telegraph*, 16 April 2005.
17. BBC, 15 April 2005: http:newsvote.bbc.co.uk
18. *Belfast Newsletter*, 19 April 2005.
19. *Irish News*, 18 April 2005.
20. *BBC Breakfast with Frost*, 17 April 2005: http://news.bbc.co.uk/hi/programmes/breakfast_with_frost/4453643.stm
21. *Belfast Newsletter*, 19 April 2005.
22. *Belfast Newsletter*, 19 April 2005.
23. *The Irish News*, 19 April 2005.
24. *Belfast Telegraph*, 19 April 2005.
25. *Belfast Newsletter*, 20 April 2005.
26. *The Irish News*, 20 April 2005.
27. *The Belfast Telegraph*, 20 April 2005.
28. *Daily Ireland*, 20 April 2005.
29. *Daily Mirror* (Northern Ireland Edition), 18 April 2005.
30. *Belfast Newsletter*, 20 April 2005.

Chapter 4
1. Ulster Unionist Manifesto, 2005.
2. *The Irish Times*, 22 April 2005.
3. *Belfast Newsletter*, 21 April 2005.
4. *The Irish Belfast Newsletter*, 21 April 2005.
5. *Belfast Newsletter*, 21 April 2005.
6. *The Irish News*, 21 April 2005.
7. SDLP Manifesto:
   www.sdlp.ie/elections05/sdlp-manifesto-2005.pdf
8. *The Irish News*, 21 April 2005.
9. *The Belfast Telegraph*, 26 January 2005.
10. UTV, 27 March 2004.
11. Statement issued by Michael McDowell TD, 13 January 2005.

12. *Belfast Newsletter*, 21 April 2005.
13. *The Irish Times*, 21 April 2005.
14. *The Belfast Telegraph*, 21 April 2005.
15. *The Irish News*, 22 April 2005.
16. *Belfast Newsletter*, 22 April 2005.
17. *The Irish Times*, 22 April 2005.
18. *The Irish News*, 22 April 2005.
19. *The Belfast Telegraph*, 12 April 2005.
20. BBC, 26 May 2005; http://news.bbc.co.uk/1/hi/uk_politics/vote_2005/northern_ireland/4433887.stm
21. See 'Peerage to Bob', 19 May 2005, www.sluggerotoole.com
22. Elliott, and Flackes, *Northern Ireland*, p. 325.
23. BBC, 'Hearts and Minds', 14 April 2005.
24. BBC, 25 April 2005: http://news.bbc.co.uk/1/hi/uk_politics/vote_2005/northern_ireland/4481343.stm
25. BBC's 'Good Morning Ulster', Wendy Austin interview with Ian Paisley 28 April 2005.
26. RTE Radio One's 'Tonight with Vincent Browne', 21 April 2005.
27. *Belfast Newsletter*, 30 April 2005.
28. *Belfast Newsletter*, 25 April 2005.
29. *Belfast Newsletter*, 12 April 2005.
30. Personal correspondence with the author, 15 April 2005.
31. Early Day Motion No. 809, tabled by Roy Beggs MP, 1 March 2005, Parliamentary Session 2004-5; www.parliament.gov.uk
32. www.feedmebetter.co.uk
33. *Belfast Newsletter*, April 26 2005.
34. *The Belfast Telegraph*, 26 April 2005.
35. *Daily Ireland*, 26 April 2005.
36. *The Belfast Telegraph*, 26 April 2005.
37. UTV Election Special from Larne, 26 April 2005.
38. 'Thinking of Voting Alliance?' Published by Concerned Citizens for a Shared Future. The leaflet said: 'Vote for your party, the Alliance Party, in the local council elections, and then for the party that can represent everyone at Westminster, the UUP. If you lend your vote to the UUP on 5 May Westminster election, then together we can win'; *The Belfast Telegraph*, 28 April 2005.
39. *The Belfast Telegraph*, 28 April 2005.
40. *The Belfast Telegraph*, 28 April 2005.

41. *The Irish News*, 28 April 2005.
42. BBCwww.news.bbc.co.uk/1/hi/uk_politics/vote_2005/ northern_ireland/4453407.stm 17 April 2005.
43. *The Irish News*, 28 April 2005.

Chapter 5
1. Interview with UUP North Antrim candidate, Rodney McCune, Westminster, 4 August 2005.
2. Interview with Roy Beggs (East Antrim MP 1983–2005), Westminster, 8 June 2005.
3. Interview with David Burnside, Westminster, 25 May 20005.
4. Interview with David Trimble, Westminster, 8 June 2005.
5. *Belfast Newsletter*, 29 April 2005.
6. *Belfast Newsletter*, 29 April 2005.
7. BBC, 30 April 2005: http://news.bbc.co.uk/1/hi/uk_politics /vote_2005/northern_ireland/4499859.stm
8. *The Belfast Telegraph*, 29 April 2005.
9. *The Belfast Telegraph*, 28 April 2005.
10. *The Irish Times*, 29 April 2005.
11. Interview with Steven King (Personal Assistant to David Trimble), Westminster, 20 June 2005.
12. *The Belfast Telegraph*, 30 April 2005.
13. *Sunday World* (Northern Ireland Edition), 1 May 2005.
14. *Ibid.*
15. BBC, 3 May 2005; http://news.bbc.co.uk/1/hi/uk_politics/ vote_2005/northern_ireland/4509109.stm
16. *The Irish Times*, 29 April 2005.
17. UTV, 1 May 2005 http://www.u.tv/newsroom/indepth. asp?pt=n&id=59737
18. *The Times*, 1 May 2005.
19. *The Irish News*, 3 May 2005.
20. Ian Paisley, Election Platform, *Belfast Newsletter*, 4 May 2005.
21. *The Irish News*, 4 May 2005.
22. *Daily Ireland*, 4 May 2005.
23. *Washington Times*, 3 May 2005.
24. *The Guardian*, 4 May 2005.
25. *The Guardian*, 4 May 2005.
26. *The Belfast Telegraph*, 3 May 2005.

27. *The Irish Times*, 4 May 2004.
28. *Daily Mirror* (Northern Ireland edition), 4 May 2005.

Chapter 6
1. See Kerr, *Imposing Power-Sharing*, Chapter 2.
2. PREM15/486 Doc 14, British Policy on Northern Ireland, 3 September 1971.
3. Private conversation with Sylvia Hermon, Westminster, 18 May 2005.
4. *Daily Telegraph*, 6 May 2005.
5. BBC online, Mark Davenport, 5 May 2005: http://news.bbc.co.uk/1/hi/uk_politics/vote_2005/northern_ireland/4514317.stm
6. *Daily Telegraph*, 6 May 2005.
7. *The Belfast Telegraph*, 4 May 2005.
8. *The Irish Independent*, 5 May 2005.
9. BBC, 6 May 2005: http://news.bbc.co.uk/1/hi/uk_politics/vote_2005/northern_ireland/4495273.stm
10. Private conversation with Lord Kilclooney, 8 May 2005.
11. Interview with Martin Smyth, Westminster, 22 June 2005.
12. *Ibid*.
13. Interview with Tim Lemon (UUP Director of Elections 2005), Westminster, 7 July 2005.
14. Interview with Alex Benjamin, Belfast, 24 June 2005.
15. Interview with David Campbell, Westminster, 8 June, 2005.
16. *The Irish Examiner*, 7 May 2005.
17. UTV, 6 May 2005: http://www.u.tv/newsroom/indepth.asp?pt=n&id=59969
18. Interview with David Campbell, Westminster, 8 June 2005.
19. *The Irish Independent*, 7 May 2005.
20. *The Irish Examiner*, 7 May 2005.
21. *The Irish Independent*, 7 May 2005.
22. *Daily Telegraph*, 7 May 2005.

Chapter 7
1. Interview with David Trimble, Westminster, 8 June 2005.
2. Interview with Brian Crowe (UUP Policy Officer), Belfast, 9 June 2005.
3. Interview with David Trimble, Westminster, 8 June 2005.

4. Interview with Tim Lemon, Belfast, 7 July 2005.
5. David Trimble on the BBC Radio Four's 'On the Ropes', 12 July 2005.
6. Interview with David Campbell, Stormont, 11 September 2001
7. Interview with David Kerr, Stormont, 5 September 2001.
8. Interview with David Campbell, Stormont, 11 September 2001
9. Interview with David Kerr, Stormont, 5 September 2001.
10. Interview with David Campbell, Stormont, 11 September 2001
11. See Kerr, *Imposing Power-Sharing*, Chapter 2.
12. BBC, 6 May 2005: http://news.bbc.co.uk/1/hi/uk_politics/vote_2005/northern_ireland/4524145.stm
13. Interview with John Hume, Londonderry/Derry, 13 September 2001.
14. BBC, 29 July 2005: www.news.bbc.co.uk/1/hi/northern_ireland/4726249.stm
15. *The Independent*, 28 July 2005.
16. Interview with Reg Empey (UUP Leader 2005), Westminster, 25 July 2005.
17. Interview with David Trimble, Westminster, 7 June 2005.
18. Interview with Lord Kilclooney, Westminster, 13 July 2005.
19. Interview with Alex Benjamin, Holywood, 24 June 2005.
20. Interview with Lord Maginnis (Fermanagh and South Tyrone MP 1983–2001), Westminster, 21 July 2005.
21. Interview with David Kerr, Stormont, 5 September 2001.
22. Interview with David Campbell, Westminster, 8 June 2005.
23. Interview with Sylvia Hermon, Westminster, 7 July 2005.
24. Interview with Alex Benjamin, Holywood, 24 June 2005.
25. Interview with David Campbell, Westminster, 8 June 2005.
26. Interview with Lord Rogan (UUP President 2003–), Westminster, 23 June 2005.
27. Interview with Lord Kilclooney, Westminster, 13 July 2005.
28. Interview with Tim Lemon, Belfast, 7 July 2005.
29. Interview with David Trimble, Westminster, 8 July 2005.
30. Interview with Steven King, Westminster, 20 June 2005.
31. See Kerr, *Imposing Power-Sharing*, Chapter 4.
32. Interview with David Campbell, Westminster, 8 June 2005.
33. Interview with Geoff McGimpsey (UUP Press Officer), Belfast, 18 May 2005.

34. Interview with Tim Lemon, Belfast, 7 July 2005.
35. Private poll conducted for the UUP on 23–26 March 2001. PriceWaterhouseCoopers interviewed 1,173 Unionist voters. The basis for this question was 371: those Unionist voters determined to vote for an anti-Agreement candidate in the forthcoming 2001 general election.
36. Interview with Alex Benjamin, Belfast, 24 June 2005.
37. Interview with David Kerr, Stormont, 5 September 2001.
38. Interview with David Campbell, Stormont, 11 September 2001.
39. Interview with Sylvia Hermon, Westminster, 7 July 2005.
40. Interview with Alex Benjamin, Belfast, 24 June 2005.
41. Interview with David Campbell, Westminster, 8 June 2005.
42. Interview with David Burnside, Embankment, London, 25 May 2005.
43. Interview with Alex Benjamin, Belfast, 24 June 2005.
44. David Trimble on BBC Radio Four's 'On the Ropes', 12 July 2005.
45. Interview with David Burnside, Embankment, London, 25 May 2005.
46. Interview with David Trimble, Westminster, 8 June 2005.
47. *Ibid.*
48. Interview with Jim Gibney, Belfast, 11 April 2001.
49. Interview with Sylvia Hermon, Westminster, 7 July 2005.
50. Interview with Rodney McCune, Westminster, 4 August 2005.
51. Interview with Roy Beggs, Westminster, 8 June 2005.
52. Interview with Steven King, Westminster, 20 June 2005.
53. *Ibid.*
54. Interview with Lord Maginnis, Westminster, 21 July 2005.
55. Interview with Steven King, Westminster, 20 June 2005.
56. Interview with David Burnside, London Embankment, 25 May 2005; private conversation with Lord Kilclooney, Westminster, 29 June 2005; Interview with Sylvia Hermon, Westminster, 7 July, 2005.
57. Interview with Lord Kilclooney, Westminster, 13 July 2005.
58. *Ibid.*
59. David Trimble on the BBC Radio Four's programme 'On the Ropes', 12 July 2005.
60. Interview with Brian Crowe, Belfast, 9 June 2005.
61. Interview with David Burnside, London Embankment, 25 May 2005.

Chapter 8

1. *Belfast Newsletter*, 30 May 2005.
2. RTE, 8 May 2005.
3. BBC, 9 May 2005, http://news.bbc.co.uk/1/hi/northern_ireland/4528843.stm
4. *Daily Telegraph*, 7 May 2005.
5. BBC, 11 May 2005: http://news.bbc.co.uk/1/hi/northern_ireland/4538319.stm
6. *The Belfast Telegraph*, 9 May 2005.
7. Letter from Lord Kilclooney to UUP Party Officers, 12 May 2005.
8. *The Irish Times*, 18 May 2005.
9. *Ibid.*
10. *The Sunday Times*, 15 May 2005.
11. *Ibid.*
12. *The Belfast Telegraph*, 19 May 2005.
13. *Ibid.*
14. *The Irish News*, 18 May 2005.
15. *Belfast Newsletter*, 24 May 2005.
16. 25 May 2005: http://www.dup.org.uk/articles.asp?Article_ID=1456
17. *Belfast Newsletter*, 30 May 2005.
18. *The Belfast Telegraph*, 1 June 2005.
19. *The Belfast Telegraph*, 1 June 2005.
20. *Belfast Newsletter*, 2 June 2005.
21. Interview with Tim Lemon, Belfast, 7 July 2005.
22. *The Irish Times*, 8 June 2005.
23. BBC, 10 June 2005: http://news.bbc.co.uk/1/hi/northern_ireland/4082328.stm
24. *The Belfast Telegraph*, 8 June 2005.
25. *The Irish Times*, 9 June 2005.
26. http://www.portadown news.com 16 June 2005.
27. BBC, 13 June 2005: http://news.bbc.co.uk/1/hi/northern_ireland/4085738.stm
28. *The Irish Times*, 15 June 2005.
29. BBC, 15 June 2005: http://news.bbc.co.uk/1/hi/northern_ireland/4097270.stm
30. Interview with Tim Lemon, Belfast, 7 July 2005.
31. *The Belfast Telegraph*, 18 June 2005.

32. *The Belfast Telegraph*, 18 June 2005.
33. *Sunday Life*, 19 June 2005.
34. *The Belfast Telegraph*, 22 June 2005.
35. See Godson, *Himself Alone*, pp 146–55.
36. Interview with Tim Lemon, Belfast, 7 July 2005.
37. *Sunday Life*, 19 June 2005.
38. Leadership letter from David McNarry to UUC delegates, June 2005.
39. Alan McFarland, UUP Leadership Election Literature, June 2005.
40. *Belfast Newsletter*, 23 June 2005.
41. Leadership election leaflet by Sir Reg Empey, *Going Forward Together: A Roadmap to Success*, June 2005.
42. Interview with David Burnside, London Embankment, 25 May 2005.
43. *The Irish Independent*, 24 June 2005.
44. *Belfast Newsletter*, 25 June 2005.
45. *The Observer*, 26 June 2005.
46. *The Scotsman*, 25 June 2005.
47. *The Irish Independent*, 26 June 2005.

Chapter 9

1. Interview with Lord Kilclooney, Westminster, 15 February 2001.
2. Interview with Alex Benjamin, Holywood, 24 June 2005.
3. Interview with David Trimble, Westminster, 8 June 2005.
4. Interview with David Trimble, Westminster, 8 June 2003.
5. Interview with David Kerr, Stormont, 5 September 2001.
6. Interview with David Burnside, London Embankment, 25 May 2005.
7. Interview with David Campbell, Stormont, 11 September 2001.
8. Interview with Reg Empey, Westminster, 25 July 2005.
9. Interview with Lord Maginnis, Westminster, 21 July 2005.
10. Interview with Alex Benjamin, Westminster, 24 June 2004.
11. Interview with David Trimble, Westminster, 8 June 2005.
12. *Ibid*.
13. Interview with Reg Empey, Westminster, 25 July 2005.
14. Interview with David Trimble, Westminster, 8 June 2005.
15. David Trimble on BBC Radio Four's 'On the Ropes', 12 July 2005.

16. See *Reports* 1-5 of The Independent Monitoring Commission, (London: HMSO, 2005).

17. Interview with Reg Empey, Westminster, 25 July 2005.

18. Interview with Denis Rogan, Westminster, 23 June 2005.

19. Interview with David Campbell, Westminster, 8 June 2005.

20. Interview with David Trimble, Westminster, 8 June 2005.

21. Interview with David Campbell, Westminster, 8 June 2005.

22. Interview with Jim Gibney, Belfast, 17 September 2004.

23. David Trimble on BBC Radio Four's 'On the Ropes', 12 July 2005.

24. Interview with David Campbell, Westminster, 8 June 2005.

25. Interview with Reg Empey, Westminster, 25 July 2005.

26. Interview with Sylvia Hermon, Westminster, 7 July 2005.

27. Interview with Roy Beggs, Westminster, 8 June 2005.

28. Interview with David Campbell, Westminster, 8 June 2005.

29. Ken Bloomfield, Craigavad, 23 August 2001; Austin Currie (Minister for Housing, Planning and Local Government 1974), Dublin, 05 January 2001; John Hume, Londonderry, 13 September 2001; Basil McIvor (Education Minister 1974), Spa, 24 August 2001; Leslie Morrell, Belfast, 4 January 2001; Sir Oliver Napier (Alliance Party Leader 1972–84 and Minister of Law Reform 1974), Holywood, 29 December 2000.

30. Interview with John Semple (Former Secretary to the Northern Ireland Executive), Helen's Bay, 9 July 2002; Mark Durkan (Deputy First Minister 2001–2, Foyle MP 2005–, SDLP Leader 2001–), Londonderry, 14 September 2001; Sean Farren (SDLP Minister of Higher and Further Education 1999–2001), Belfast, 15 May 2001.

31. O'Leary, B., *Consociation: What We Know or Think We Know and What We Need to Know* (Paper presented to the Conference on National and Ethnic Conflict Regulation at the University of Western Ontario, 8–10 November 2002).

32. Interview with David Campbell, Westminster, 8 June 2005.

33. Interview with Reg Empey, Westminster, 25 July 2005.

34. Interview with David Burnside, London Embankment, 25 May 2005.

35. Northern Ireland Life and Times Survey, 2003.

36. Northern Ireland Life and Times Survey, 2001–4.

Interviews

David Adams (UDP Negotiator 1996–98) Lisburn, 9 May 2001

Lord Alderdice (Speaker of the Northern Ireland Assembly 1998–2002, APNI Leader 1987–98) Stormont, 24 August 2001

Glen Barr (Assembly Member for Londonderry 1973–74; Chairman of the UWC) Londonderry/Derry, 22 August 2001

Alderman Roy Beggs (East Antrim MP 1983–2005) Westminster 8 June 2005

Alex Benjamin (UUP Director of Communications) Holywood, 24 June 2005

Sir David Blatherwick (British Ambassador to Ireland 1991–95) London, 25 July 2001

Sir Ken Bloomfield (Northern Ireland Executive Secretary 1974; Head of the Northern Ireland Civil Service 1984–91) Craigavad, 23 August 2001

Lord Brooke (Secretary of State for Northern Ireland 1989–92) London, 6 July 2001

David Burnside (South Antrim MP 2001–5) London Embankment, 25 May 2005

Lord Robin Butler (Private Secretary to Margaret Thatcher 1982–85) Oxford, 9 October 2001.

David Campbell CBE (UUP Vice-Chairman) Stormont, 11 September 2001 and Westminster, 8 June 2005

Brian Crowe (UUP Policy Officer) Belfast, 9 June 2005.

Austin Currie TD (SDLP Minister for Housing, Planning and Local Government 1974) Dublin, 5 January 2001

Mark Durkan MLA (Deputy First Minister 2001–2, Foyle MP 2005–, SDLP Leader 2001-) Londonderry, 14 September 2001

Jeffery Donaldson MP (UUP Negotiator 1996–8 Lagan Valley MP 1997–2003; DUP MP 2004–) Lisburn, 14 August 2001

Lord Archbishop Dr Robin Eames (Church of Ireland Primate) Armagh, 3 August 2001

Tom Elliott MLA (UUP Fermanagh and South Tyrone MLA 2001–) Westminster, 25 July 2005

Sir Reg Empey MLA (UUP Leader 2005–) Westminster UUP, 25 July 2005

David Ervine MLA (East Belfast MLA 1998–; PUP Leader) Stormont, 9 May 2001

Dr Sean Farren MLA (SDLP Minister of Higher and Further Education 1999–2001) Belfast, 15 May 2001

Dr Robert Fisk (*The Independent*) Beirut, 13 May 2002

Garret FitzGerald (Irish Foreign Minister 1973–77; Taoiseach 1981–March 1982; December 1982-87) Dublin, 12 September 2001

Jim Gibney (Sinn Féin Negotiator 1996–98) Belfast, 11 April 2001 and 17 September 2004

Denis Haughey MLA (SDLP Junior Minister 1999–2001) Castle Buildings, 8 May 2001

Sir Edward Heath (British Prime Minister 1970–74) London Victoria, 7 February 2001

Lady Sylvia Hermon (North Down MP 2001–) Westminster, 7 July 2005

John Hume (SDLP Leader 1979–2001; Foyle MP 1983–2005) Londonderry/Derry, 13 September 2001

David Kerr (Former Personal Assistant to David Trimble) Stormont, 5 September 2001

Lord Kilclooney MLA (Strangford MP 1983–2001 Home Affairs Minister 1970–73, MEP 1979–89) Westminster, 15 February 2001 & 13 July 2005

Dr Steven King (Personal Assistant to David Trimble) Westminster, 20 June 2005

Tim Lemon (UUP Director of Elections 2005) Belfast, 7 July 2005

Denis Loretto (Former Alliance Party Chairman) Leatherhead, 12 December 2000

Rev. Dr Roy Magee (Fitzroy Presbyterian Church) Dundonald, 5 September 2001

Lord Maginnis (Fermanagh and South Tyrone MP 1983–2001) Westminster, 21 July 2005

Peter Mandelson (Secretary of State for Northern Ireland 1999–2001)

Westminster, 2 July 2001

Dr Martin Mansergh (Adviser to the Taoiseach 1997–) Dublin, 10 September 2001

Lord Mayhew (Former Secretary of State for Northern Ireland 1992–97) Westminster, 17 July 2001

Rodney McCune (North Antrim Candidate) London, 4 August 2005.

Alan McFarland (UUP North Down MLA 1998–) Westminster 25 July 2005

Basil McIvor (Education Minister 1974) Spa, 24 August 2001

Mitchell McLaughlin MLA (Londonderry/Derry MLA 1998– Sinn Féin Chairman 1998–) Londonderry/Derry, 4 January 2001

Gary McMichael (Former UDP Leader) Lisburn, 8 May 2001

Lord Molyneaux (South Antrim MP 1970–83 and Lagan Valley 1983–97, UUP Leader 1979–95), Westminster, 30 January 2001.

Leslie Morrell (UUP Agriculture Minister 1974) Belfast, 4 January 2001

Dermot Nally (Irish Diplomat at Sunningdale) Dublin, 10 May 2001

Sir Oliver Napier (Alliance Party Leader 1972–84 and Minister of Law Reform 1974) Holywood, 29 December 2000

Sean Neeson MLA (Alliance Party Leader 1998–2001) Stormont, 8 May 2001

Sean O'Callaghan (Former Head of the IRA's Southern Command) London, 18 October 2004

Ambassador Sean Ó hUiginn (former Irish Ambassador to the US) Dublin, 6 August 2001

Albert Reynolds (Taoiseach 1992–94) Dublin, 20 September 2001

Father Gerry Reynolds (Clonard Monastery Mediator) Belfast, 25 August 2001

Lord Rogan (UUP President 2003–) Westminster, 23 June 2005

Sir John Semple (Former Secretary to the Northern Ireland Executive) Helen's Bay, 9 July 2002

Rev. Martin Smyth (South Belfast MP 1982–2005) Westminster, 22 June 2005

Dick Spring (Tánaiste and Foreign Minister 1993–97) Dublin, 6 September 2001

Paddy Teahon (Senior Irish Negotiator) Dublin, 31 November 2001

Rt. Hon. David Trimble MLA (First Minister of Northern Ireland 1999–2002; UUP Leader 1995–2005; Upper Bann MP 1990–2005) Westminster, 8 June 2005

Select Bibliography

Aughey, A., *Under Siege: Ulster Unionism and the Anglo–Irish Agreement* (Belfast: Black Staff Press, 1989).

Bardon, J., *A History of Ulster* (Belfast: Black Staff Press, 1992).

Brian, R., *Behind the Lines: The Story of the IRA and Loyalist Ceasefires* (Belfast: Black Staff Press, 1995).

Buckland, P., *A History of Northern Ireland* (Dublin: Gill and Macmillan, 1981).

Cochrane, F., *Unionist Politics and the Politics of Unionism since the Anglo–Irish Agreement* (Cork: Cork University Press, 2001).

Faulkner, B., *Memoirs of a Statesman* (London: Weidenfeld & Nicolson, 1978).

Fisk, R., *The Point of No Return: The Strike that Broke the British in Ulster* (London: Andre Deutsch, 1975).

FitzGerald, G., *All in a Life* (London: Macmillan, 1991).

Godson, D., *Himself Alone: David Trimble and the Ordeal of Unionism* (London: Harper Collins, 2004).

Harbinson, J., *The Ulster Unionist Party, 1882–1973: Its Development and Organisation* (Belfast: Black Staff Press, 1973).

Kerr, M.R., *Imposing Power-Sharing: Conflict and Coexistence in Northern Ireland and Lebanon* (London: Irish Academic Press, 2005).

McGarry, J. and O'Leary, B. (eds), *The Future of Northern Ireland* (Oxford: Oxford University Press, 1990).

McGarry, J. and O'Leary, B., *Explaining Northern Ireland* (Oxford: Blackwell, 1995).

McGarry, J. (ed.), *Northern Ireland and the Divided World* (Oxford: Oxford University Press, 2001).

Millar, F., *David Trimble: The Price of Peace* (Dublin: Liffey Press, 2004).

Select Bibliography

Miller, D., *Queen's Rebels: Ulster Loyalism in Historical Perspective* (Dublin: Gill and Macmillan, 1973)

O'Leary, B. and McGarry, J., *The Politics of Antagonism: Understanding Northern Ireland* (London: Athlone Press, 1996).

O'Clery, C., *The Greening of the White House* (Dublin: Gill & Macmillan, 1996).

O'Leary, B., 'The Nature of the British–Irish Agreement', *New Left Review*, 233, 1999, pp. 66–96.

O'Leary, B. and McGarry, J., (eds), *Northern Ireland and the Divided World* (Oxford: Oxford University Press, 2001).

O'Neill, T., *Autobiography* (London: Rupert Hart Davies, 1972).

Rees, M., *Northern Ireland: A Personal Perspective* (London: Methuen, 1985).

Rose, R., *Governing Without Consensus* (London: Faber & Faber, 1971).

Ruane, J. and Todd, J. (eds), *After the Good Friday Agreement* (Dublin: UCD Press, 1999).

Stewart, A.T.Q., *The Narrow Ground: Aspects of Ulster, 1609–1969* (Belfast: Black Staff Press, 1977).

Stewart, A.T.Q., *The Ulster Crisis* (London: Faber & Faber, 1967).

Walker, G., *A History of the Ulster Unionist Party: Protest, Pragmatism and Pessimism* (Manchester: Manchester University Press, 2004).

Whyte, J., *Interpreting Northern Ireland* (Oxford: Clarendon, 1990).

Index

252

Index